AF512262

Challenges of Arms Control in South Asia

Challenges of Arms Control in South Asia

Dr. Charu Lata Singh

Gaurav Book Centre Pvt Ltd
Delhi

Publisher
GAURAV BOOK CENTRE PVT LTD
4832/24,Prahlad Lane,S-207 Ansari
Road, Daryaganj, Delhi-110002
Ph.: 43570976, 23278261
Email: gauravbookcentre@gmail.com

Edition: 2016

© Publisher

ISBN: 978-93-83316-48-9

Laser Typesetting
JEE-VEE Graphics, Delhi

Price: 1295/-

Printed
Vikas Computers, Delhi

Preface

Arms control is an old idea—almost as old as war itself. Since antiquity, it has been used as an instrument to prevent war. Arms control in modern times is also pursued to contain damage if war were to occur and to reduce the political and economic costs of defense. Human history is replete with numerous arms control initiatives. However, efforts to control arms have only a mixed record. Many arms control efforts were successful, while others were not, resulting in, in some cases, widespread and disastrous destruction.

Global, verifiable and non-discriminatory nuclear disarmament is a national security objective. India shall continue its efforts to achieve the goal of a nuclear weapon-free world at an early date. Since no-first use of nuclear weapons is India's basic commitment, every effort shall be made to persuade other States possessing nuclear weapons to join an international treaty banning first use. Having provided unqualified negative security assurances, India shall work for internationally binding unconditional negative security assurances by nuclear weapon states to non-nuclear weapon states.

Nuclear arms control measures shall be sought as part of national security policy to reduce potential threats and to protect our own capability and its effectiveness. In view of the very high destructive potential of nuclear weapons, appropriate nuclear risk reduction and confidence building measures shall be sought, negotiated and instituted.

Finally, at the global level, India is only likely to play a more positive role if it can be convinced that nuclear arms control reinforces its security interests and accepts that it need not weaponize its nuclear capability. China, as India's largest neighbour

Contents

and a nuclear weapon state, can contribute on both scores. Still, India's choice between the alternatives of nuclear arms control and nuclear armament will not ultimately be the result of a threat from China, or even of relations with Pakistan, but of considerations of international power and influence. An arrangement beyond Sino-Indian bilateral relations is necessary to the Indian role in the post-cold war nuclear order.

As the book addresses this crucial issue quite deftly, it is hoped that it would prove to be a source of great information for the reader.

—*Author*

1

Small Arms in South Asia

The proliferation and illicit use of small arms in South Asia can never be understood in isolation. This is as much a theoretical position, as it is a practical one. In view of recent developments at the local and global levels, particularly with the arrival and reproduction of globalisation, small arms had a qualitative transformation with respect to its proliferation and use. Never did the world see such an easy availability and at the same time grandeur yet demonic use of weapons that have been conventionally categorised as 'small.' It seems that the humane call of Bhupen Hazarika that 'We are in the same boat, brother!' has come to haunt us-from Chicago to Chittagong, from Jaffna to Johannesburg, from Bosnia to Baghdad-indeed, more dramatically yet more painfully. But lest we make a mistake in understanding the dynamics informing, influencing and reproducing the proliferation and illicit use of small arms, it is important that we take a critical account of the meaning of globalisation and its practical implications locally, nationally, regionally, and of course, internationally.

Globalisation, mainly because of its birth from a complex combination of multiple interactions, has given rise to a multiversity or multiple universes of knowledge and practices. Three precise modes could easily be identified. First is economic globalisation, second is reverse globalisation, and the third is subaltern globalisation. In each of these modes small arms play a precise and distinctive role. A closer exposition will make this clear.

ECONOMIC GLOBALISATION

The Globalisation meaning has been best captured by an OECD publication which, while crediting the term to Theodore Levitt who first used it in 1985 in his book, The Globalisation of Markets, sees globalisation as 'a seamless or borderless, global economy.' More concretely, it is informed by precise sets of economic activities with precise characteristics on a world scale. There exists a subtle difference between the 'internationalisation of economy' and 'globalisation' according to this perspective. While the former primarily refers to the internationalisation of trade and later on, the internationalisation of finance and investment, each coming in the wake of precise historical moments of capitalism, globalisation refers to the complex combination of all these but more importantly one that is inclusive of a thoroughly transformed production structure. The latter can be best described as the organisation and development of a denationalised form of production.

That is, multi-national or rather transnational companies now collect resources in several countries, process them in another several countries and finally, export the finished products to the rest of the world. A fully finished product, therefore, no longer has one single birthmark; it has multiple birthmarks since several countries have gone to produce it. A Compaq computer, in that sense, is no longer entirely American, or a Toyota car fully Japanese. The final product of both these items will have components made in several countries of the world. Put differently, unlike the previous internationalisation of things, in the globalisation phase of capitalism the thing itself is the product of the international or global market.

In this newer configuration, the non-state enterprises are often more critical than the state-oriented or state enterprises in the reproduction of capitalism. The need for safeguarding the non-state enterprises, therefore, is as vital as protecting the state enterprises. The outcome has been greater policing and diffusion of licit weapons, which often for reasons of pilferage and structural leakage end up in the market as illicit commodities.

Reverse Globalisation

The second meaning of globalisation is very much intrinsic to the developing country's craze for modernity, principally the organisation of the (post-colonial) nation state in the image of the modern 'Western' state. In some respect this has been well described by Nirad C. Chaudhuri as early as 1926 when Chaudhuri, while referring to 'a clash of civilisation' between the East and West, sarcastically noted that 'the real cultural role of the (colonised Indians) is to assimilate the ways of Europe' (1996:1,5). Put differently, if OECD's definition could be referred to as economic globalisation, the modernist aspirations of the developing or less developed countries could be referred to as reverse globalisation.

The global reach of Bollywood (India's film industry) and Indian restaurants are good examples of reverse globalisation, where the non-state forces of the East or that of the South are no less critical in channelising the development of the (culturally and intellectually colonised) less developed or developing countries. One critical outcome of reverse globalisation has been to develop militarily in the image of the modern West, bringing with it not only the military hardware, including small arms, developed in the West but also the impetus to produce such weapons at home. Often this has taken the form of joint collaboration between developed and developing countries with many of the small arms like AK-47, M16, G3, and even grenades produced and marketed as globalised items. Again, for reasons of pilferage and structural leakage many of these weapons end up in the market as illicit commodities.

Subaltern Globalisation

There is yet another type of interaction informing and reproducing globalisation. This is a complex mode and therefore requires greater care in its exposition. Critics have already referred to the mushrooming of global networks resisting economic globalisation as 'globalisation from below'. The latter includes a diverse group of people environmentalists, NGOs, religious groups, small farmers, labour unions (incidentally of both the developed and developing countries), women's movement, consumerists,

African debt relief campaigners, anti-sweatshop activists, and the like, all one way or another either critical of or directly suffering from and struggling against the impact of economic globalisation. Here the forces of the seemingly disempowered non-state have creatively joined hands to overcome the exploitation of the empowered non-state, i.e. the forces of economic globalisation. The subaltern nature of the resistance movements, particularly the networking, can hardly be minimised.

But then, there is a further subaltern variant to the whole notion of globalisation from below. This refers to the deepening of relationship between and amongst the 'dubious groups' and 'shadowy activities' ranging from smuggling of goods and people, illicit production and trading of small arms, money laundering, narco-production and trading, terrorism, and the like, and that again, across and beyond national, ethnic, racial, and even religious affiliations. The subalterns, particularly the poverty-ridden and marginalised population, become easy target of such groups and activities, but more importantly the state of being itself becomes a factor for certain groups of (relatively well off) people to rally support and even clandestinely work for their cause.

A protracted nature of poverty and marginality and a lack of substantive global concern also push them to seek informal or even criminal means to reproduce their lives or redress the situation. The complex networking at this level and in combination with the resistance movements against economic globalisation could be best referred to as subaltern globalisation. Here the subalterns, including their ardent supporters and sympathisers, are no less creative and empowered when it comes to organising and reproducing their activities at the global level, and that too often by challenging the overly empowered forces of economic globalisation.

Two things are worth pointing out here. First is the subtle connivance of the state machineries with the dubious forces in reproducing subaltern globalisation. In fact, the state machineries go on to empower the subaltern networks almost to their own peril, which brings us to the second point. Indeed, if economic globalisation is in the business of weakening the power of the state, the practices of subaltern globalisation are no less menacing and destructive to the state. According to Mittelman : '(Criminal) groups are alternative social organisations that, in some respects, challenge the power and authority of the state to impose its standards, codified as law. These groups constitute an alternative system by offering commerce and banking in black and gray markets that operate outside the regulatory framework of the state; buying, selling, and distributing controlled or prohibited commodities, such as narcotics; providing swift and usually discreet dispute resolution and debt collection without resorting to the courts; creating and maintaining cartels when state laws proscribe them; and arranging security for the so-called protection of businesses, as well as sheltering them from competitors, the state and rival criminals. There is no reason to doubt the destructive potential of subaltern globalisation. Even those resisting economic globalisation and joining ranks with the subalterns may find themselves at risk if and when the destructive potential of subaltern globalisation is played out with full ferocity and demonic intent. The use of small arms can hardly be underestimated here. A quick look at some of the practices of subaltern globalisation would provide credence to our contention.

SMALL ARMS TRADE

In the age of nuclear and other weapons of mass destruction, the vast majority of all warfare continues to be conducted using conventional weapons: machine rifles, grenades, landmines, explosives, and light rockets. These small arms, and the ability to obtain them, are the operational means of warfare. The much-touted efficiency of "high-tech" warfare based on computer-guided rockets and remote-controlled war machinery has been generally successful only as bombardment in advance of ground-based attack which ultimately depends on soldiers wielding hand-held weapons. Thus, even when blessed with unlimited war capability and unlimited weaponry options, militaries such as those of the United States and Russia depend on small arms to subdue populations and control territory. So do guerilla revolutionaries and those defending themselves against their own violently abusive governments. This essay will consider the issue of the global trade in small arms, examining its scope, its global economic underpinnings, its relationships to the economies of conflict-plagued countries, its particular connections to the current war in Sudan, and finally possible initiatives for reform of the global small arms trade.

The Scope of the Problem

As recently as World War II, the ability to prosecute war depended on developing the industrial capacity to produce these "small arms." During the Cold War, the United States and the Soviet Union provided conventional weapons for their respective client states fighting "proxy" wars. The high-geared military-industrial economies of the two leviathans have stimulated France, China, Germany, the UK, Italy, Ukraine, and Israel to compete in the lucrative worldwide business of weapons export. In 2002 these nine weapons-selling countries exported $14.8 billion in conventional weapons to the rest of the world. Forty percent of this staggering volume of weapons flows from Russia; 27% is shipped from the USA. The USA, UK, and France earned more in small arms sales to developing countries in 1998-2001 than they gave in aid.

The gigantism of this industry renders it a force in national economic policies. It is in the national interest of these nations, to some degree, to promote violent conflict and war around the world. As is apparent in the case of Sudan, the economic leverage of the weapons industry, including the small arms industry, may determine whether major first-world nations support or impede peace processes in war-torn countries. This positive self-interest that weapons-supplying first-world nations have in the negative interest — the active destruction and resulting impoverishment — of third-world nations is a very dark side of the economic colonialism that typifies neo-liberal economic globalization.

Classic game-theory analyses of arms race determinants assume arms development and production to come at the expense of a nation's economic well-being. While that may actually be true in terms of benefit to an entire nation's economy, it is *always* true that war yields positive economic benefit to national military industries, and that military industries hold disproportionate power over their governments' decision-making processes. In result, the world is flooded with weapons, and the potential to pursue violence is immediately and endlessly available to all. As Mary Kaldor notes, "violence is increasingly privatized both as a result of growing organized crime and the emergence of paramilitary groups." There are reported to be more than 639 million small arms in the world today; in the case of South Asia, 80% are in civilian (non-governmental) hands.

The availability of small arms is further assured through the worldwide financial deregulation that is a cornerstone of neo-liberal economic globalization. The deregulation of financial transactions has effectively rendered the financing of war exempt from national or international governance. Arms merchants and, significantly, diaspora supporters of civil conflicts are easily able to move funds instantly and covertly behind the screens of small states specializing in such banking services, thanks to the blessings of deregulated economic globalization. Weapons procurers are similarly enabled to operate with impunity, even when supplying arms illegally to the perpetrators of humanitarian crimes and genocides. Even when legal "controls" are in effect, sales and movement of small weapons to parties in conflict can proceed unabated. The illegal arms trade is estimated at more than (perhaps much more than) $1 billion per year. Conflict entrepreneurs — weapons manufacturers, gun-runners, merchant middle-men, and the weapons users themselves, profit both from the supply of weapons and from their use in protracted conflict.

During the Cold War massive supplies of conventional and more sophisticated weapons systems were pumped into client states by the Cold War powers, providing vast stores of machinery for ensuing post-Cold War wars. Weapons fed into the Afghanistan and Cambodian conflicts have been the foundation of supply for current South Asian violence. Massive supplies of weapons supplied to the Congo and Angola wars provided the stockpile for succeeding West African wars. The killing lives of such weapons may last many years. During the Cold War, the Coordinating Committee for Multilateral Export Controls (CoCom) operated as the Western self-regulation of which weapons and technologies were to be restricted. By 1989, however, the appeal of economic gains effectively overwhelmed security concerns. CoCom was disbanded in 1994, and first-world weapons producers have since fed arms to parties in conflict with unrestricted, free-market eagerness.

CAMPAIGN AGAINST ARMS TRADE

Campaign Against Arms Trade (CAAT) is a UK-based NGO and campaigning organisation working towards the abolition of the international arms trade. Founded in 1974 by a broad coalition of peace groups, CAAT is united in opposition to the military industrial complex and the growth of the private military industry. It argues that these organisations reinforce global militarism whilst undermining attempts by civil society and the United Nations to resolve disputes peacefully. CAAT's main focus is to end the influence of arms companies over the UK government, and works together with similar organisations in other countries to the same end. CAAT has grown in stature in recent years as a result of several high profile campaigns, particularly its legal challenge against the Serious Fraud Office's decision to suspend a corruption investigation into BAE Systems in 2007.

Current Issues

BAE Systems and Saudi Arabia Corruption Inquiry

BAE Systems formerly British Aerospace, is the world's third largest weapons trader. In September 1985 BAE was a signatory to the UK's largest ever arms deal, the Al Yamamah contract to provide military planes as well as servicing provisions to the government of Saudi Arabia. This ongoing contact has evolved through several phases to the present day and has thus made the company £43 billion pounds.

Shortly after the contract was signed however, corruption allegations began to surface concerning bribes paid to Saudi officials through a £60 million pound slush fund. On 12 September 2003 the Serious Fraud Office began an investigation into possible corruption. BAE are also the subject of four active SFO investigations for its dealings in Romania, the Czech Republic, South Africa and Tanzania, calling into question the general operating conduct of its agents. However on the 14th December 2006 the Government discontinued the Al Yamamah probe on the grounds that its conclusions may embarrass the Kingdom of Saudi Arabia and threaten Britain's national security.

CAAT in conjunction with the Corner House, an anti-corruption NGO, mounted a legal challenge to this decision, to assess if in curtailing the Serious Fraud Office's investigation the Government had acted illegally. Thus on 9 November 2007 the High Court in London granted a request for a judicial review of the decision. Subsequently, on the 10 April the conclusion of this review stated that the Government had indeed acted illegally in stopping the corruption investigation. Lord Justice Moses and Mr Justice Sullivan ruled that the Government had capitulated under intimidation from the government of Saudi Arabia and that "no-one whether within this country or outside, is entitled to interfere with the course of justice." BAE Systems continue to deny any impropriety stating the court had failed "to distinguish between a commission and a bribe."

Subsequently the SFO launched an appeal that was heard before the Appellate committee of the House of Lords on 7 and 8 July 2008. On the 30th July the House of Lords overturned the High Courts' ruling, and decreed that the SFO had acted lawfully in the interest of national security. Senior Peer Lord Bingham of Cornwall stated that "the director's decision was one he was lawfully entitled to make" but the ruling incited a chorus of condemnation from Nick Clegg in the House of Commons. The leader of the Liberal Democrats characterised the verdict as "a legal licence for international blackmail." The ruling also provoked considerable ire among anti-corruption campaigners and a string of NGO's. CAAT spokesman Symon Hill commented "BAE and the government will be quickly disappointed if they think that this ruling will bring an end to public criticism. Throughout this case we have been overwhelmed with support from people in all walks of life. There has been a sharp rise in opposition to BAE's influence in the corridors of power. Fewer people are now taken in by exaggerated claims about British jobs dependent on the arms trade. The government has been judged in the court of public opinion."

In response to the judicial review the Government has drafted a controversial clause of the Constitutional Reform Bill. This will grant the attorney-general the power to quash any further such investigations with immunity from judicial interference. CAAT and the Corner House have both condemned any such legislation as a perversion of justice which will erode the accountability of the executive and threaten the rule of law.

Closure of DESO

The Defence Export Services Organisation was an adjunct of the Ministry of Defence concerned with procuring contracts for private military companies to export arms to foreign governments. The closure of DESO had been a core campaigning aim of CAAT since its inception in 1974, and was their main focus in 2006. CAAT brought considerable pressure on the government concerning the ethics of some such trading, given that in 2004, UK arms export licenses were granted to 13 of the 20 'major countries of concern' identified by the Foreign and Commonwealth Office in its 2005 Human Rights Annual Report. CAAT also alleged that DESO unfairly privileged the interests of the arms companies and helped facilitate bribes to foreign officials. In response to this on 25 July 2007 Gordon Brown announced that DESO would indeed be shut down.

Chief Executive of BAE Systems Mike Turner condemned the decision by citing the damage it would do to Britain's export trade. CAAT argued that the closure of DESO is a step forward in transparency for the government. As a result it will be less hamstrung by lobbyists seeking to manipulate its human rights and budgetary policies.

In future export promotion will be the responsibility of UK Trade and Investment, the body that supports all UK exports. On 1 April 2008 the UKTI Defence and Security Organisation, which will be responsible for some of DESO's previous functions, was formed. The current head of UKTI DSO is Richard Paniguian CBE, a former BP executive. CAAT has pledged to monitor UKTI to make sure that military exports, (less than 2% of total UK exports in 2004), do not monopolise a disproportionate amount of its resources.

DSEi: Reed Elsevier Campaign

Defence Systems and Equipment International is one of the largest arms fairs in the world which takes place in London bi-annually, the last occurring in September 2007. From 2003 to May 2008 the DSEi was organised by Reed Elsevier, a publishing and information company, who acquired the previous organisers Spearhead in 2003. As CAAT is opposed to the existence of arms fairs, it campaigned to encourage Reed Elsevier to extricate itself from the arms industry.

There followed a sustained and concerted effort from academics, doctors and writers that use the company's products, who demanded they end their involvement with arms fairs on ethical grounds. This culminated in Reed's decision to sell its arms fairs to Clarion Events in June 2007, a sale which was completed in May 2008. However, CAAT intends to continue campaigning for the overall closure of DSEi and other arms fairs.

Clean Investment Campaign

From universities to local authorities CAAT has consistently sought to highlight areas where public bodies hold shares in companies trading in arms. On 9 July CAAT released research that 75 local authorities in the UK held such investments through their pension funds. It has argued that many council employees reject the notion that they should help to prop up such companies and continues to advocate a more ethical investment strategy.

The long standing Clean Investment campaign has had many successes in the past, one of the most significant occurring in 2001. In response to pressure from the CAAT Christian Network the Church of England redefined its investment criteria and confirmed it will no longer invest in arms companies. Despite excluding arms company holdings, the Church remained, in 2005, the second best performer of more than 1,000 funds over the previous decade.

Furthermore, from 2005 the CAAT Universities Network has met with considerable success in its campaign to advocate ethical investment across the UK. A report entitled 'Study War No More' has highlighted military funding and involvement within 26 British universities. CAAT facilitates research into the details of university investment portfolios which has helped students to mount their own campaigns for clean investment. This has resulted in many universities divesting their shares in the arms industry, whilst many more campuses continue to campaign for similar action to be taken.

Private Military Companies

Since the invasion of Iraq in March 2003, the use of 'private military companies' has become standard practice for countries such as the UK and the US. CAAT considers these contractors to be modern-day mercenaries.

The Geneva Convention may classify as a mercenary a civilian contractor who is "motivated to take part in the hostilities essentially by the desire for private gain and, in fact, is promised, by or on behalf of a party to the conflict, material compensation substantially in excess of that promised or paid to combatants of similar ranks and functions in the armed forces of that Party". Private military companies have become big business, with an estimated turnover world wide of $100 billion, and their use is set to rise.

The UK Government's Green Paper of 2002 on Private Military Companies prompted a debate on the privatisation of a whole range of military services which has been taking place with little comment, high profile cases such as Sandline in Sierra Leone notwithstanding. CAAT seeks an end to all mercenary activities. If this cannot be achieved at this point, the following controls are its minimum immediate requirements:

- a ban on all combat activities
- all dealings between Government departments and agencies and the military companies, other than operational details, to be in the public domain

- any contract entered into between a military company and a foreign government to stipulate a cash fee and no other benefit. No other business sharing directors or offices with the providers of security should be allowed to have any dealings with the foreign government concerned for a period of, say, five years. The ownership of the military companies should be made transparent.
- companies to be made responsible under UK law for any breaches of human rights or the laws of war that may be committed by their employees

CAAT is also committed to publishing research on the issue in order to raise public awareness of the ever increasing role mercenaries play in modern conflict zones.

Structure and Funding Network

CAAT has no formal membership structure. Individuals and affiliated groups (local branches of peace organisations, trade unions, churches, etc.), donate whatever they can afford towards the cost of running the campaign and receiving *CAAT News*, a bi-monthly magazine. There are also sponsoring groups who either took part in founding CAAT or have taken a major supporting role since. However 80% of CAAT's funding comes from individual donations.

CAAT is made up of grass-roots groups who come together to campaign for a variety of causes and issues surrounding its overall aims. In addition to local groups, CAAT also has a Christian Network, which looks at arms trade issues involving churches and mobilises Christians against the arms trade, (although CAAT as a whole includes members from many diverse faiths and those of no faiths). CAAT also has a Universities Network which involves students and university staff in campus-based campaigning. Potentially, other new networks can be formed at any time.

SUBALTERN GLOBALISATION AND THE ARMING OF THE NON-STATE

The element of subalternity in the resistance movements against economic globalisation (and the case could also be stretched to reverse globalisation) cannot be denied. The anti-globalisation protests in Seattle, Rome, Prague or Washington all tend to indicate that the subalterns or marginalised forces have been put into a dire situation because of economic globalisation. The protests are otherwise meant to highlight the grievances of the subalterns worldwide.

The resistance movements however in and by themselves do not reproduce the life and living of the subalterns. Mittelman has already indicated that 'where poverty is severe, criminal gangs flourish'. The link between poverty and criminality is less linear than what is seemingly suggested here. A state of subalternity in fact creates conditions that make people disinterested in the business of reproducing the power of the state. Mis-governance otherwise becomes the (dis)order of the day. People, particularly the subalterns, increasingly start depending on informal, often criminal, means for reproducing their livelihood. Even when requiring business or personal security they fall back on the power of the 'godfathers,' hired goons, mastans, and the like, than on the otherwise inept, often corrupt, governmental machineries.

A shadowy network of things and transactions gets reproduced and in the process destabilises not only the power of the state but also the power of the subalterns, indeed, making them more vulnerable and disempowered. This further creates grounds for fresh recruits and creative but demonic ventures for organising and reproducing subaltern globalisation.

Narco-terrorism

Narco-production and trading is a lucrative business in this region. In 2001 Myanmar surpassed Afghanistan as the largest producer of illicit opium and heroin in the world. To provide some knowledge of the amount, 865 metric tons of opium was produced in Myanmar in 2001, almost all of which were processed into heroin and sold to the illicit market both within and outside the region. This is more than double the amount of illicit opium that is available in other heroin-producing countries, such as India, Columbia, Mexico, or Laos. It may be mentioned that there exists a vibrant but complex relationship between opium growers and heroin producers, drug dealers and consumers, security and custom officials, high-risk investors and money launderers, and that again, not only nationally but also regionally and globally. As the following U.S. Drug Enforcement Agency report suggests :

'Opium poppy cultivation and heroin refining take place in remote, mountainous border regions. Armed ethnic groups such as, the United Wa State Army, the Kokang Chinese, and the Myanmar National Democratic Alliance Army control the cultivation areas, refine opium into heroin, and also produce methamphetamine. Associates of these organisations from other Asian nations have shipped tons of heroin from Burma to the United States within the past decade. The largest single heroin seizure in the United States consisted of 486 kilograms of Burma-produced heroin that the US Customs Service discovered in a containerised shipment of plastic bags from Southeast Asia, via Taiwan, en route to a warehouse in Hayward, California, in May 1991'.

But Myanmar, apart from being a member of the infamous 'Golden Triangle', is also close to yet another major narco-producing region, the 'Golden Crescent.' In smuggling heroin from Myanmar beyond the region and the continent both India and Bangladesh are used as transit points. This further exacerbates problems related to narco-terrorism in the region. In fact, one critical problem arising out of the confluence of two major narco-producing and trading regions is the cementing of a diabolic relationship between insurgent groups, arms dealers and narco-terrorism. Such a relationship is quite common in and around Thai-Myanmar, Indo-Myanmar and Bangladesh-Myanmar borders. Not that all the insurgent groups engage in narco-production or narco-trafficking but it has been found that almost all of them have regularly taxed and exhorted money from the traffickers while providing protection to the latter for conducting trafficking in drugs. There are several critical implications of this.

Firstly, the transnational narco-networks, now backed by armed insurgents, make anti-narco-production or anti-narco-trafficking drive immensely difficult. And given the terrain (both physical and topographical) in which the insurgents and the traffickers operate there is now all the more reason to believe that the nationally-organised military or coercive solutions may not be the correct way of overcoming the menace of narco-terrorism.

Secondly, weapons, particularly small arms, in the hands of both the insurgents and traffickers become more rampant, indeed, to the point of threatening the law and order situation in the vicinity. A large portion of the money received from taxing and extorting the narco-traffickers goes on to purchase small, at times sophisticated, arms for the insurgents.

Finally, subaltern aspirations get entwined between insurgency and narco-terrorism, almost to the point of blurring the distinction between the two. While this becomes handy for the state machineries in the strategy of depicting the insurgents as narco-traders and winning back the support of the members of the dissenting communities, it often leads them to quick-fix remedies with little or no results. As the World Bank-sponsored study on Indo-Bangladesh border smuggling once pointed out that 'Ordinary men, women and even children participate in smuggling as couriers, porters and rickshaw pullers', which only indicates that the subalternity of smuggling or even narco-terrorism is far more complex than what is readily understood. There is therefore no guarantee that the narco-menace would discourage the subalterns from joining the trade.

Money Laundering

Narco-terrorism would not make much headway without the practice of money laundering. It is the latter that provides the required funds for the production and later on, shipments of the narcotics across regions and continents. The weakness and corruption prevalent in the banking system of the region remain easily susceptible to money laundering. Often drug traffickers invest their drug profits in the country's infrastructure and legitimate businesses. The drug trafficker cum money launderer otherwise with the connivance of the bank and the state end up running legal businesses! When such a structure comes into being it becomes impossible to eradicate narco-trafficking and all the corroborating agencies, including money laundering and terrorism, unless and until the state itself goes through a sustained period of reforms and restructuring.

At times certain other structural factors are also responsible in reproducing money laundering, as is the case with the stateless but relatively well off Rohingyas living abroad. As stateless and few licit areas to invest, these Rohingyas have no option but to launder money to various Rohingya nationalist or insurgent groups, mainly to fulfil their subaltern aspirations in the northern Arakan region of Myanmar. That a part of this money would be used in purchasing arms and later on in insurgent or terrorist activities can never be ruled out.

Let me at this stage clarify one point. Once a subaltern struggle takes a military or violent turn, it cannot escape from being linked to the various networks of subaltern globalisation. This is because in order to sustain the subaltern movement through military means there is a dire need for both cash and arms, indeed, over and above the committed recruits of fighters. Often the funds as well as the arms come via the network of dubious groups and shadowy activities.

In recent times, more so in the post-cold war era, this has been the case practically with all the militant groups, including those directly involved in subaltern movements. Tamil Tigers is a good instance, which despite having being funded by the Tamil diaspora, did not hesitate to enter into the business of selling heroin and hashish for financing arms purchases. Again, take the case of Kachin Independence Organisation, a militant group fighting for the interests of the Kachin people within Myanmar, which with five thousand regular 'armed' soldiers remains 'heavily involved in the heroin trade'. This is not something unexpected in view of the protracted nature of these movements and the cost that is involved in sustaining them. Even a modest costing will show that the need for cash is quite substantial. For instance, if we take that a militant group is made up of 3000 fighters or terrorists and that each is paid a monthly allowance of Rs. 5000, the need for cash just for paying the terrorists every month comes to Rs. 15,000,000 (or USD 319,148 at the current exchange rate), which is quite substantial in local standards. Often the militant groups for the sake of maintaining their freedom and this is more so in the aftermath of the cold war shy away from a particular source of funding. Instead, they now prefer diversifying fund-raising, which at times includes money from taxing the narco-traders or even joining in the business of selling drugs and arms. The following report is a good indicator of the militant groups' involvement in arms trafficking and making money from it :

Around 100 AK-47 rifles reached different gangs of criminals in the port city (of Chittagong) and its surrounding areas from the insurgents of Arakan state of Myanmar staying in deep forests across the Bangladesh border.... Arakan insurgents sold the rifles and some other sophisticated weapons to these gangs through a clandestine channel of local kingpins of arms dealers and smugglers on various occasions in the past few years. This brings us to the third and final area, the issue of illicit small arms.

2

Small Arms Proliferation: The Arms Control Challenge

Over the course of the past decade small arms have become the primary choice of weapons for political and criminal groups in fueling armed conflicts, wars, massacres, ethnic cleansing and human rights violations. That, in no small measure is due to the fact that small arms are too readily available and too inexpensive, while at the same time requiring only minimal training, logistics and support to maintain and operate. 300 manufacturers in 74 countries produce small arms, of which well over 500,000,000 are believed to be in circulation, inside or outside of state regulatory controls. Between 1985 and 1995, there has been a twenty-five per cent increase in the number of producers. Moreover, low-end sell-offs or give-aways of "surplus" small arms increase supply as well. As a result, there is an overabundance of inexpensive small arms glutting the world market. Yet, to date the international trade in small arms remains largely unregulated.

Principal sources of small arms include: small arms acquired for legal purposes and misused (e.g. human rights violations and external aggression), small arms acquired for legal purposes and sold/stolen; small arms for crime and unintentional injuries (gray market), and illegally manufactured or trafficked small arms (black market). Whatever the perspective, i.e. peace-building versus crime prevention or arms control, draining these supply sources is imperative. Measures must be devised to limit the access to small arms (licensing, storage, embargoes), to reduce the supply of small arms (control of manufacture, identification, tracing etc.) and to reduce the demand for small arms (amnesties, buy-backs). The weapons of violence must be brought back into the control of the state, with the state itself being made accountable for its deeds. This essentially means empowering the state at one level, and using all tools available to induce more responsible behaviour on its part, at another. The two approaches must be mutually compatible.

The permanent members of the UN Security Council alone are responsible for 85% of the global arms trade. 40% of the worldwide flow of small arms is attributed to illicit trafficking and the majority of illicit weapons are proven to originate in the licit trade. Getting these governments to tighten national controls and to accept strengthened international standards for legal arms transfers should lend itself to reducing supply, significantly. Small arms transfer policies should be designed to support transfers that do not destabilize or threaten regional peace and security. With production monitored and limited and exports restricted and tighter controlled a reduced supply should restrict access and decrease overall circulation.

Given that small arms are produced, acquired and exported for legitimate purposes it is not, as opposed to the global campaign to ban landmines, appropriate to seek a ban. Rather, EPG's overall objective is to assist in efforts to curtail the supply of illicit small arms. Such an objective will require a constructive parallelism among a range of politically and legally binding instruments, involving operative and normative measures which pertain both to the licit as well as the illicit trade, and which address both conflict prevention and conflict resolution. As one building block toward this overall objective, the group's goal is to promote a cooperative regulatory approach built around a small arms control regime (SACR), broad in scope and global in reach and to consist of, on the preventive side, (1) a Small Arms Register, (2) strengthened national export controls, and (3) an international code of conduct. On the reduction side, to consist of weapons collection programs as integral to peace agreements and post-conflict demobilization and reconstruction programs as well as to conflict prevention strategies. Universal, comprehensive and non-discriminatory SACR would integrate current efforts based on a variety of approaches: crime prevention, arms control, firearms regulation, human rights, development, gun safety etc. It should, therefore, not be viewed as detracting from or interfering with ongoing, local, national or regional efforts. Rather, SACR can be said to provide a set of common standards around which these efforts can be harnessed.

Cooperative arms regulation and disarmament must address security and developmental concerns as functional corollaries and must be integrated into national programs as well as into international cooperation efforts. While the task is a daunting one, many international development agencies have already taken steps to incorporate security sector reform and other conflict prevention strategies into their assistance programs. Integral to cooperative disarmament, preventive measures must pursue two objectives: first, to limit and control availability and access to small arms (supply side) and secondly, to reduce the demand for such weapons (demand side). On the supply side such an approach necessitates measures aimed at effectively regulating legal transfers between states based on a principle of responsible restraint, controlling the availability, use and storage of small arms within states, preventing and combating illicit transfers, collecting and removing surplus arms from both civil society and regions of conflict, increasing transparency and accountability, support for research and information sharing.

Correspondingly, on the demand side, the international community must commit to helping reverse cultures of violence through support for the reform of the security sector (both police and military) in affected states as fundamental to good governance, through the promotion of norms of civilian non-possession and of government restraint, by enhancing demobilization and reintegration programs for ex-combatants, by halting the abhorrent use of child fighters and by effectively combating the culture of impunity that fuels the illicit arms trade. Also, reduction measures must be devised to secure, destroy or otherwise responsibly dispose of small arms that are already in circulation, inside or outside of legal possession. The international donor community should establish collection and buy-back programs as well as other mechanisms to identify and promote best practices and to ensure adequate financial support. This is of particular importance with respect to "surplus" military weapons during a peace process. Integral to peace accords, combatants must be demobilized, disarmed and weapons surrendered safely destroyed. There are important lessons to be learned from small arms collection and destruction (Mozambique, Mali, Liberia) reintegration of ex-combatants into productive civilian life (Cambodia, Philippines), post-conflict reconstruction (Cambodia, Bougainville) and the reform of police, judicial and penal systems (Cambodia, Papua New Guinea). Law enforcement efforts in States where the illicit use of small arms is particularly severe should be supported as well. The international donor community should cooperate with affected states in the establishment of incentive-based weapons collection programs as well as other mechanisms to identify and promote best practices and to ensure adequate financial support. The UN can develop centres for excellence pertaining to certain aspects of the problem area, such as arms collection programs, security sector reform and security arrangements for post-conflict development. Technical and financial resources are needed and the UN can play a role in mobilizing these resources.

SMALL ARMS PROLIFERATION

The proliferation of small arms is a complex and increasingly international issue. There are important linkages between the non-proliferation, arms control and disarmament dimensions of small arms problems, on the one hand, and firearms regulation (i.e., gun control and criminality) dimensions, on the other. The problems caused by small arms are primarily regional, sub-regional and internal (i.e., within states) in nature. As a result, while useful things may be done on a global level, a primary focus for practical solutions would appear to be in regional, sub-regional and internal action. It is important, therefore, to develop a body of relevant case studies of the impact of small arms proliferation in particular regions as a basis for policy action. This project will examine the extent of small arms trade and proliferation in two geographical areas of East Asia – Southeast Asia and the Russian Far East. These two areas have significant possibility of experiencing small arms proliferation problems because of ethnic, cultural and political diversity, decades of post-colonial violence, and inadequate policing in both regions, and the emergence of major organized crime in the latter. The general problem of sub-state weaponry is not unique to the two regions, of course, but it is a particular aggravation to government and social order there. From Canada's perspective the problem may become larger as arms sales directly affect maritime trade and state stability in the regions, enter or pass through our territory, or involve criminal organizations within Canada.

The topic of our research is illicit trafficking of small arms and light weapons, as defined by the UN General Assembly. However in some cases it is hard to draw a distinct line between illicit and "legal" arms proliferation, in cases when high-rank state structures are involved in the above activity. The latter cases are also included into the scope of this research.

The Case of Southeast Asia

Southeast Asia saw a perverse "peace dividend" of small arms proliferation as early as 1975, with the end of the Vietnam War. An unknown quantity of weapons flowed out of Indo-China at that time into surrounding states, to guerrilla groups and pirates who plied the waters of Southeast Asia. The uneven development between major cities in the region and the more traditional rural regions, combined with the relatively weak presence of state police and military power in rural areas, and the mobility of watercraft, provided opportunities for arms traders to carry on their commerce undisturbed. Reports of rogue Chinese military trading in small arms must also be examined. Fallout from the recent "financial meltdown" in the region may also exacerbate crime growth in the near future.

The Case of the Russian Far East

The end of the Cold War has had a direct effect on the phenomenon of small arms proliferation in Asia and elsewhere.

The arms buildup in the Soviet Union was both in nuclear and conventional weapons, and with the end of Communism, the rationale for the heavy armaments declined precipitously. Moreover, the demoralization and impoverishment of Russian society and the Red Army has weakened government control over weaponry, which has become a commodity of trade in many cases. The socalled Russian Mafia, which had existed throughout the Soviet period, was lured by the illicit arms trade to facilitate the export of weapons.

Implications

The widespread demand for small weapons has been exacerbated by breakdown of local security and easy access. Relatively simple technology also means that manufacture and assembly does not require advanced industrial techniques. The model of the drug trade may be applicable, and indeed, one of the findings of the research is the linkage of the drug and small arms trade through the same trafficking routes and criminal organizations (not unlike the Latin American experience). Drugs and arms share some of the following characteristics in the two regions under study:

1. Widespread demand for the product;
2. Relatively high value per unit;
3. Relative ease of transportation;
4. Relative difficulty of detection;
5. High profit margin;
6. Corrosive effects on law enforcement within states;
7. Manufacture, shipment, and distribution requires illicit networks, which further undermine law and order; and
8. Long-range harm to society in the diversion of scarce resources to non-productive ventures.

Arms and drugs both have legitimate roles in society, when controlled and used for positive ends – police and defence in the former, and medical purposes in the latter (opiates are used for painkilling and sleep inducement). To the extent that the drug trade model is applicable to small arms proliferation, the above eight characteristics can provide entry points for reducing small arms flows, as follows:

1. Reduce supply and demand for the product;
2. Interdict transportation;
3. Improve detection capability and technology;
4. Clean up police and government corruption; and,
5. Improve enforcement capabilities, including international cooperation.

The Japanese have been successful in practically eliminating small weapons from society, and some lessons for Asia can be learned there. Unless the problem of small arms proliferation is brought under control, civil disorder and violence may become more widespread in the East Asian region. Drugs and small weapons are criminalized because they encourage and facilitate further crimes. Drugs create a dependency which can drive persons to engage in robbery and prostitution to acquire illegal substances, moving out of productive and responsible habits necessary to sustain social integrity. Guns decrease the vulnerability of criminals who undertake greater risks and anti-social actions, knowing that their weapons escalate the cost of challenging their actions.

But drugs also have major differences with small arms. Some trade in the latter is legitimate, as long as there is government sanction, while the illicit drug trade is practically proscribed universally.

Also, illicit drugs have accelerated the spread of diseases such as hepatitis and HIV, affecting individuals far beyond users. The indirect effect of small weapons is much more limited. Finally, the end users of weapons are usually men, and these tend to have profiles of greater criminality and aggressiveness than the average population, while drug users tend to be more passive and of both sexes. Most importantly, the trade in small weapons is an area which lends itself best to detection and reduction in the experience of arms control and verification. The legitimate production, distribution, and deployment of large and small weapons has been the jurisdiction and central interest of the arms control community. Accounting for disposition of large as well as light weapons, for example, has been one of the activities of the Neutral Nations Supervisory Commission (NNSC) under the 1953 Military Armistice Agreement in Korea. Other arms control agreements in other areas of the world have also included small weapons in their provisions.

SOUTHEAST ASIA

Scope of Research

The illicit movement of small arms and light weapons into, within and out of Southeast Asia, predominantly through illegal channels and the black market, is a dangerous phenomenon. Borrowing the definition used by the United Nations, illicit trafficking is the movement of weapons that is "contrary to the laws of States and/or international law." This phenomenon is of growing concern because it has the potential to undercut government efforts at establishing stability and order. Also, its potential disruption towards legitimate commercial activities can cause serious harm to economic and social development within the region. The illicit movement of small arms is a human security concern since it has the potential to fuel increased numbers and levels of violent crimes. This perception mainly arises from the fear that there would be a surge in criminal activities resulting from increased economic hardship, which is induced presently by the region's financial turmoil. Violent crimes, in turn, could present a destabilizing force undermining state sovereignty. Governments in Southeast Asia (and the rest of Asia, in general) are worried about the growing illicit trade in small arms because a number of factors have allowed it to flourish steadily:

- inadequate controls against illicit weapons production, exports and imports at the national level due to poorly trained and/or corrupt officials;
- financial and technological difficulties in implementing effective controls;
- lack of coordination and cooperation among regional states in monitoring the circulation and supply of weapons from within and outside of the region; and,

- non-existence of international or regional agreements on controlling the small arms trade (licit and illicit).

The security impact of illicit small arms movement is not confined to the region. Regional ports are becoming popular sites for transshipping weapons around the world, including destinations in the Middle East and possibly North America. Taking this argument into consideration, the small arms proliferation in Southeast Asia could have significant implications for Canada.

China

The People's Republic of China (PRC) may be one of the major sources of small arms proliferation in Southeast Asia. According to media reports, Chinese arms manufacturers are known to be involved in illegal production. The central government determines levels of production for each manufacturer, but many of the factories have produced quantities beyond these levels. Surplus arms are sold through illicit channels for the sake of profits. Officials in Beijing blame this condition on the lack of centralized regulations. However, regulations alone will not solve the problem. Although China recently adopted strong laws against the illicit possession, production and transfer of small arms, such laws may only limit the growth of "cottage" production (which has been growing rapidly). The laws' ability to make an impact against the wellconnected, larger state manufacturers remains doubtful. For example, two firms, Poly Technologies and China Northern Industries (Norinco), are connected to central government officials. The former is a defence conglomerate controlled by the General Staff of the People's Liberation Army (PLA) while the latter reports to the State Council under the Prime Minister. Having entered an era of capitalism, small arms production in China is also increasingly governed by the market — the demand for such weapons within China and in neighbouring states have grown as well as the profits to be had. Current conditions in the arms manufacturing industry contribute to this trend:

- factory managers resort to illicit sales to make up for capital shortages resulting from a decline in "legal" demand for small arms;

- the lack of competitiveness, which result from outdated technology, leads to dumping of weapons; and
- corruption among officials and lack of supervision of surplus weapons result in increased thefts. Beijing attempts to manage the problem through identifying and halting proliferation at its sources, increasing border and port controls as well as launching a campaign to seize banned weapons. Nevertheless, the obstacles are daunting.

North Korea

Weapons from North Korea have also circulated throughout the region and beyond. Some have been confiscated in Hong Kong and most of these were believed to be destined for the Middle East. North Korean weapons range from small arms (machine guns, rifles and grenade launchers) to high tech missile components. Specific information about arms production in the DPRK is scarce, and efforts to assess small arms transfers from North Korea are difficult. North Korea has the additional incentive of needing weapons sales to earn hard currency to buy food to alleviate the ongoing famine as well as other goods.

Russia

Many of the small arms that have been intercepted and confiscated point to Russia as another major source of supply. Some of these weapons were left over from past conflicts in Indochina (Cambodia and Vietnam), but there are signs that new Russian small arms are also in circulation. Cambodia and Vietnam import Russian weapons for defence purposes, but there is a possibility that theft and corruption among military officials have allowed weapons to fall into non-military hands. Such conditions may be more prevalent in Cambodia, where stability has been uncertain since last year's coup.

Vietnam and Cambodia

Vietnam is another source of small arms in the region. Seizure of weapons from Vietnamese trawlers (some of the Vietnamese "fishermen" appear to be former military personnel) in the South

China Sea raises the possibility that Vietnamese military stores are being looted by soldiers and that weapons leftover from past conflicts are making their way into neighbouring states. There is demand for small arms in Vietnam, but the country is increasingly becoming a transshipment area for weapons originating from China and Russia. The weapons enter Vietnam through its porous northern borders and move to its ports before they are loaded onto cargo ships. Russian weapons are also arriving directly at Vietnamese ports where they are further dispersed throughout the region and possibly beyond. Cambodian weapons originate from left over caches of the war against Vietnam as well as continued Khmer Rouge insurgency which had made the country a "killing field" from the mid 1970s until early 1990s. Last year's coup, the ensuing violence and the breakdown of the UN peace-building mission may not have changed these conditions. The demand for small arms has probably risen as the sense of national security diminishes and Cambodians seek personal security through the possession of firearms.

Establishing Patterns of Proliferation

Patterns of proliferation described in this chapter should not be assessed as hard data, and are based on analysis of media reports of intercepted small arms movement throughout the region. According to one source, in general the proliferation of small arms is "not random but highly patterned" and it can be controlled effectively through identifying likely channels of supply. Another characteristic of weapons movement through a particular channel is that such a movement often goes in both directions. For example, when illicit Chinese-made machine guns are confiscated in Vietnam, it is apparent that Vietnamese weapons could enter China through the same channel of supply. By keeping these factors in mind, our understanding of the small arms proliferation in the region would be more comprehensive. Small arms proliferation in Southeast Asia is often linked to the drug trade. It is believed that drug cartels in Myanmar are receiving small arms from Chinese sources. This claim may be valid considering that the southwestern corner of China is known as the "Dark Channels" of illicit activities.

It is possible that Chinese weapons are traded for drugs; although information on this remains sketchy. Burmese drug lords have also been receiving small arms from Cambodia. These weapons are usually transported overland through Thailand. The Thai government has attempted to step up controls but high levels of corruption among customs and security officials has undermined such efforts. Chinese weapons are also making their way into Vietnam. However, it is unclear whether the weapons are intended for Vietnamese markets, or if Vietnam is only used as a transshipping site. This is important considering that Vietnam is already saturated with small arms left over from past conflicts as well as those which recently occurred in neighbouring Cambodia. Furthermore, Chinese sources claim that the Vietnamese are smuggling weapons into China, reinforcing the "dual-direction" argument of small arms smuggling.

Small arms from Vietnam have been found on fishing trawlers off the coast of Malaysia on the South China Sea. Malaysian officials argue that these cases do not represent a serious threat because the coastal guards have only confiscated fourteen small weapons from 1990 to 1994. Malaysian optimism is countered by the fact that such confiscations occurred on several occasions, indicating a patterned movement. Actual interception may indicate only the tip of the iceberg. Vietnamese small arms have also been reported circulating in the Philippines, with weapons making their way through methods similar to those in the Malaysian case above. In most cases, illicit weapons were found after the Vietnamese trawlers had been detained for illegal entry. Manila points to rebels in the southern island of Mindanao as the most likely recipients of these weapons. One of the rebel factions, the Moro National Liberation Front (MNLF), admits to obtaining small arms from abroad but has not identified a country source. These patterns of small arms proliferation do not exhaust those in the region, but do indicate some of the better-known channels of supply.

East Asian Ports

The region's ports play a major role in facilitating proliferation. The lack of controls on the movement of goods often allows the ports to be used as sites for transshipping small arms. Arms dealers see these ports as effective channels for dispersing their merchandise throughout the region and beyond. Hong Kong, Taiwan and many of the ports in ASEAN countries share this problem because of the following characteristics:

- the large volume of goods passing through the ports daily;
- frequent corruption and lack of professionalism among customs and security (the military, police, coast guard) officials;
- states' reluctance to impose harsh controls for fear of losing competitiveness;
- financial and technological deficiencies which prevent the development of effective control measures; and
- lack of coordination and cooperation among the region's customs and security officials.

In the case of Hong Kong, former British security officials have noted the problem. Although the demand for small arms in Hong Kong is not high, the territory is a magnet to weapons because its docks are used for licit and illicit transshipment. Hong Kong is strategically located at the crossroads of Northeast and Southeast Asia as well as being the region's gateway to Europe, North America and the Middle East. Although officials claim that Hong Kong's shipping controls are very effective, the port's high volume of traffic is enough reason for arms dealers to take the risk. A tight security net around Hong Kong is neither viable nor seen as desirable because it would severely restrict legitimate trade. The weapons that are transshipped here not only originate from mainland China but also from neighbouring countries such as North Korea. In 1995, a third of the Chinese weapons confiscated originated from PLA sources and have ranged from small arms to high-tech missile components. The situation is worsening because China's harsh internal crackdown on illicit small arms trade has resulted in a surge of weapons movement from the rest of the country to the southern provinces and into Hong Kong. In Guangdong and other areas around Hong Kong violent criminal activities have been on the rise in the last two years.

In addition to Hong Kong, small arms are making their way to Taiwan. Suspected weapons carrying ships from mainland China have been reported unloading cargoes at several ports on the island. It is still not clear whether Taiwan is the final destination of these weapons or if it simply serves as a transshipping site or both. There have been examples of Taiwan serving as a transit point: the 2,000 AK-47 machine guns that were confiscated in San Francisco about two years ago had been transported by Chinese and Taiwanese citizens. The demand for small arms in Taiwan is high among criminal elements and a report in 1996 also suspects that the Chinese government may be supplying prointegration groups on the island. In addition to the discovery of Chinese weapons, the Taiwanese security apparatus has also found caches of small arms that originate from Sabah, Malaysia. The existence of weapons supplier other than just the Chinese supports the view that Taiwan is a possible hub in a network of illicit small arms trade in the region.

Ports in Southeast Asian countries have been identified as having some of the least effective antismuggling controls in the world (especially against drugs and small arms). The United States has pressured members of the Association of Southeast Asian Nations (ASEAN) to increase control mechanisms at their ports. However, the ASEAN countries have not been responsive. As in the situation in Hong Kong and Taiwan, the lack of effective anti-smuggling controls is a result of the factors. Most of the ASEAN states, especially Singapore, argue that increased controls would seriously hamper legitimate trade and make their ports unattractive to shipping companies.

PROLIFERATION OF SMALL ARMS AND LIGHT WEAPONS IN SOUTH ASIA

According to the UN Deputy Secretary General, Louise Fréchette, 'No region, no country is immune from the devastating consequences of the proliferation of small arms and light weapons..., [which] severely hampers social and economic development.' South Asia is no exception to how SALW poses a non-traditional security threat. Regardless of age, gender, status or location, all are targets.

Moreover, even children can be trained on how to use them. Private ownership of SALW is widespread and they can be obtained very cheaply. The SALW firearms in South Asia mostly originate from western nations. The spread of SALW grew in the wake of Afghan War during the 70s and 80s as refugee communities and volunteers were co-opted along side the regular cadres to fight the Soviet Army, and they had to be armed. Similarly, the end of declared war in Cambodia made available large numbers of small weapons that eventually found their way into Sri Lanka and northeastern India.

There are now an estimated 75 million firearms in South Asia, 63 million of which are in civilian hands. India and Pakistan overwhelmingly account for most of the weapons (40 million and 20 million respectively) where there is local production as well, while civilians in Nepal and Sri Lanka own an estimated 3 million weapons. Non-State actors are getting hold of government weapons and re-exporting them to armed groups fighting insurgencies in other countries.

The possession of small arms by politicians is also a growing problem across the subcontinent as owning private militia has become both a status symbol, as well as political clout against adversaries. Despite state regulations, several political leaders have not surrendered their arms to their government and still hold unlicensed arms. Politicians use these weapons to intimidate opponents and voters, patronise the underworld and criminal syndicates in order to protect themselves and thus pose a serious threat to the democratic process itself.

In Bangladesh, most of the weapons in circulation are those that were not collected after its 1971 independence war. Bangladesh is also being used as a corridor for smuggling firearms. Currently, Bangladesh has more than 200,000 small arms and most of these are with various organised criminal gangs and their political godfathers. There are about 80 crime syndicates around the country of which more than 28 are active in Dhaka alone. Politicians, too, use armed private militia to protect themselves, as well as to intimidate opponents. Law-makers are also turning a blind eye both to border patrol agents who are poorly equipped and to police officers who rent out their arms to criminals and terrorists. Clandestine manufacturers operate small operations that can be set up, dismantled and relocated overnight. In 2002, Bangladesh introduced tighter controls on firearms, but the problem remains.

Indian's record of small arms is the highest in the region which accounts for around 40 million contraband firearms. In India, all possible problems associated with the proliferation of small arms are to be found: illegal manufacture, theft from State arsenals, licensing loopholes, lax enforcement, cross-border smuggling, political violence, unregulated private security and a movie culture that often glorifies firepower and revenge by those defiant of authority. In India, small arms have eroded human rights, weakened democratic institutions, and polarised ethnic, religious, economic and political differences between citizens. Tensions between Hindu and Muslim groups in India under state patronage are one of the country's major sources of violence. In early 2002, up to 2000 Muslims were massacred in India in state of Gujarat. India also banned 32 organisations under the Prevention of Terrorism Act (POTA) for their activities. Although the Government of India (GoI) has taken several steps it still faces the problems of proliferation of SALW. Currently New Delhi is in the process of drafting a proposal to the United Nations seeking a global ban on small-arms sales to non-state actors. According to reports from a senior Home Ministry official, 'If a global ban is achieved, it would help to improve the security situation in the country.'

Nepal has been suffering from destabilising effects of SALW in the hands of its Maoists. About a decade ago, an aerial fire or the use of tear gas in Nepal would have caused a national hue and cry and national/international coverage of the news. Now, even two digit death statistics have become routine news. Deaths and injuries from small arms have become like an 'epidemic' in Nepal. While the main sources of proliferation of small arms are the Maoist insurgency, criminality and the political elite are no less responsible.

The Maoists rebels have stolen their weapons from police outposts and other government arsenals, while other criminal gangs are engaged in smuggling drugs for guns and money-laundering along the Indian border. Women are often used as carriers of small arms in illicit trafficking. It is estimated that one-third of the Maoist fighters are women. At the community level it is often known who owns arms and where they are kept. After the restoration of democracy in 1993, politicians resorted to all available means to win elections, including armed intimidation. Although a tentative ceasefire agreement was signed between the Government and the Maoists, but the proliferation of SALW remains unabated.

The ratio of SALW proliferation in Pakistan is the second highest in the region. In Pakistan there is a close linkage between organised groups, narcotics, money-laundering, terrorism activities and illicit trade in SALW. The proliferation of SALW and terrorism emerged as one of the main problems after the 1979 Soviet invasion of Afghanistan, when the US covertly armed thousands of 'Mujahedeen' with millions of SALWs, a great number of which eventually found their way into Pakistan along with the refugees who sought asylum. Pakistan's indigenous arms manufacturing cottage industry in the northwest tribal areas named as 'Darra Adamkhel' has fuelled-up the conflict-prone legacy of society with millions of small arms.

Darra's 'father-and-son' arms industry has existed for generations as a family legacy and traditionally, as a cottage arms production industry, has been outside the jurisdiction of central authorities. According to recent estimates, Darra employs more than 400,000 people. Prior to the Soviet invasion of Afghanistan in 1979, these shops produced mainly repeating rifles. The steady influx of weapons from various sources during the war enhanced the local manufacturer's knowledge, skills and production capacities.

The Darra region annually produces approximately 20,000 units of all kinds of weapons, including AK-47. It is estimated that in the past 20 years as a result of on going antagonisms between tribes, sectarianism, ethnicity, terrorism, organised crimes and poor law and order situation have sharpened into ethnic and community divides. Gun-related violence has resulted in more than 500,000 killings around the country. In 2001, the Government of Pakistan (GoP) launched a country-wide anti-arms drive in a bid to curb the 'Kalashnikov culture.' The Government devised a multi-pronged and phased 'de-weaponisation' strategy which includes: banning the display of weapons in public, the buying back of arms, recovering illicit arms and regulating production in the tribal areas. Initially a public awareness campaign was launched with an amnesty period for the surrender of illicit SALWs. After the expiry of the amnesty period, campaign for weapons collection and recovery were launched. Until 2003, around 250,000 illicit SALW firearms of different categories and types were recovered or confiscated, in addition to large amount of ammunition. While this ambitious effort has been praised nationally and internationally, Pakistan civil society is calling for a broader policy framework to address the underlying challenges of under-development which lead to proliferation, namely: the need for economic incentives as an alternative for 'culture of weaponisation'. Despite the official ban on sale and purchase of non-licensed weapons, unauthorised arms and ammunition remain in circulation and the illegal arms trade and gunrunning continues.

The status of proliferation of SALW in Sri Lanka can be attributed to many factors such as the internal armed conflicts, arms and political campaigns, arms held by deserters and criminals, as well as arms owned by private security firms and deteriorating public safety due to criminal activities. One of the main primary sources of SALW proliferation is the internal conflict between Government and the LTTE which has caused more than 65,000 deaths. Although a ceasefire was signed in February 2002, between Government and the LTTE, the circulation of weapons will continue to be a security threat to ordinary Sri Lankans. Meanwhile, it has now become common practice for politicians to raise private armies to literally fight elections for them; and, the generous funding these mercenary armies receive are drawing even government soldiers to join their ranks. Furthermore, politicians offer protection to members of criminal gangs who become allies thus impeding the efforts of police to combat the growing problem of organised crime in the country. According to some rough open source estimates there are more than 2 million firearms in circulation in

Sri Lanka. 90% of the illegal arms in circulation are said to come from the Government. Finally, all smuggling from outside Sri Lanka comes by sea routes, and coastal patrols are lacking. The Sri Lankan Government has taken several steps to address the problem through the implementation of relevant legislation, namely amnesty for surrender of illegal arms, registration of existing arms, and attempts to collect weapons and so forth. In January 2002, an amnesty for surrender of illegal arms was offered by the Ministry of Interior but did not produce the expected results. In 2004, disarmament, demobilisation and reintegration (DDR) of ex-combatants, including in many cases child soldiers, started in Sri Lanka which still has to yield its results.

IMPACT OF SMALL ARMS PROLIFERATION

The persistence and the complication of wars in Africa are partially due to small arms proliferation. The consequences of small arms on African people due to international conflicts within Africa, rebel group activities, mercenary groups, and armed gang activities have yet to be fully measured. The International Action Network on Small Arms, Saferworld, and Oxfam International put it in perspective when they reported that armed conflict cost Africa $18 billion each year and about US$300 billion between 1990-2005. During this period, 23 African nations experienced war: Algeria, Angola, Burundi, Central Africa Republic, Chad, Democratic Republic of Congo (DRC), Republic of Congo, Cote d'Ivoire, Djibouti, Eritrea, Ethiopia, Ghana, Guinea, Guinea-Bissau, Liberia, Niger, Nigeria, Rwanda, Senegal, Sierra Leone, South Africa, Sudan, and Uganda.

Although proliferation of small arms generates a lot of money for those who manufacture and trade them, African people pay a heavy price due to a lack of accountability or international regulations to address the abuses those products cause. According to the Global Facilitation Network Security Sector Reform, nations such as France, Russia, China, UK and USA – the five permanent members of the UN Security Council – together account for 88 percent of the world's conventional arms exports. These exports contribute regularly to gross abuses of human rights in Africa and elsewhere. Some of these are legal arms sales to irresponsible governments who use them to oppress the people. Other supplies are made available to rebel groups by some countries in an effort to overthrow dictatorial regimes which in many cases become worse or as bad as the previous regime. The United States and France, for example, assisted Chadian President Idriss Deby in removing his predecessor, Hissene Habre, from power. Deby then became another dictator who still has not stabilized his country.

Is violence the only tool we have to bring about change? Whoever said "who wants peace, prepares for war" was wrong in this case. Violence is not the answer to the root causes and triggers of instability in Africa. Nonviolence still stands in the forefront as a means of bringing about true peace. While the root causes of violence in Africa vary, it is unquestionable that small arms are a major challenge to security. The United Nations Security Council's report on small arms, S/2008/258, expresses it well by saying that "[T]he dividing lines between underdevelopment, instability, fragility, crisis, conflict and war are increasingly blurred; the small arms issue is therefore intertwined with the security, development, and human rights preconditions for sustainable peace. Present-day conflict prevention, conflict resolution, and peacebuilding require multidimensional interventions."

In fact, more than ever before, strong measures and appropriate attention must be given to this issue. The United Nation's General Assembly resolution (A/C.1/63/L.39*) on the arms trade treaty aims to establish common international standards for the import, export and transfer of conventional arms. It states that the absence of these standards is "one of the contributory factors to conflict, the displacement of people, crime and terrorism, thereby undermining peace, reconciliation, safety, security, stability and sustainable social and economic development." In addition to finding a solution to the proliferation of small arms, manufacturers and traders of small weapons should bear partial responsibility for the abuses and crimes that are committed as a consequence of use of these arms. Among nations that are culpable, let us single out the United States, as Africa Faith and Justice Network's mission is to advocate for just and fair U.S.-Africa relations. The same way

U.S military policies in Africa have promoted dictatorship rather than democracy, the presence of American made weapons on the African continent has hurt the African people more than it has helped. The U.S. is aware that some of their legally transferred weapons contribute to feeding the illegal arms market. It was U.S. made weapons that supported the rebel groups RENAMO in Mozambique, UNITA in Angola, RPF in Rwanda and CNDP in the Democratic Republic of the Congo (DRC). In the UN experts' report on the crisis in the DRC, S/2008/773, paragraph 28 connects the origin of military uniforms shipment destined to the rebel group CNDP from the United States in these terms: "In October 2008, Rwandan security services seized a shipment of uniforms destined for CNDP at Kanombe airport in Kigali. ... The shipment reportedly originated in Boston, Massachusetts, United States." Although this shipment contained uniquely military uniforms, it does not rule out the possibility that weapons were shipped from the U.S destined to CNDP.

Political instability in Africa continues to create more demand for small arms. Manufacturers of weapons know best the link between politics and weapons markets and are therefore often linked to these political instabilities to take advantage of the weapons business it creates. For example, former Congresswoman Ms. Cynthia McKinney of Georgia, in her opening remarks before the Subcommittee on International Operations and Human Rights of the Committee on International Relations of the US House of Representatives on May 17th, 2001, stated that " [W]hat we do know is that the U.S. Special Forces and U.S funded private military companies have been arming and training Rwandan and Ugandan troops to deadly effect. The U.S. taxpayer should be directly assisting the military efforts of Rwanda and Uganda, the aggressors in this tragic conflict and who are confirmed by Amnesty International and Human Rights Watch as the authors of terrible atrocities against Congolese civilians. Our efforts in Africa have amounted to nothing more than bankrolling belligerent and mass murders." War creates a demand for weapons. This is why manufacturers and traders are opposed to international standards for small arms trade.

In addition to the illegal arms sales network, there is a link between the legal and the illegal trade that consists of illegally selling legally obtained arms. This is the core of the problem of small arms proliferation which violators are not interested in solving. As of September 26, 2008, the United States of America, France, Russia, and permanent members of the UN Security Council had not signed the protocol against the illicit Manufacturing of and Trafficking in Firearms, Their Parts and Components and Ammunition, a supplement to the United Nations convention against Transnational Organized Crimes. Africa Faith and Justice Network, in its advocacy effort to the US government for peace and stability in Africa, calls upon President Obama's administration to take a leadership role on this long overdue issue. We recommend that the U.S. signs the international Arms Trade Treaty by the United Nations, passes legislation to hold violators accountable, and reforms its arms production and export policy. Such legislation should include ways to track down U.S. weapons wherever they are used to prevent illegal arms trade from the U.S. to Africa and elsewhere.

SOUTH ASIA AND THE MIDDLE EAST: PROLIFERATION LINKS

While an analysis of proliferation in the Middle East is outside the scope of this study, it is necessary to highlight existing and potential links between the Middle East and South Asia, apart from the A.Q. Khan network mentioned above. Khan's network provided significant know-how to Iran in the late eighties and early nineties (including centrifuge technology), though the full extent of these transfers has still not been confirmed. While nuclear links between Iran and Pakistan have ended for now, Islamabad's nuclear connection to the Middle East remains, such as through possible collaboration with Saudi Arabia.

From the South Asian proliferation perspective, the close ties between Saudi Arabia and the development of Pakistan's nuclear program is a crucial development. News reports as well as official U.S. government analyses have claimed that Riyadh provided considerable financing for Pakistan's nuclear and missile program in the past, but some reports now suggest a more proactive role by Saudi Arabia-in terms of nuclear energy development itself. This is in line with the announcement in November 2006 by six Arab states-Saudi Arabia, Morocco, Egypt, Algeria, Tunisia, and the United Arab Emirates-that they would develop civilian nuclear programs. Earlier, in 2005, Saudi Arabia applied for and was granted exemption from nuclear inspections through the IAEA's 'small quantities protocol.' Before that, a widely quoted 2003 report in The Guardian stated that Riyadh was considering three nuclear options: (a) building a nuclear deterrent, (b) allying with a nuclear power, or (c) working toward a nuclear weapon free zone in the Middle East. Recent developments suggest that a combination of the first two options might be adopted given that it is highly unlikely that Iran and Israel relinquish their nuclear programs in the near future.

This is where Pakistan's role could be significant. German news reports stated in early 2006 that Pakistani scientists assisted Saudi efforts to develop a nuclear program and that this was done under the guise of pilgrimages to Saudi Arabia between 2003 and 2005. Several high-ranking Saudi royals as well as government officials are among the few non-Pakistanis who have toured Islamabad's nuclear facilities.

These include defence minister Prince Sultan (now also crown prince) who visited the Kahuta uranium enrichment facility in 1999, and a son of the current Saudi ruler, King Abdullah, who attended a test of the nuclear-capable 950-mile range Ghauri missile in 1999. These developments suggest that if Riyadh decides to acquire nuclear weapons, the spotlight could be on Pakistan as one of the sources. A factor that could prompt Saudi Arabia to pursue nuclear weapons would be if Tehran unambiguously builds it own nuclear weapon, prompting Israel to shed the opacity over its arsenal.

While disincentives for Pakistan to go along this route are considerable (most notably, U.S. opposition), there are also incentives for Islamabad to aid the Saudis in their quest-cheap oil from Saudi Arabia, and a favorable endorsement for the Musharraf regime (or a successor regime) from powerful conservative Sunni religious and political groups within Pakistan. A 2003 news report quoted an anonymous Pakistani official who claimed that Riyadh and Islamabad had concluded a secret agreement under which Pakistan would receive subsidized oil in exchange for transferring nuclear technology. In 2004, Iranian government sources also claimed that they had information that confirmed this agreement, but there was no further corroboration of this from other sources. Therefore, even if there is no immediate possibility of such a transfer, Saudi Arabia could pursue this with Pakistan in the future to hedge against nuclear developments in the Middle East.

A key incentive for Pakistan could also be to use Saudi Arabia for strategic depth purposes. Islamabad's traditional geographic buffer against Indian military campaigns was Afghanistan, but that was lost after the fall of the Taliban in 2001. Ostensibly, Pakistan requires strategic depth to protect its forces (conventional and nuclear) from an armored offensive by the Indian military, which could cut off the country similar to the 1971 war. Saudi Arabia could provide a base for stationing Pakistani nuclear devices that would be safe from the reach of Indian missiles and give Islamabad a semblance of second-strike capability. This idea of looking towards the Middle East for strategic depth is not new. In the 1990s, former Prime Minister Benazir Bhutto, skeptical of the reliance on Afghanistan, recommended Iran as a more useful ally for purposes of strategic depth.

Apart from the Pakistan-Saudi Arabia link, concerns have also been expressed (especially in the U.S. Congress) over India's ties to Iran, at a time when the IAEA and western powers led by the United States are working toward controlling Tehran's uranium enrichment program. These concerns have arisen during the broader debate in Washington on the nuclear agreement with India. In particular, attention has focused on India's long-standing political and diplomatic relationship with Iran as well as the imposition of sanctions on two private Indian companies suspected of transferring chemicals meant for rocket fuel as well as chemical weapons. The Indian government claimed that both companies (Balaji Amines Ltd. & Prachi Poly Products) were doing legitimate business with Iranian firms. Balaji Amines insisted that they had been supplying products used for manufacturing life-saving drugs such as ampicillin and other antibiotics, but nevertheless, New Delhi ordered the company to stop all trade with Iran.

Both India and Pakistan have attempted to ensure that they are in compliance with the latest international regulations against Tehran's nuclear program. In February 2007, Pakistan froze assets of several individuals and other entities connected to Tehran's nuclear and missile projects in accordance with UN Security Council resolution 1737. In the same month, New Delhi banned exports of equipment and technologies to Iran that could be used in nuclear and missile development projects.

The Iran nuclear issue has been an important point of discussion in context of the Indo-U.S. nuclear agreement. The Hyde Act, passed by the U.S. Congress in December 2006, endorses nuclear cooperation between India and the United States, but it also states that New Delhi should assist the international community in clamping down on Iran's nuclear program. Furthermore, in May 2007, a group of U.S. senators sent a joint letter to Indian Prime Minister Manmohan Singh articulating their dissatisfaction over India's military ties with Iran, especially a 'joint defence working group' between the two countries. Nuclear ties between India and the United States are not limited to nuclear trade between the two, but also extends to discussions over restricting proliferation elsewhere.

Prime Minister Manmohan Singh has stated in the past that New Delhi does not favour another nuclear power in the neighbourhood, and India voted against Iran at the IAEA in September 2005 and February 2006. However, two factors have restrained the Indian government from opposing Iran's nuclear weapons program more forcefully. First, the scramble for energy resources has made the Iran-Pakistan-India (IPI) natural gas pipeline a crucial economic issue for India. Stern Indian opposition to Iran's nuclear program would jeopardize the proposed IPI pipeline from Iran to India. The pipeline is considered to be of crucial importance to India in order to sustain high economic growth rates in the coming years. Thus, economic imperatives, specifically the need for energy sources, are an important factor in nonproliferation positions of countries such as India and China. In this context, New Delhi has reiterated that the construction of the pipeline will proceed in spite of pressures from Washington to cancel the project.

Second, for New Delhi, another variable is satisfying domestic political constituencies that are skeptical of the nuclear overtures from Washington that come at the cost of long-standing ties with Tehran. Since the Congress Party-led coalition government depends on parliamentary support from Communist parties, the government is obliged to periodically hold positions on contentious issues such as the Iranian nuclear program.

The Manmohan Singh government has stated that it would be guided by India's national interest on the Iran nuclear issue, but this does not clarify to what extent India would be willing to go along with the United States on this issue. Some recent reports have also stated that New Delhi could play a more formal role in mediating the growing tensions over Iran's nuclear program in conjunction with the UN Security Council. However, it is unclear what form this would take.

In sum, nuclear issues in South Asia cannot be examined in isolation from developments elsewhere. Historically close political ties have existed between the South Asian subcontinent and the Middle East, and therefore, regional rivalries and bilateral relations play an important role in shaping decisions that impact broader nuclear issues, including horizontal proliferation.

Indo-U.S. Nuclear Cooperation

Since July 2005, when the U.S. and Indian governments unveiled their nuclear cooperation agreement, a debate has risen over its impact on the global nonproliferation regime. This agreement will allow India to acquire nuclear technology and materials from the United States and other suppliers. In return, New Delhi will designate which of its nuclear facilities are for civilian use and which are for military use. The former list would be opened up for international inspections. Prior to implementation, New Delhi will have to conclude a safeguards agreement with the IAEA, while the Nuclear Suppliers Group (NSG) will have to effect changes in its rules to enable nuclear cooperation between its member states and India.

The Hyde Act passed by the U.S. Congress in December 2006, authorized the Bush administration to bring into place a nuclear cooperation mechanism with India, after concluding a bilateral agreement under Section 123 of the U.S. Atomic Energy Act. Negotiations on the '123' agreement began in early 2007, but as of early June, talks were stalled on a few contentious issues. The disagreement is over five main items; (i) the right to reprocess spent fuel, (ii) the conversion of a voluntary moratorium on nuclear testing into a legal commitment by India, (iii) the assured supply of fuel by the United States, (iv) the return of all equipment to the United States if India conducts a nuclear test, and (v) the level of inspections of Indian facilities.

The nuclear deal reflects an influential view in India that the nonproliferation regime embodied in the NPT is defective. According to Indian Prime Minister Manmohan Singh, the regime is ineffective and that the international community should introduce measures that restrict nuclear proliferation more effectively without suppressing peaceful uses of nuclear energy. At the same time, the contention is that India is a responsible nuclear state that has adhered to the guidelines of nonproliferation (without legally being part of the NPT regime) through strict export controls and denying nuclear assistance to other states, unlike the record of some nuclear weapon states.

A basic feature of this agreement is that by acquiring uranium from foreign sources (to free up domestic supplies) and by placing a set of nuclear facilities on the military list, India can increase its fissile material production for weaponization purposes. However, a different line of analysis examines the implications of increased uranium supplies in the context of India's fledgling nuclear submarine project. This perspective views that rather than increasing nuclear warhead production, New Delhi would use the expansion of its uranium supplies and enrichment capability to fuel its nuclear submarine project, a key element of India's desire to achieve a secure second strike capability under its credible minimum deterrence doctrine.

There are two separate lines of criticism of the deal; the first focuses on the nonproliferation objective, and the second on India's strategic needs. The first perspective is that the agreement will weaken the global nonproliferation regime by condoning India's nuclear weapons program.

The argument is that by introducing India-specific changes to global as well as domestic U.S. nonproliferation laws, it will be more difficult to prevent nuclear transfers involving other countries such as China-Pakistan and Russia-Iran.

A further objection is that even with 14 reactors under safeguards, 8 others will remain on the military list, free to manufacture plutonium for several nuclear weapons annually. Additionally, critics have stated that the agreement so far does not commit India to eschew nuclear testing formally, or to end fissile material production.

The second criticism comes most notably, from members of the nuclear scientific community in India, who contend that elements of the agreement would in effect cap India's nuclear program and constrain its thorium-based three stage nuclear project.

They argue that while New Delhi has maintained a unilateral moratorium on nuclear testing, it does not want such a clause legalized in a bilateral treaty. The argument here is that India might have to reconsider its moratorium in the event that China or Pakistan conducts a nuclear test.

In addition, India's scientific community and government have insisted that it be explicitly granted the right to reprocess spent fuel for the three stage nuclear project that exploits the ample thorium reserves in the country (about 30% of the global supply). The Indian government wants to retain reprocessing rights as part of an advanced nuclear fuel cycle. This would involve recycling uranium oxide fuel while the consequent plutonium would be used with thorium in fast breeder reactors. However, some Indian scientific experts have stated that even if reprocessing rights and technology are not granted under the 123 agreement, it is likely that the initial reactors bought by New Delhi will come from

Russia and France, rather than the United States. It is entirely possible that trade with these two countries, especially Russia, will involve reprocessing rights and sale of reactors and fuel. On the other hand, Indian analysts criticize the reported objective of the U.S. government of insuring that India's nuclear trade with other supplier states has equally rigorous conditions attached. Finally, Indian analysts have faulted the U.S. position of not allowing assurances of fuel supplies and of prohibiting India from stockpiling nuclear fuel.

Thus, the nuclear agreement between India and the United States has been criticized on the grounds of its potential impact on the global nonproliferation regime as well as its impact on India's strategic nuclear program.

It must also be noted that since the bilateral 123 agreement between India and the United States is still under negotiation, it is too early to assume the eventual direction of the nuclear agreement framework. Even if the two countries conclude the 123 agreement satisfactorily (for both sides), India still must obtain approval for nuclear trade from the NSG and has to negotiate a safeguards agreement with the IAEA.

The China Issue

Several rationales have been offered as justification for the nuclear agreement (such as economics, strategic alliance, and nonproliferation benefits), but perhaps the most intriguing is one has been left largely unstated by the two governments-that of balancing China.

Both India and the United States are concerned about the future direction of Chinese foreign and security policy. For the United States, aiding India through nuclear cooperation as well as a strategic partnership, Washington would be able to balance China more effectively in the region. In the process it would divert China from its main security issue-Taiwan. For India, the agreement is a significant diplomatic and strategic addition to its capabilities vis-à-vis China, with both the possible increase in fissile material production and a strengthened strategic partnership with the United States.

One argument supportive of the Indo-U.S. agreement stresses that China has built up Pakistan as a counter to India for several decades, a policy that involved transfers of nuclear and missile technology. It must also be noted that more than a year before the Indo-U.S. nuclear agreement was first announced in July 2005, there were reports in March 2004 that China was planning to provide Islamabad with a nuclear reactor.

The implication is that that the Beijing-Islamabad nuclear partnership might have continued in any case. Nevertheless, it is important to consider the current pattern of nuclear cooperation between China and Pakistan in the light of the Indo-U.S. deal. Regardless of the pros and cons of the deal, it can be used by Beijing to lay the grounds for legitimizing continued nuclear collaboration with Pakistan. A sign of this has been China's argument that any changes in the NSG rules should be criteria-based rather than country specific.

In December 2005, China began construction of the 300 MW second phase of the Chashma Nuclear Power Plant (contracted in May 2004), subsequent to the commissioning of the first phase in September 2000. Parallel to the Indo-U.S. deal, China and Pakistan also reportedly agreed to a nuclear cooperation arrangement under which as many as six nuclear reactors of at least 600 MW capacity would be provided to Islamabad. As of now, no other details are available so it is not clear what kind of safeguards will be installed, though some sources have stated that this initiative is being opposed by the NSG.

Reports of a possible Beijing-Islamabad nuclear agreement gained ground ahead of Chinese President Hu Jintao's visit to Pakistan in November 2006. However, no such deal was announced during the visit, leading to a conclusion that Beijing is possibly waiting to see the final shape of the Indo-U.S. agreement to gauge its impact on China. However, one influential Pakistani analyst stated that the lack of a public nuclear cooperation agreement between Beijing and Islamabad does not mean that such an arrangement will not come about; China can supply Pakistan with the required nuclear technology at a more politically convenient time.

Pakistan's desire for a stronger and more public nuclear relationship with China is in part because Islamabad failed to obtain a similar arrangement with the United States. Some Pakistani commentators have in fact argued that their country needs nuclear cooperation with the United States (and other suppliers, for that matter) more than India because the gap between existing energy supplies and future energy requirements is far more serious for Pakistan that it is for India.

A senior Pakistani official connected to the nuclear program, stated in October 2006 that Washington's nuclear policy should be guided by a "criteria-based" approach rather than one geared toward a single country. However, U.S. government officials have stated that they have no intention of considering a similar agreement with Pakistan.

It is likely that this refusal has much to do with the activities of the A.Q. Khan network as well as Islamabad's reluctance to allow a full interrogation of Khan by U.S. experts that would shed light on some unanswered questions related to the network.

Islamabad has cited the fact that Washington declined to offer Pakistan a nuclear cooperation agreement as a motivation for increased self-reliance on nuclear energy, through indigenous fuel manufacturing capabilities.

In this context, government officials in Pakistan stated in April 2007 that the country would set up an installation for fuel testing for use in nuclear plants in a quest for "complete technological capability." As highlighted previously, Pakistan's overall agenda is to redress the perceived widening of the nuclear imbalance with India. Nevertheless, Pakistani experts have admitted that Islamabad's quest for increased nuclear capability is a result of the tacit rivalry between Beijing and New Delhi and the latter's desire to catch up with China. Apart from the impending nuclear technology transfers from Beijing, recent reports have also stated that the Musharraf regime has commenced construction of a 1,000 MW heavy water reactor that will potentially produce adequate plutonium for as many as 50 warheads per year. In addition, Islamabad is setting up a commercial scale nuclear reprocessing plant to allow production of weapons grade plutonium. Such activities would enable Islamabad to stockpile as much fissile material as possible before a future FMCT comes into force.

These developments suggest that Islamabad is attempting to diversify its nuclear weapons program through plutonium, as opposed to its traditional reliance on uranium as fissile material. Plutonium allows for more compact weapons and provides increased flexibility for the arsenal. For Islamabad, this is critical for developing a second strike capability against India. However, some Indian scientific experts have stated that even with the new Pakistani reactor, India will still be able to maintain an insurmountable lead in fissile material production through unsafeguarded reactors under the nuclear agreement.

Chinese support is key to Pakistan's quest for some strategic benefits vis-à-vis India, especially if the U.S.-India nuclear agreement reaches the implementation stage. In a possible attempt to reduce Chinese opposition to the nuclear deal with Washington, New Delhi has committed itself, in principle, to civilian nuclear cooperation with Beijing, a declaration announced during President Hu's visit to New Delhi in November 2006.

This could be viewed as an incentive from Beijing to dissuade India from a potential anti-China partnership with Washington. Nuclear trade between India and China is not necessarily an empty proposal; it has a precedent.

In 1995, India acquired low enriched uranium from China for the Tarapur nuclear reactors. The official Chinese position is opposition to any NSG amendments that would adversely effect the non-proliferation regime, and that they would consider viable arrangements at the NSG, and not bilaterally. Beijing's response reiterates its view that any exceptions should not be India-specific and should include other states.

Interestingly, Indian Foreign Minister Pranab Mukherjee stated in November 2006 that New Delhi does not have any problem with a similar nuclear agreement between Pakistan and China. If this attitude is indeed the Indian government's position, the implication could be that New Delhi is confident that the benefits it will accrue from the agreement with the United States far outweigh the possible increase in nuclear cooperation between China and Pakistan.

Commercial Issues

The Indo-U.S. nuclear agreement also demonstrates that changes in the nuclear supplier regimes will not be restricted only to bilateral nuclear trade between the United States and India. Nuclear energy firms from several countries other than India are already lining up to negotiate commercial nuclear deals with India. NSG member states such as Australia are considering approval of changes in the group's rules to permit nuclear cooperation with New Delhi. Even though Australia (a major uranium producer) has not yet agreed to revoke the prohibition of supply to India, Australian companies such as BHP Billiton are anticipating lucrative sales. Other important members of the NSG have also supported civilian nuclear cooperation with India, within the appropriate IAEA safeguards framework. French and Canadian companies have also contacted the Nuclear Power Corporation of India (one of the main government nuclear energy entities), in connection with the supply of light-water nuclear power related equipment.

Thus, nuclear energy companies are important players in the future of this agreement as well as the broader nonproliferation regime. Firms such as General Electric and Bechtel have lobbied the Bush administration in favour of the agreement. Besides deals in the nuclear energy sector, the expectation is also that such cooperation will facilitate contracts in the conventional military sector, especially with respect to the impending deal for 126 fighter aircraft for the Indian Air Force, a deal worth about $9 billion. Aerospace giants such as Lockheed Martin and Boeing are among the contenders for the contract. Therefore, the implication is that the incentives go well beyond the nuclear energy sector.

Finally, it is instructive to consider the scenario if the nuclear agreement between India and the United States is scrapped, either because of insurmountable differences over the 123 agreement or later in the implementation stage. In India, several members of the influential atomic energy scientific community have expressed reservations over the agreement as have the communist parties and the opposition Bharatiya Janata Party (BJP). In the United States as well, there has been considerable opposition from nonproliferation experts as well as sections of the political establishment.

It is not certain if the reservations expressed by the Indian government towards certain clauses of the December 2006 Hyde Act will be rectified in New Delhi's favour in the bilateral 123 agreement, which again has to be approved by the U.S. Congress. Given these complicating factors, the implications of scrapping the agreement are immense; affecting broader bilateral ties between India and the United States, the nonproliferation regime in general, and the global nuclear energy market.

3

Challenges in South Asia to Nonproliferation Regimes

The nuclear tests conducted by India and Pakistan in May 1998 put the nuclear nonproliferation regime under great stress. For the first time in 34 years, a state openly declared itself to be a nuclear weapon state. Unlike India's 1974 test a single event, carefully defined by the government of the day as a peaceful nuclear explosion, and not followed by declarations regarding nuclear status the 1998 event involved a series of tests, followed by the Prime Minister asserting that India was now a nuclear weapon state and that it would not hesitate, if it chose to do so, to deploy nuclear weapons. Pakistan followed suit toward the end of May.

While leaders in India and Pakistan stressed the strategic and political considerations that informed the decisions in both capitals, the general view from outside the region is that overt nuclearization has created uncertainty and risk for both countries and made the region a more dangerous place. The 1999 military clash over Kashmir, involving insurgents crossing into Indian-held Kashmir from Pakistan, and the downing of Indian jet fighters over Pakistani Kashmir, only serves to heighten those concerns.

Although as of July 1999 neither side has deployed nuclear weapons, that may not always be the case. Assembly, induction, and deployment of nuclear weapons by both sides will negatively impact regional stability and security. Moreover, tacit international acquiescence in such embedded proliferation may have significant negative spillover effects on the nuclear nonproliferation regime. These considerations underscore the importance of developing and maintaining focused policies to mitigate the consequences of the events that have taken place and to restrain the future course of nuclear development, and encouraging the Indian and Pakistani leadership to support measures that advance nonproliferation and nuclear arms control and disarmament, even if they are not prepared to adhere to the NPT.

Reactions to the tests in the P-5, the UN Security Council, and the group of eight advanced industrial nations (G-8) converged on common themes, which focused on averting a nuclear arms race on the subcontinent and protecting the nonproliferation regime. In addition to condemning the tests, responses included calls for:

- no further testing;
- adherence to the CTBT;
- non-deployment of nuclear weapons and nuclear-capable ballistic missiles;
- support for a fissile material production ban, and a moratorium on production while a treaty is being negotiated;
- tightening export controls over materials, equipment, and technology that could contribute to the development of WMD or missiles capable of delivering WMD;
- exercising restraint in the development of ballistic missiles capable of delivering nuclear weapons; and
- taking political steps to address and resolve long-standing differences that could lead to military hostilities between the two states.

STATUS OF NUCLEAR NONPROLIFERATION IN THE REGION

Progress toward these goals has been slow and halting, and in some cases subject to backsliding. Initial expectations of early signing of the CTBT, based on public statements by Indian and

Pakistani leadership, remain unfulfilled. India's declared interest in achieving an as-yet-undefined minimal deterrent forecloses any rollback possibilities in the foreseeable future, and raises doubts about how effectively fissile material production, and nuclear weapons and missile development and deployment, can be curbed. A fissile material production cut-off remains a distant prospect. In the area of export controls, it initially appeared that measures to strengthen and broaden controls would be undertaken with dispatch. Yet the view has emerged in some quarters in India that there are no problems to be fixed, and that if strengthened controls are what the United States and other states want, then India should expect something in return. This raises the question whether nonproliferation is valued in its own right, or is an appropriate matter to be held "ransom." Missile tests have continued on a tit-for-tat basis, ratcheting up in range and provocative character. Proliferation is not an all-or-nothing affair, but rather a matter of steps and degrees. And there is little evidence from the past year to give comfort that South Asian proliferation is in anything more promising than a holding pattern.

Proliferation in South Asia is the consequence of a convergence of three classes of motivations: security perceptions, domestic political considerations, and particularly in the case of India concerns and frustrations about international equity. The nonproliferation regime can affect the first of these issues, and provide support to domestic constituencies opposed to proliferation insofar as the second is concerned. But it has a more limited effect on the third, especially as the regime acknowledges (but does not create or legitimate on a permanent basis) differential status between two classes of states. For India, unlike Pakistan, the question is not only one of national security but also of international status and position, which, looking at the permanent membership of the UN Security Council, India equates with nuclear status.

Thus, the issue of proliferation in South Asia cannot be addressed by the nonproliferation regime and the NPT alone. More attention needs to be given to political incentives and intentions than has traditionally been the case, as reflected in the supply-side constraint strategies articulated by NPT leadership states. In the post-Cold War environment, in which local and regional interests, considerations, and concerns have risen in priority, closer attention needs to be given to the factors that motivate states. As long as nuclear weapon states maintain doctrines and postures that confirm the relevance of nuclear weapons to national security, and as long as the perception endures that nuclear status buys political standing, it will be difficult to move India away from its current positions on the NPT, a regional nuclear-weapon-free zone for South Asia, and implementation of some form of deterrence. This is true despite the fact that the security attained by such a unilateral deterrent is problematic at best, while the potential for negative spillover is high.

This situation calls for a policy agenda aimed at blunting the effects of South Asian proliferation, mitigating its potentially damaging impact on the NPT and nonproliferation regimes, and fostering an environment that amplifies incentives to inhibit, if not, at least in the near term, reverse, proliferation behaviour. Steps in this direction have to be such that they neither reward nor are seen to reward proliferators for their behaviour. This places outside the realm of plausible options:

- engaging in nuclear-specific cooperation on anything other than the terms and conditions established by the NPT and the nuclear supplier consensus;
- considering granting status such as a permanent seat on the UN Security Council to a state that has crossed the nuclear proliferation threshold;
- acquiescing in "the new reality" by giving priority to "other" interests rather than to nonproliferation;
- assisting the proliferators with transfers of relevant equipment and technology to stabilize their newly acquired nuclear weapons against risks of misuse, miscalculation, or accidental launch.

These postulates can be subject to some flexibility, in the context of packaged agreements that do not sacrifice the regime to momentary expediency. For example, it would be appropriate to consider flexibility on limited nuclear cooperation (e.g., on nuclear safety), in the context of South Asian participation in the CTBT and FMCT, and acceptance of international safeguards on all their peaceful nuclear activities.

Policy Options

There are no silver bullets, no quick and easy solutions, and no clever strategies that will survive the discerning eyes of Indian and Pakistani politicians and bureaucrats. Rather, a mix of incentives and disincentives is required. The following approaches will not be surprising or show-stopping, and are consistent with UN Security Council Resolution 1172 of 1998, the G-8 communiqué, and other multinational communiqués and statements. If the nonproliferation treaty and regime are not to be compromised, then these goals, including eventual universalization of the NPT, should remain paramount for the international community.

Focus on global nuclear arms control and disarmament measures, in particular the CTBT and FMCT negotiations. These are major building blocks for nuclear disarmament and nonproliferation. They are non-discriminatory, universally applicable arrangements that respectively cap qualitative and quantitative dimensions of nuclear development and acquisition. They should not be proposed as end points, but rather as building blocks in a long-term process leading toward the ultimate elimination of nuclear weapons an objective that the P-5 should collectively reaffirm, as they did at the 1997 NPT PrepCom. Thus the issue of existing stocks, which is a sticking point in FMCT, can be compartmentalized and addressed subsequently in the context of treaties that are universally adhered to and effectively verified.

A first step toward progress on the CTBT is for those of the five weapon states that have not yet done so to ratify the treaty themselves. Preaching what one does not practice is a poor recipe for successful leadership. The United States has a special responsibility in this regard.

In the case of the FMCT, China is the only nuclear weapon state that has not formally asserted that it no longer produces fissile material for weapon purposes. Given Indian security concerns, a first step would be for China to make such a formal declaration. A second step would be for the five de jure weapon states to codify their position on fissile material production, affirm a moratorium while an FMCT is being negotiated, and call upon India and Pakistan to do likewise and to work constructively for successful negotiation of a treaty in the UN Conference on Disarmament.

Implicit in all of this is a need to ensure sustained commitment to nonproliferation among the nuclear weapon states. Breaks in the ranks reflected in export policies, nuclear cooperation with proliferants, or tacit political support for them in areas suggesting their behaviour is legitimate will undermine nonproliferation in the long run.

Although in the foreseeable future it is not even remotely plausible that India or Pakistan will reverse the actions that they have taken, Indian emphasis on the lack of progress toward nuclear disarmament underscores a concern shared by many NPT adherents. Indian pressure for negotiation of nuclear disarmament in the CD on the basis of a time-bound framework is not a plausible option from the point of view of the nuclear weapon states. But resistance to even allowing discussion of nuclear disarmament in the CD is overwrought: even given the principle of slippery slopes, discussion will not lead automatically to negotiations.

While there has been little progress toward nuclear disarmament in the past year, over the past decade the bilateral negotiations and reciprocal unilateral measures taken by the United States and the Russian Federation have constituted considerable progress.

Getting START back on track is more important than enlarging the number of players in the dialogue; that process has worked and is the only tenable approach for the present. Multilateralization can complicate the process and even be counter-productive. However, it should be possible for the nuclear weapon states to discuss disarmament, and to agree on and implement one or two measures to demonstrate another step toward nuclear disarmament in the NPT review conferences. These could include not only measures to reduce numbers, but also to increase transparency and to lock in irreversibility.

Revitalized bilateral or bilateral-plus arms control and disarmament negotiations, coupled with discussion of the general issue in the CD, would remove a point of leverage for India with the non-aligned states. It could also serve to remove one rationale for whatever actions toward "weaponization" or development of a "minimal deterrent" that India might take. At the very least, it would provide ammunition to cooler heads in New Delhi regarding the pace at which nuclearization proceeds. It could also bear on the important issue of deployment of nuclear-armed missiles, and could help dampen the process of further development and refining of medium-range and especially intercontinental ballistic missiles.

Confidence-building measures aimed at addressing legitimate security concerns that serve as an incentive to acquiring nuclear and other weapons of mass destruction need to be developed and implemented. These should include not only the regional players, but also China. Outside states may play a constructive role in assisting in the identification, development, and implementation (through technological assistance) of confidence-building measures that reinforce commitments such as those made in the Lahore Memorandum of Understanding. Missile proliferation restraint is critical. India has substantial indigenous capability in missile development and production, and Pakistan has become increasingly self-reliant. Both, however, remain reliant to some degree on external assistance, as demonstrated by India's effort to acquire cryogenic engine technology from Russia and Pakistan's long-standing cooperation program with China. This underscores the importance of strengthening the MTCR. But equally important is the need for increased efforts to persuade India and Pakistan to exercise restraint in missile activity, especially deployment of nuclear-capable missiles.

Both India and Pakistan have ratified the CWC and BWC, and India has made a frank declaration of its past CW production activities. Full adherence to all aspects of these treaties would not only reinforce the global regimes they represent, but also remove any concern between the two parties that treaty-prohibited activities are taking place. This is an added element of a confidence-building regime that can help dampen proliferation-oriented behaviour.

CROSS-CUTTING CHALLENGES TO NONPROLIFERATION REGIMES

Systematic examination of the diverse challenges to the nuclear, biological, chemical, and missile nonproliferation regimes reveals that although manifested in different ways and degrees of severity, most types of challenges are common to all the regimes. None enjoys universal adherence or compliance. All are of limited efficacy in meeting their established goals, yet it remains uncertain whether even the complete fulfillment of their objectives would be sufficient to sustain nonproliferation.

Moreover, security and political imperatives overshadow the influence of nonproliferation regimes in key regions of the world, while exogenous national and international developments have significant negative consequences for the regimes. Linkages between sensitive technologies, nonproliferation regimes, and conflict-ridden regions create vicious cycles in which progress toward one nonproliferation goal may undermine prospects for success in another. Despite the evident need to address the full diversity and gravity of these challenges to nonproliferation regimes, meager political will among potential leaders of the international community, as well as disagreement regarding tactics, strategies, and goals, hinders the international cooperation that is necessary to sustain the regimes.

The remainder of this summary report considers these overarching challenges in further detail, as they are manifest across the nuclear, biological, chemical, and missile regimes.

Universality

Although it is the most widely subscribed security treaty in history, even the NPT is bedeviled by four holdouts: Cuba, India, Israel, and Pakistan. In terms of the total number and of the importance of some states that have not signed and ratified the CWC and BWC, these regimes remain even farther from enjoying universal adherence. Limited membership is inherent to the MTCR as an arrangement among leading suppliers, but the refusal of some important suppliers to participate fully likewise limits the scope of its contribution to missile nonproliferation.

Efficacy

The efficacy of nonproliferation regimes in meeting their stated objectiveseither among states party to the regimes or with regard to targets of the regimesare challenged by problems related to compliance, verification, resources, and organization.

The linchpin of nonproliferation regimes, the NPT, is at risk of becoming a "hollow" regime insofar as it proves unable to resolve the challenge posed by defiant proliferants and treaty violators, notably Iraq and the DPRK, or to contribute to the disarmament of the nuclear weapon states. Similarly, nagging questions about Russian compliance with the BWC, due to inadequate transparency regarding current operations of former biological weapon facilities, cast doubt on the regimes efficacy. The expulsion of UNSCOM inspectors charged with verifying Iraqs biological and chemical disarmament undermines the effectiveness of the BWC. The lack of adequate international or national enforcement of the MTCR similarly undermines its efficacy.

Without universal acceptance and full implementation of the IAEAs 93+2 program of enhanced nuclear safeguards, considerable doubt will remain as to the ability of the agency to verify state parties compliance with the NPT. Negotiations to conclude a BWC protocol on verification show no promise of early conclusion, and it is unclear whether negotiating parties will grant access sufficient to justify confidence that the regime can be verified. Challenges to the verification of the CWC range from incomplete reporting by national authorities to national security and commercial exemptions unilaterally decreed by some member states. Lacking an implementing agency, the MTCR lacks any verification capability beyond that provided ad hoc by member states.

Resource constraints plague international efforts to support nonproliferation regimes. Despite increasingly demanding responsibilities, notably with regard to undeclared nuclear facilities, the IAEAs budget has remained consistently inadequate. US-Russian Cooperative Threat Reduction programs to address Soviet nuclear legacies are likewise under-funded. Insufficient resources are a primary reason why Russia will almost certainly fall short of fulfilling its commitment to destroy chemical weapon munitions according to the schedule set for CWC implementation.

Organizational factors are one source of the incapacity of the NPT review process to fulfill states parties expectations that it would contribute to nonproliferation and disarmament. The OPCWs organizational culture of secrecy may be detrimental to the regime, insofar as it complicates judgments regarding compliance by member states. The lack of international legal obligations and inconsistent criteria for membership limit the MTCRs effectiveness.

Adequacy

Some extant challenges to nonproliferation regimes fall outside their scope or cast doubt on their fundamental principles. The ongoing diffusion of sensitive nuclear, biological, chemical, and missile technologies makes it increasingly difficult to sustain international cooperation, creates new types of proliferation threats, and may allow ever more actors to circumvent the regimes. Normative deficits imperil nuclear and especially missile nonproliferation, while the allure of weapons of mass destruction continues to motivate some actors to reject or subvert the regimes.

Denying proliferation-relevant technologies is increasingly problematic due to the commercially driven diffusion of dual-use technologies. The uncertain security of fissile materials produced by the Soviet Union calls into question a fundamental assumption underpinning international safeguards: that access to fissile material is the primary hurdle to nuclear weapon capability. Commercial interests in biotechnologyand technological developments that constitute a veritable revolution in the fieldreduce confidence that a reliable control regime can be established, even as they create the possibility of biological weapons of greater utility for military and terrorist use. The latter threats may include, for example, "innovative" attacks on agriculture. The pace, scope, and sophistication of missile proliferation appears to be simply outstripping the MTCR, with eight states in the Middle East region alone currently deploying Scud-B or even longer-range ballistic missiles.

Disintegration of the military-industrial complex of the former Soviet Union, Russias deep economic crisis, and the ensuing risk of a "brain drain" of nuclear, biological, chemical, and missile knowledge and technologies to potential proliferants, constitutes a background threat of uncertain proportions and no obvious remedy.

The nonproliferation regimes lack sufficiently strong norms against weapons of mass destruction. This normative deficit is manifest both in relatively weak opposition to WMD acquisition and to a lesser degree to WMD use, as well as by the enduring international allure of nuclear weapons and especially ballistic missiles. Tepid international response to the South Asian tests both reflected and further contributed to the weakness of the norm against nuclear proliferation, while the slow implementation of the NPT by parties to the treaty limits the regimes legitimacy. Continued reliance by the P-5 on nuclear weapons to assure their security, as well as renewed US interest in the military utility of nuclear weapons to confront biological and chemical weapon threats and Russian interest in tactical nuclear weapons to compensate for conventional military shortfalls, demonstrate that some leading states believe their possession is both licit and wise.

International norms against the use of chemical and biological weapons are certainly stronger, though of unclear potency in curbing their acquisition. However, the international normative context of missile proliferation is unfavourable to nonproliferation regimes: ballistic and cruise missiles are commonplace and almost universally accepted components of advanced arsenals and military conflict. Even within the regime, working definitions of missiles and missile-relevant technologies are problematic. For those outside of the MTCR, its "cartel" nature creates, moreover, perceptions that the regime is discriminatory and thus illegitimate.

REGIONAL IMPERATIVES AND REGIME LINKAGES

In at least two senses, regional dynamics "trump" nonproliferation regimes. First, security and political factors outweigh the influence of global regimes in East Asia, the Middle East, South Asia, and arguably Europe. Second, nonproliferation policies and security arrangements designed to address particular regional circumstances may undermine the credibility and effectiveness of the regimes in other contexts or at the global level. Linkages between types of proliferation within regional contexts, as well as exogenous developments, compound these challenges. Despite the nonproliferation regimes contributions to global security, resolving the challenges to the regimes that result from regional dynamics will require a clear understanding of the security needs and other considerations that motivate states within the regions.

To date, the NPT regime lacks a fully credible response to nuclear proliferation challenges emerging in the Middle East, Northeast Asia, and South Asia.

Most immediately, the 1998 nuclear tests in South Asia were driven by regional security and political causes, but their ensuing consequences may unfold in the Middle East, the NPT review process, and the UN Security Council. International perceptions of positive or negative changes in status afforded India and Pakistan will be particularly important in determining the cumulative impact of the weapons tests. In the Middle East, Israels possession of nuclear weapons may lead to an intense near-term challenge if Egypt seeks to use it to block agreement at the 2000 NPT Review Conference. Causal linkages among nuclear, biological, chemical, and missile proliferation also afflict the region, such that efforts to promote nonproliferation in any one area may unintentionally encourage another form of WMD proliferation. Missile arms races in all three of these regions indicate the extent to which negative regional dynamics overshadow the positive contributions that nonproliferation regimes can make in promoting national and international security.

With regard to policy responses, the United States-DPRK Agreed Framework exemplifies the tough challenge of devising measures that can work within a regional context without setting precedents that undermine nonproliferation regimes. Less obviously, compromises on the implementation of verification provisions of the CWC that may be made to meet certain national and regional demands could well have negative consequences in other contexts, and for standards and expectations that will be established for the BWC.

While linkages between regions, regimes, and types of proliferation are evident, they are difficult to grasp analytically and even harder to address through consistent, integrated policy. The most important and ironic example is that the success of the nuclear nonproliferation regime may provide incentives for states to seek biological and chemical alternatives. Arguably at least, difficulties in strengthening nonproliferation regimes may be traced to the stalemate on efforts to negotiate measures toward disarmament in the UN Conference on Disarmament. And as noted above, successfully addressing one type of proliferation in the Middle East, and thus shoring up one nonproliferation regime, may unwittingly exacerbate pressures for the acquisition of alternative weapons of mass destruction. Hopes that all challenges in this or other key regions could be resolved simultaneously, however, remain dim.

Finally, exogenous events and trends affect the nonproliferation regimes. For example, Russian economic problems and NATOs recent conflict with Yugoslavia are among the factors undermining US-Russian cooperation on nonproliferation. These types of challenges cannot be addressed by the regimes, but their consequences must be mitigated.

Insufficient Political Will

Scant political will and inconstant attention among potential leaders of the international community pose an across-the-board challenge to sustaining and strengthening all of the nonproliferation regimes, and to related arms control measures such as the CTBT and START. The paucity of high-level commitment is a product of the dominance of domestic factors in setting the agendas of key states, the low priority of nonproliferation among foreign and security affairs, and commercial incentives overriding efforts to control technological diffusion.

Public statements about the severity of the WMD threat notwithstanding, the United States and other influential states do not have a coherent, long-term strategy to sustain the regimes.

Instead, new policy initiatives lag behind trends and emerge sporadically only in response to crises. Senior US policymakers rarely devote serious or sustained attention to the regimes, with predictably negative consequences for the long-term health of the regimes. In these respects, nonproliferation is allocated a low priority among foreign and security issues.

Despite the pace of international change in the post-Cold War era, domestic political factors ranging from electoral schedules to bureaucratic interests to sectoral interests dominate agenda setting among key states. The Russian Dumas obstructionism with regard to START is perhaps the most obvious example. However, the US agenda is likewise plagued by such "provincial" pressures, ranging from policy stagnation during the presidential electoral cycle, to bureaucratic drift on negotiations on a BWC protocol, to pressures to reduce controls on sensitive technologies. The traditional US penchant for unilateralism in its foreign relations, in the context of a militarily unipolar world, allows immoderate influences at home while provoking opposition to nonproliferation regimes among domestic polities and decisionmakers abroad. Similar examples of domestic factors dominating national agendas can be identified in many other states today.

International commercial competitionoften real if sometimes overblownposes a serious challenge to sustaining political support for controlling sensitive technologies. This negative factor is manifest in negotiations on the BWC verification protocol, and in wilful US delay in implementing the CWC. Industry reluctance to support effective implementation of nonproliferation regimes must be overcome if the regimes are to be sustained. Member states must avoid fixation on narrow commercial interests as well as unilateral action in fulfilling their commitments to the CWC. Similarly, commercial space-launch interests of MTCR members and non-members pose a serious impediment to sustaining the missile control regime.

Lack of Consensus

The viability of nonproliferation regimes is challenged by international and national discord on specific tactics, general strategies, and even fundamental goals of nonproliferation. In some cases, the disputes result in part from the sheer difficulty of the problem: e.g., in coping with the Iraqi and North Korean challenges to the regimes. In other areas entrenched differences impede cooperation, as evidenced by the perennial debates over Article VI of the NPT. With respect to some key issues, including missile defences and BWC verification, the United States and other key actors have yet to decide upon their priorities with respect to the regimes.

Tactical disagreements make it difficult to sustain and strengthen nonproliferation regimes. With regard to all four regimes, many states have shown a predilection for technical and unilateral solutions, giving scant attention to political dimensions or the need for international collaboration to successfully meet challenges to the regimes. In some cases, the "best" solution has been at odds with a "good" approach to sustaining a regime. For example, some state parties have sought to employ the NPT Review Conference process primarily as a vehicle for promoting disarmament. While the Review Conference may contribute to disarmament, it also fulfils other regime objectives, and the NPT may be unable to bear the weight of some members aspirations to promote disarmament. Likewise, negotiation of the BWC verification protocol must be carried out with regard to the trade-off between taking time to build consensus on a technically sound protocol, against the risk that indefinite delay could result in no protocol whatsoever. A merely symbolic protocol, however, might well be worse than none at all.

Disagreements over strategies to sustain the nonproliferation regimes are sharpest and most vexing with regard to the hardest cases: how to cope with defiant proliferants that cheat on their nonproliferation commitments. In this regard, Iraq and North Korea have demonstrated an impressive and lamentable capacity for sowing dissent among the leaders of the nonproliferation regimes. US deployment of national missile defences or of theatre missile defences in East Asia may play a damaging role by furthering disagreement over strategies to sustain non-proliferation regimes. National missile defences will likely have a significant and negative impact on the ABM Treaty, and perhaps on the NPT. Regional systems provide incentives for increased acquisition of ballistic missiles, and may provoke defiant countermeasures that could include irresponsible WMD exports by suppliers who believe their political or security interests are harmed by missile defences. While the potential contradictions between missile defences and nonproliferation regimes are sometimes overdrawn, and potentially complementary aspects under-recognized, their cumulative impact may be quite negative and due to political as much as security factors.

Effective multilateral nonproliferation regimes depend as much or more on effective leadership as they do on inclusive and meaningful participation by all parties. While strong leadership by the United States is by itself insufficient, its absence provides little confidence for the success of the regimes. Despite the importance of US leadership in meeting challenges to the regimes, many in the nonproliferation community believe that in some important ways the United States itself may pose threats to the regimes. There is no consensual judgment why this is the case, however. Depending on ideological, political, and professional perspective, analysts make divergent attributions of responsibility: Republicans or Democrats, myopic isolationists or export-oriented free marketeers, the "military-industrial complex" or the arms control "theocracy."

Like many international endeavours, nonproliferation regimes serve as means to divergent ends, ranging in this case from peace to prestige to security to power. The predominant motivations in specific cases may be quite contradictory, which may call into question the long-term prospects for the regimes. Some states, such as Japan, South Africa, and Sweden, may see nonproliferation as an institutional and normative means to promote international disarmament. Others, such as Argentina and Brazil, may see their participation in the regimes primarily as means to gain credentials in the international community that serve other foreign policy objectives. A few, notably Iraq and North Korea, have viewed nonproliferation commitments as instruments for deceitas smokescreens for the clandestine pursuit of weapons of mass destruction. Key sectors in at least one actor, the United States, view the nonproliferation regimes in part as means to sustain the nations conventional military dominance and to enhance its operational capacity for foreign military intervention.

There is no reason, a priori, why divergent motivations cannot indefinitely sustain the support of many countries. But in practice, divergent objectives may cause friction or even lead some states to withdraw support from nonproliferation regimes. For example, increasing US reliance on nuclear weapons to address CBW threats helps to sustain the international legitimacy of possessing and threatening to use nuclear weapons. Increased Russian reliance on tactical nuclear weapons to meet perceived conventional security threats could likewise be of pernicious effect in demonstrating how sharply some key states diverge over the purpose of the nonproliferation regimes. Most profoundly, key supporters of the NPT regime disagree whether it is threatened by the lack of progress or by the risk of progress toward nuclear disarmament.

NORTHEAST ASIA 1999: CURRENT THREATS TO NONPROLIFERATION REGIMES

Northeast Asia stands out as a region of significant concern regarding the proliferation of weapons of mass destruction and their delivery vehicles. North Korea and China continue to engage in activities inconsistent with international nonproliferation norms. In the last year, North Korea became increasingly intransigent about its suspected nuclear weapon program and even threatened several times to abandon the United States-North Korea Agreed Framework and restart its nuclear program. Furthermore, North Korea and to a lesser extent Chinaremain countries of concern regarding transfers of sensitive technologies to known proliferators, and both nations have pushed the limit of or even violated widely accepted nonproliferation norms of the international community.

Moreover, these security problems are unfolding in the context of a significant regional economic downturn and in the absence of an effective regional security mechanism to ameliorate and resolve many of the underlying economic and security issues. The acute economic problems enveloping the region create uncertainties regarding political stability and regime continuity that could, in the future, generate new proliferation risks. Indeed, the lack of a regional security mechanism means that the region as a whole is not adequately prepared to address effectively the increasingly complex arms control and nonproliferation agenda that confronts it.

China

In the last decade, China's overall participation in arms control and nonproliferation has increased dramatically. China signed the NPT, the CWC, and the CTBT. (It has been a BWC member since 1984.) China has also agreed to abide by the MTCR, and Beijing supports FMCT negotiations. However, many concerns persist regarding Beijing's interpretations of its commitments and its ability to implement and enforce them. China's missile, nuclear and chemical exports merit particular attention. Prospects for resolving these problems are uncertain, because China's positions on arms control and nonproliferation are increasingly being politicized by Beijing and, therefore, are being tied to shifts in Sino-US relations.

First, regarding missile nonproliferation, China is not yet a full member of the MTCR and its current commitments to the regime are vague and weak. China has only committed to abide by the MTCR's original 1987 guidelines and parameters; it has not agreed to accept the 1993 revisions. China has also never accepted the MTCR's annex that outlines the technologies controlled under the accord. Without acceptance of the MTCR's annex, meaningful implementation of MTCR restrictions is difficult to carry out. In addition, China has never openly published export controls covering MTCR-controlled technologies, making it unclear how and the extent to which Beijing controls the export of MTCR items.

These ambiguities have allowed China to maintain its exports of missile-related equipment and technologies to Iran, and possibly to Pakistan. China continues to provide Iran with missile sub-systems and production technologies for short-range missiles not covered by the MTCR, yet these items could also be used for Iran's medium- and long-range programs. Moreover, China provides Iran with many dual-use technologies (e.g., titanium-stabilized duplex stainless steel), which are also likely used for proscribed missile programs.

Although China's past missile assistance to Pakistan was extensive and involved the export of complete M-11 missiles, Chinese missile aid to Pakistan may have ceased following the May 1998 nuclear tests in South Asia. In a June 1998 United States-China Statement on South Asia, China pledged to stop all missile and missile technology exports to Pakistan. China's adherence to this pledge requires continued monitoring and verification. But in any case, prospects for China's full membership in the MTCR are bleak. Chinese officials state they are "actively studying" MTCR membership, but little progress is expected due to China's concerns about the US sale of theatre missile defense systems to Taiwan.

Second, Chinese exports of nuclear equipment, materials, and technologies to Pakistan remain of concern. Although the Chinese government promised in 1996 to halt nuclear assistance to unsafeguarded facilities, China's longstanding nuclear weapons-related assistance to Pakistan has created technical relationships and channels of communication that will be difficult to limit. Some Chinese entities may continue to export dual-use nuclear items to Pakistan that could be diverted to the country's military nuclear program. Such assistance could also be provided under the guise of China's ongoing civilian nuclear cooperation with Pakistan. Furthermore, the ongoing restructuring of China's nuclear industry has created managerial uncertainty that in the short term could facilitate illicit nuclear exports to Pakistan.

Third, China is a member of the CWC and has taken several steps arguably more than has the United States to implement its commitments, including the promulgation of a series of export control laws covering CWC items. China, however, has had difficulty implementing and enforcing the CWC's export prohibitions. According to the US Central Intelligence Agency, in 1998 Chinese entities exported CW-related chemicals to Iran, Syria, and possibly Iraq. In 1997, the United States imposed sanctions on seven Chinese entities for engaging in CW-related exports. China's large and sprawling domestic chemical industry has made it difficult for the central government to control the business activities of its chemical industry. Often, Chinese companies are simply unaware of the CWC's export prohibitions. Another source of concern has been China's position on the Australia Group. China rejects the AG on the grounds that it is not a multilateral treaty like the CWC, it interferes in the operation of the CWC, and it unfairly targets countries like Iran. As a result, Chinese companies continue to export dual-use chemicals that are controlled by the AG, but not the CWC. China's position on the AG has been the source of several bilateral disputes with the United States, and resulted in the imposition of US sanctions in 1997.

Lastly, one overarching factor that will likely influence China's participation in a host of global arms control and nonproliferation accords is the US plan to deploy NMD and TMD systems in Northeast Asia. Chinese officials and analysts fear that NMD deployments will significantly undercut China's strategic deterrent and, as a result, they contend that China will need to reconsider its existing and future commitments to the CTBT and the FMCT. NMD deployment by the United States may also catalyze vertical proliferation of China's missile arsenal (possibly including development of MIRVed missiles) in an effort to overcome the perceived strategic imbalance created by a US missile defense system. Furthermore, Chinese officials see TMD as a form of missile proliferation that, at a minimum, will delay their consideration of MTCR membership. TMD deployments in Japan or Taiwan, moreover, could lead China to reconsider its previous MTCR commitments and prompt resumption of exports of complete missile systems to countries in the Middle East.

North Korea

North Korea's extensive domestic WMD development programs and its flagrant missile export activities arguably rank it as the world's "Number One Proliferator." Pyongyang's activities represent a serious and immediate threat to global nonproliferation efforts. Yet measures to resolve these multiple WMD issues are largely tied to broader issues of the scale and pace of US diplomatic engagement with North Korea, as well as Washington's approach to Korean reunification.

North Korea's nuclear program remains a persistent threat to nuclear nonproliferation efforts. Pyongyang signed the NPT in 1985, but has not signed the CTBT. Nor is the North in complete compliance with its NPT obligations: the IAEA has not been able to verify the North's initial declaration of the amount of nuclear material it possesses. Based on inspections in 1991, the IAEA calculated that the North produced more than the declared 90 grams of plutonium, but the IAEA does not know how much more. The US intelligence community estimates that the North may have enough plutonium for one or two basic, implosion-type nuclear devices. It is currently not clear when or whether the IAEA will be able to verify the North's initial declaration, because the inspections necessary to resolve this issue are tied to implementation of the 1994 Agreed Framework (AF), which continues to experience delays. If these delays persist, the IAEA may not be able to determine conclusively North Korea's past plutonium production, possibly allowing the North to keep a small cache of weapons-usable material.

Moreover, the North's implementation of the AF has been inconsistent. Since 1994, North Korea has maintained its freeze on the operation of several key nuclear facilities and halted the construction of two larger reactors. However, the construction at Kumchangri of an underground facility possibly intended for production of nuclear materials raises questions about the North's intentions. Although inspections in May 1999 revealed that the facility was little more than a concrete shell, the North most likely initiated the construction as a political signal of objection to the perceived shortcomings in US implementation of the AF, and as an attempt to extract concessions from the United States. Alternatively, factions in North Korea may still harbor nuclear ambitions and seek to secretly reconstitute the North's nuclear weapon program. North Korea has not relied on outside suppliers for its nuclear programs, and there have not been any reports of North Korean exports of nuclear materials, equipment, or technologies.

North Korea is not a signatory to the CWC and has not expressed any interest in joining the treaty. Since the late 1980s,

North Korea has been capable of producing large quantities of chemical weapon agents, including blister, nerve, choking, and blood agents. Many of these CW agents have been weaponized in artillery, aerial bombs, and missile warhead munitions. Beginning in the early 1990s, the North expanded and accelerated its CW production efforts, and according to US intelligence it currently posses "a sizeable stockpile of chemical weapons."

Moreover, although North Korea signed the BWC, it may possess an operational biological weapons program. Over the past few decades, Pyongyang has had an active BW research and development program, and its current bio-technical infrastructure is sufficient to produce limited amounts of BW agents. The North is not known to have exported chemical or biological weapons-related items to other countries.

North Korea is notorious for its exports of complete missiles and missile production technologies. The North's ongoing missile sales to Iran and Pakistan represent the most immediate and direct challenge to global missile nonproliferation efforts. The North can almost single-handedly undermine global missile nonproliferation efforts with its export policies.

In the past North Korea sold missiles and related technologies to Egypt, Syria, and possibly Iraq, and most significantly the North even supplied Iran and Syria with production and assembly technologies for Scud-B and Scud-C missiles. Pyongyang also sold Iran the Nodong missile, for which Tehran reportedly provided advance funding. More recently, North Korea may have sold Nodong missiles to Pakistan, which Islamabad calls the "Ghuari" and claims as indigenous.

North Korea's principal motivation for exporting missiles has been to earn hard currency to help its faltering economy. The United States has twice engaged the North in talks about missile proliferation and the MTCR, but North Korean officials say they will only halt missile exports if the United States offers compensation at the level of $1 billion per year. The United States has categorically rejected that offer as blackmail. North Korea is not a member of the MTCR and has expressed no interest in joining the regime.

North Korea's domestic missile development program is also of proliferation concern, because Pyongyang has shown a proclivity to export any item in its inventory. North Korea's August 1998 test flight of the Taepodong-1 suggests that this system could be deployed or available for sale at some point in the near future. Export of this new system could be particularly likely if its development was funded by another country, such as Iran or Pakistan.

Taiwan

Given the threat Taiwan faces from China, combined with the Chinese military's overwhelming numerical superiority, Taiwan's development of chemical weapons to deter or to rebuke an invasion would seem a reasonable option for military planners. Taiwan is not a member of the CWC and may possess an active CW program. It is unclear from open-source information whether Taiwan possesses chemical weapons. The Taiwanese government denies that it has an offensive CW program, and claims that it only engages in defensive CW activities. In fact, even though Taiwan says that it wants to join the CWC, it is not allowed to join. China has objected to Taiwan's membership in the CWC because it would signal Taiwan's status as a sovereign entity rather than part of mainland China. When CWC members implement export-import restrictions to non-members, Taiwan's chemical industry stands to suffer, as it will be unable to purchase certain CWC-controlled chemicals. A series of creative, legal solutions to this problem may exist (such as joint inspections) but they would likely require a degree of cooperation between China and Taiwan that is difficult to envision during the currently tense period in cross-strait relations.

Japan

Japan's possible future development of nuclear weapons and ballistic missiles is an issue of medium- to long-term proliferation concern. Japan possesses the technical capability and the materials to develop nuclear weapons and ballistic missiles. Japan operates an extensive civilian plutonium production program that has allowed it to amass a large stockpile of weapons-usable plutonium, and the country's highly advanced space launch vehicle program could easily facilitate the development of ballistic missiles, possibly of intercontinental ranges.

It is unclear, however, what changes in the international security environment would lead Tokyo to revisit its current nonproliferation pledges. Possible developments include the emergence of a number of new nuclear weapon states such as India, Pakistan, and possibly Ukraine. Other, more dramatic changes could include a weakening of the US security commitment to Japan, or the emergence of China as a highly aggressive actor in the East Asian theatre.

Neither of these developments is likely to occur in the short to medium term, however, especially given the recent redefinition of the United States-Japan Defense Guidelines and expanding missile defense cooperation between Washington and Tokyo. In addition, Japan would have to overcome several internal legal barriers and much domestic and international opposition to develop nuclear weapons or ballistic missiles. Most notably, Japan would be forced to undertake the complex legal step of amending its constitution. Nevertheless, given Japan's latent capabilities, attention to debates within Japan is warranted, as well as continuing consideration of the impact of non-Asian proliferation developments (such as the nuclear status of India, Pakistan, and Ukraine) on attitudes in Japan.

4

Nuclear Arms Control: Prospects and Challenges

Over the last 15 years, India and Pakistan have engaged in operationalizing their respective strategies of 'credible minimum deterrence.' Thus, they focused on building stockpiles of nuclear warheads and testing and inducting delivery systems of varying ranges. The two countries are believed to have accumulated a roughly equal number of nuclear warheads—though Pakistan's stockpile is believed to contain a couple dozen more than India's. Regarding nuclear delivery systems, while Pakistan has tested missiles ranging from 60 km to 2,500 km, India has done the same for 150 km to 5,000 km. These vectors, however, are at different stages of operationalization. A look at the pattern of testing reveals that Pakistan focuses on either very short range (*Nasr* and *Abdali*) or long range missiles of over 2,000 km. In India, the spotlight currently appears set on IRBMs (*Agni* IV and V).

In this process of capability enhancement, little if any thought has been given to nuclear arms control (NAC), which would include explicit unilateral or negotiated measures designed to regulate some aspect of capability or potential capability. In fact, the India-Pakistan relationship suffered from a huge trust deficit from 1999 - 2009. Soon after the nuclear tests in 1998, both governments crafted a number of very forward looking confidence building measures (CBMs) as part of their February 1999 bilateral memorandum of understanding (MoU) signed in Lahore. Most of the CBMs, however, were never implemented. Within three months of the MoU agreement India found that Pakistan mounted a covert operation across the line of control (LoC) in Kargil. In the summer a mini-war broke out between the two countries in which scores of Indian soldiers lost their lives. The biggest casualty of the crisis was the trust built up earlier in Lahore. A trust deficit has always dominated relations between India and Pakistan, especially after the repeated acts of terrorism planned in and supported by Pakistan—the latest being in Mumbai in November 2008.

India's problems thus are that it must face China, which is modernizing its military forces and compels parallel Indian modernization. Yet, on the other hand India must contend with an asymmetric strategy emanating from Pakistan. A further perceived danger is the possibility, however remote, of a two-front war enabled by Sino-Pak cooperation. Under these circumstances constructing an arms control regime is a huge challenge for India.

Given this background of mistrust and parallel military modernization programs, it is hardly surprising that Pakistan and India have not placed serious thought on NAC. In fact, the first reaction to suggestions of NAC amongst many in Delhi's strategic circles, and possibly Islamabad's, is to question whether their country has enough nuclear weapons or capabilities. The general belief is that building credible deterrence remains a work in progress. Hence arms control is viewed as premature.

A second reaction that dismisses NAC is the lack of conducive political conditions. Of course, the dilemma over whether the right political atmosphere exists to foster arms control or whether arms control can create cordial conditions has never been resolved conclusively—not even during the Cold War. Several analysts concluded that efforts toward arms control during the 1970s and mid-1980s never made much progress because of the "depth of disagreement between East and West. There were constant antagonisms between NATO and the Soviet Union, with frequent allegations of violations of the existing CBMs that hindered and detracted from relations between the two blocs.

The situation changed only in April 1986 with new initiatives from Soviet President Mikhail Gorbachev. These initiatives radically altered the political atmosphere and opened the way for nuclear and conventional arms control. If the above is true, how can the countries of South Asia be expected to engage in NAC and CBMs with such strained political relations?

This chapter argues that nuclear learning in South Asia has been affected by the absence of any progress in arms control and suggests that irrespective of the state of political relations between India, Pakistan, and China, the time for creation of NAC and CBMS architecture has arrived. The deeper the political mistrust, the greater the need for NAC in order to minimize, if not obviate, chances of miscalculation or accidental escalation. As Hedley Bull pointed out in the 1960s, the United States and Soviet Union being locked in a political and ideological conflict "did not mean that they could not recognize common interests in avoiding a ruinous nuclear war, or cooperate to advance these common interests."

Given that nuclear weapons are here to stay until universal nuclear disarmament can occur, and given that existential risks of their inadvertent use and concerns over nuclear security accompany nuclear weapons, it is only prudent that countries try to identify and accept measures that can help alleviate these concerns to the extent possible. This is even more necessary as countries move towards acquisition of a mix of offensive and defensive capabilities, where every act of one side evokes a response from the other. Consequently, as arsenals grow, capabilities increase, and infrastructure expands, so will the risks of events triggered by improper leadership judgment and involuntarily offence-defense spirals. NAC can provide one way of stabilizing deterrence by redressing crisis instability caused by pre-emptive pressure and arms race instability.

This chapter examines the need, rationale, and mechanics of NAC. It is broadly divided into three sections. The first examines the purpose and prerequisites of NAC in a general manner derived from Cold War experiences of the superpowers. The second applies these generic conclusions to the specific context of the India-Pakistan nuclear relationship. This chapter establishes the unquestionable relevance of NAC and examines the significant challenges standing in its way, which has stymied positive nuclear learning. Finally, the chapter concludes with some suggestions on possible future nuclear CBMs and arms control measures, which will augment the learning curve for the region.

PURPOSE AND PREREQUISITES OF NUCLEAR ARMS CONTROL

Countries build nuclear weapons to deter against an adversary's nuclear weapons through the threat of retaliation. However, deterrence stability is prone to two problems – probabilities of nuclear use and prospects of nuclear arms race. The first problem derives from a doctrine of deliberately use and the risk of an inadvertent use through miscalculation or misperception. The second problem arises from a desire to stay ahead of an adversary's offensive or defensive nuclear capability, which eventually leads to an unstable arms race.

NAC can be an effective tool to address these two problems because it enables mutually agreed measures to alleviate mutually perceived risks. NAC can range from efforts at increasing transparency such as through an exchange of doctrines, to more specific elimination of classes of weapons or their uses, or even a regulation of certain military activities or deployments. The basic objective is to enhance the understanding of each other's nuclear doctrines and capabilities, reduce the aspects of unpredictability, and help avoid nuclear war. In fact, the very process of arms control negotiations creates better communication and understanding, reduces hostilities, and helps improve political relationships. For successful implementation of NAC, certain pre-conditions are necessary. One of the most important is a shared interest between negotiating nations on the need to avoid deterrence breakdowns and recognize that nuclear war brings no benefits. In the absence of a shared mutuality of interest, NAC is certain to flounder.

A second prerequisite is the acceptance of NAC as a worthy objective by national leaderships. In a democracy, this would imply a broad consensus between the major political parties to acknowledge NAC as a matter of the highest national interest and accord it requisite priority. This acceptance is critical if negotiations are to steer clear of party politics. At the same time, political consensus is also essential to imbue the arms control process with a certain confidence that outlasts changes in government. In a more military-dominated system, acceptance of the logic and rationale for arms control as a worthwhile pursuit is equally important. By their very nature militaries are reluctant to limit their fighting capabilities. Therefore, forging consensus within diverse political parties as well as convincing national military leadership to accept the centrality of arms control is an uphill task. Unless all stake-holders consider it worthwhile, NAC can quickly degenerate into a futile exercise.

Thirdly, having accepted NAC as a national objective, the nation must exhibit a readiness to invest in negotiations and decision-making. NAC is negotiated in relationships that are difficult and even hostile, which is certain to make the exercise a complex, drawn-out process. Hence, the state must commit time and manpower to maneuver through political negotiations and technical issues. The following paragraphs apply these lessons to the context of India-Pakistan nuclear relations. As will become evident, the need for NAC between these two countries is unquestionable. The risks that afflict this relationship demand the highest level of priority in their mitigation, but the challenges are numerous and difficult.

CHALLENGES TO INDO – PAK NAC

India and Pakistan share a six-decade-long history of confrontation. Territorial disputes remain unresolved and without a clear-cut demarcation of the international boundary, border skirmishes occur frequently across the line of control. The danger of these escalating to a larger conflict always exists. In fact, chances of conflict are exacerbated and the prospects of arms control are dampened if there is a pervasive belief that states are complicit in the use of terrorism as an instrument of state policy. Continuation of such acts has the potential of breaching India's tolerance threshold, which would lead to a viscous circle of escalation. India's concept of 'limited war' or the calibrated use of military force is amongst the several options that India might be forced to choose as result of India's persistent hypothesis of Pakistan's complicity. But the presence of nuclear weapons obviously makes the military option a risky game.

The challenges to South Asian NAC appear enormous and can be divided into two categories: general and nuclear specific. Amongst the general problems, the most obvious is the deep rooted mistrust that has existed between the two countries since partition. The wars in 1947, 1965, 1971, the Kargil conflict in 1999, and major terrorist incidents in 2001 and 2008—in addition to the myriad smaller ones—have only aggravated this mistrust.

Meanwhile, there is a long history of failed CBMs. Yet, both countries are not new to the concept of confidence building. They negotiated at least two significant documents in the last 65 years. The first was the Simla agreement in 1972, which established the "commitment to peaceful coexistence, respect for each other's territorial integrity and sovereignty and non- interference." Both sides also agreed to "refrain from [the] threat or use of force," to respect the LoC and not to "unilaterally alter the situation."

In 1999, more specific nuclear CBMs were concluded as part of the Lahore MoU but have ultimately not been executed. Among others, these included agreements to exchange information on nuclear doctrines and security concepts, provide advance notification of ballistic missile flight tests, provide prompt notification of nuclear accidents or unauthorized or unexplained incidents, engage in bilateral consultations on security, disarmament and non-proliferation, and establish communication hotlines to avert crisis situations. The only Indo-Pak agreement not yet violated is the 1988 agreement prohibiting attacks on each other's nuclear facilities. Every year on January 1 both sides exchange a list of their nuclear installations. The overall atmosphere, however, is still one of low trust and confidence.

Yet another challenge to NAC arises from divergent threat perceptions. Pakistan has often expressed concern with India's size and the Pakistani military harbors a sense of injustice regarding the allocation of resources and military assets at partition. Put simply, Pakistan resents India for having forced it to "start its independent career as a weak nation." Hence, for the last six decades Islamabad has looked for ways to equalize its perceived power asymmetry with India. Over the years Pakistan even used this sentiment to keep the threat of India alive as the socio-economic, technological, and political trajectories of the nation veered in opposite directions. This tendency distracts Pakistan's population from the dismal state of affairs within their country. Today, this dynamic not only seriously damages Pakistan's own progress and economic growth but also dims the prospects for bilateral arms control.

In the nuclear-specific domain, challenges to NAC are linked with five asymmetries. The first is an asymmetry in the role of nuclear weapons. Indian nuclear doctrine defines a narrow role for nuclear deterrence, where weapons are meant to safeguard the country against nuclear coercion and blackmail but not seen as useful for other purposes. On the other hand, India believes Pakistan's weapons are less for deterrence and more meant to provide immunity so the country can pursue other modes of conflict including covert aggression through sub-conventional means. Deterring Indian use of nuclear weapons is actually the least important function of Pakistan's weapons, which are meant more as a shield against conventional attack. Therefore, nuclear weapons provide Pakistan with immunity to indulge in aggressive military strategies that harbor political ambitions.

A second asymmetry exists amongst Indian and Pakistani nuclear doctrines. India's written doctrine opts for a retaliation-only policy. Deterrence in this case is premised on the threat of assured retaliation causing unacceptable damage and enables India to adopt a more relaxed force posture. By placing the onus of escalation on the adversary while retaining the initiative of punitive nuclear retaliation, India abjures nuclear brinkmanship and even releases the adversary from pressures to use its nuclear forces quickly lest they be lost due to pre-emption. In contrast, India believes Pakistan professes a first use doctrine. Pakistan is focused on developing tactical nuclear missiles as a "quick reaction weapon." In order for Pakistan's weapons to provide any advantage they must be used first; however, a decapitating or disarming first strike is made virtually impossible as each side has a credible second-strike capability. Nonetheless, Pakistan's doctrinal perception pressures it to acquire more warheads and establish a more delegated C2 structure that can incorporate battlefield nuclear weapons. This doctrinal asymmetry carries the risk of pushing both countries into crisis and arms race instability.

Thirdly, there is an asymmetry in the desire for strategic stability. This is a huge challenge since a common desire for stability is an essential pre-requisite for NAC. Yet, Pakistan perceives greater utility in keeping its nuclear relationship with India unstable. As put by one analyst, Pakistan "is not searching for nuclear stability but for managed instability.

The purpose of this instability is to keep India off balance, to resist agreement, to underpin uncertainty, and to generate ambiguity." Besides targeting India, instability is meant equally to magnify fears within the international community by suggesting the possibility of a nuclear exchange. The Pakistani Army presumes that a concerned international community (especially the United States) would restrain India from using military force. Evidently, Pakistan's confidence in managing instability is far greater than India's.

A fourth asymmetry lies in the objective sought from arms control by the two countries. While India seeks strategic stability by addressing weapons or capabilities that exacerbate first strike fears and crisis instability, Pakistan perceives a greater threat from India's conventional superiority and is keener to link conventional arms control to NAC. Islamabad has always argued that since India's conventional capability is superior to that of Pakistan, it has no option but to increase its reliance on nuclear weapons to deter India. In such a situation, it seeks parallel conventional arms control. However, a new twist has been added since India's threat perception of China impinges on its calculation of required conventional capability. Moreover, the Sino-Pak strategic nexus adds to India's security concerns. In fact, the complex state of the political relationship between China, India, and Pakistan produces a tough case for creating a tripartite arms control agreement. Constructing NAC that simultaneously addresses threats at all levels of conflict—sub-conventional, conventional, and nuclear—has never before been attempted.

Lastly, there is an asymmetry in the decision-making authorities of India and Pakistan. In India, the democratic political establishment controls all foreign policy. India's military is only asked to provide inputs where necessary and execute tasking. In Pakistan, on the contrary, all decisions related to nuclear policymaking and especially those related to India are taken by the military.

SUGGESTIONS FOR NAC AND CBMS IN SOUTH ASIA

The current state of nuclear affairs in South Asia leaves much to be desired. In fact, the challenges enumerated on earlier can only be surmounted if the relevant participants share an equal sense of the dangers presented by nuclear weapons and urgency of lengthening the fuse of any crisis. It is with the hope that such a day will dawn, sooner rather than later, that some suggestions are offered below. These range from reciprocal measures aimed at enhancing confidence by facilitating conceptual clarity, to more specific suggestions on weapon systems. Each recommendation would be useful for addressing either first strike instability, arms race instability, or both.

Clarity on Nuclear Doctrines and Force Structures

While India formulated a written nuclear doctrine and put it in the public domain in 1999, Pakistan never reciprocated. Greater transparency in nuclear doctrines and force structures can be useful for achieving arms race stability. Confidence in understanding the nature and direction of the other side's forces provides a certain amount of transparency and predictability. Thus, it alleviates concerns of arms racing. For instance, the character of India's nuclear forces, per its doctrine, is "effective, enduring, diverse, flexible, and responsive." Such a clear statement provides notice on the capabilities and aims to remove ambiguity. It announces that India focuses on operationalizing its delivery capabilities via mobile long range missiles, including SLBMs, and the establishment of a robust command and control system. As countries improve their space surveillance technology, a certain transparency of the force structure is inevitable. But a negotiated approach is useful to understand the future trajectories of development plans so that both sides need not hedge against presumed adversary capabilities.

Transparency in Survivability Measures

A secure second-strike capability forms the bedrock of stable deterrence. Hence, development of, and transparency regarding, survivable capabilities, can alleviate pressures for preemption. This improves crisis stability by credibly promising assured retaliation. The construction of missile silos, operationalization of sea based deterrence, and increased C2 robustness for also do so. Countries moving in the direction of these developments and maintaining a certain transparency about them foster strategic stability and lower the chances of deterrence breakdown.

Formalizing Low-Alert Statuses

Washington and Moscow's NAC agenda includes measures that lower the alert levels of their nuclear arsenals. Since both countries maintain a significant part of their force on hair-trigger alert, de- alerting and de-mating warheads increases crisis stability. Fortunately, China, India, and Pakistan's arsenals are already in such a state. However, an agreement that formalizes the low-alert status of each country's arsenal could be a further step towards stability. If verification could be part of the agreement, it would also be a huge confidence booster. Yet, the political and logistical feasibility of such an agreement poses significant hurdles.

Exchange of Information on Nuclear Safety and Security

Given that the threat of nuclear terrorism looms large over the region, South Asia's nuclear states have an opportunity to enhance confidence by exchanging information on their practices and procedures for maintaining nuclear safety and security. Adherence to the many international conventions in these areas as well as a joint regional center focused on the threat is a possibility worth exploring. This center could distribute region wide information on safety and security best practices.

Joint Study on Effects of Nuclear Explosions

No significant attention has been paid to the likely effects of a nuclear weapons exchange in any of the three countries identified above. Given the regions' high population density and the fact that modern mega cities use material that could maximize the thermal and blast effects of a nuclear explosion, it may be useful to conduct a joint study to assess the damage that nuclear arsenals would inflict on population centers. Such a study could be an effective method of calculating the cost- benefit aspects of nuclear war. This would enhance deterrence by making China, India, and Pakistan understand and appreciate the likely extent of damage if nuclear weapons were used.

Limits on BMD

Defense and deterrence have long been thought mutually exclusive. The ability to defend against another's nuclear strike is believed to lessen its sense of vulnerability, tempt it toward nuclear pre-emption, and thereby degrade the other's deterrence. Consequently, during the Cold War years, the United States and Soviet Union agreed to keep each other mutually vulnerable by severely restricting their deployment of anti-ballistic missile (ABM). For instance, the ABM treaty of 1972 mandated that both sides defend no more than one site each with no more than 100 interceptors.

Turning to South Asia, one sees that BMD is beginning to make its presence felt. Given Pakistani doctrine and the danger of inadvertent use, India perceives BMD as an insurance measure to reduce damage should the worst happen. At the same time, China's ABM capability is deployed with America's nuclear arsenal in mind. This development obviously casts a shadow over Indian doctrine and makes Indian BMD a sort of necessary evil. In Islamabad, however, the Indian step has been perceived as destabilizing: it degrades Pakistan's nuclear deterrence posture and fears arise that BMD enables India to engage in limited nuclear war. Pakistan's obvious response has been to increase the number and sophistication of its missiles so as to saturate Indian BMD. In turn, Pakistan's actions raise Indian threat perceptions, especially given the reality of the Sino-Pak strategic nexus. This three way nuclear relationship and the induction of BMD complicates the situation.

Despite BMDs complicating effects, NAC can still be attempted. At one level with China, an ABM treaty that allows BMD over a fixed number of mutually agreed upon sites should be explored. Given that both countries have similar nuclear doctrines premised on no-first use and deterrence by punishment, BMD should logically be used for retaliatory capabilities—including command and control structures. Such an agreement would not only stabilize deterrence but also help alleviate arms race instability. If BMD can be mutually deployed to improve the survivability of retaliatory assets and nuclear command authorities, an agreement could increase deterrence stability by ruling out the possibility of a disarming first strike. At the same time, all sides would evade the defense-offense spiral. With Pakistan, NAC in an environment where BMD exists could occur through the fostering of better understanding and clarity on nuclear doctrine. For instance, it is important for India to explain that an NFU doctrine with BMD in no way increases the chance of pre-emption. Also, an India-China agreement on the subject could go a fair distance in psychologically alleviating Pakistani concerns on the matter.

Controls on MIRVed Missiles

China is believed to have MIRV technology but it is unclear whether Beijing has deployed it. Meanwhile, India is certainly moving toward MIRVs and it is only a matter of time until Pakistan also develops or acquires MIRV missiles. Once China, India, and Pakistan deploy MIRVs, strategic stability will suffer because this capability produces a temptation for pre-emption. With their greater accuracy, multiple warheads become essentially first strike weapons. For the attacking state, a MIRV provides the promise of being able to carry out a disarming counter-force strike. Meanwhile, missiles with many warheads also become attractive targets for the adversary too, creating an urge to strike MIRV missiles before they are launched. Therefore, the use or lose dilemma is heightened. Moreover, in a crisis, the states with MIRV technology might be tempted to strike first in hopes of gaining a war-winning advantage.

An agreement whereby all sides agree not to develop MIRV missiles would contribute to fostering crisis stability. Single warhead missiles present much less tempting targets: a pre-emption strategy would require more warheads be expended than could be destroyed. It would be far more worthwhile for India, China, and Pakistan to arrive at a mutual understanding on this technology rather than follow the dangerous path taken by Washington and Moscow. The three South Asian powers would only arrive at the realization that the United States echoed in its latest Nuclear Posture Review, which mandates the de-MIRVing of its missiles as a step towards strategic stability.

The case for mutual agreement on MIRV missiles may appear unfeasible because countries with 'minimum deterrence' doctrines might find it more useful to have smaller numbers of MIRV missiles. But some strategic stability must be established. In this case, it may be worthwhile to link MIRV capabilities with NFU. Doing so will rule out pre-emption since it reduces risks generated by the existence of MIRV arsenals and functions as effective NAC.

THE ROOTS OF POLITICAL INERTIA

Since China exploded its first nuclear device in 1964, hawkish opinion has insisted on acquiring nuclear weapons for India. The demands became more strident as the Chinese nuclear arsenal grew. Against this background, Dr. Vikram Sarabhai, head of the Department of Atomic Energy in the 1960s, drew up his ambitious 'Profile' for India's nuclear programme. Peaceful nuclear explosions formed a part of that programme.

The Indian elephant moves slowly and often in an uncoordinated manner. After the initial panic generated by China's nuclear weapon programme, things lapsed into a relaxed pace. It seemed that the Indian Government had learned to live with China's rapidly developing programme. China had scrupulously avoided saying anything that could have been construed by India as a nuclear threat. The 'Sarabhai Profile' finally did produce a nuclear device in 1974 but a parallel programme of the Indian Space Research Organization (ISRO) to build carrier rockets lagged far behind.

Meanwhile, in the UN as well as in other forums, India continued to press its original proposal for a test ban, first made in 1954. Before the Chinese nuclear explosion of 1964, India had been an enthusiastic supporter of non-proliferation. Jawaharlal Nehru, then India's Prime Minister, asked his Ministry of External Affairs to seek to be the first to sign the PTBT. Nehru died before the Chinese explosion and India's nuclear policy changed radically after that. After negotiations for the NPT began, India toyed with the idea of signing the NPT if positive assurances about protecting India against a presumed Chinese nuclear threat were available, but the assurances which were offered by the USA and other Western powers were not found satisfactory.

India's nuclear policy, if not exactly volatile, has been an oscillating one. On one issue, however—that of the comprehensive test ban (CTB)—it was steady. By labelling the explosion of 1974 a peaceful one, India could claim that it was not going against the banning initiative, which it conceived only in terms of tests for the purposes of developing weapons. Continuing with this logic, India could have carried out a series of peaceful explosive tests if the international reaction to the 1974 test had not been extremely adverse. Its visible manifestation was the Canadian cancellation of all nuclear technology assistance to India's nuclear power industry; Canada was the chief provider of technological assistance to India's reactors. The other, less direct, manifestation was the setting up of the Nuclear Suppliers' Group, which made it impossible for India to acquire any, even dual-purpose, technology on the international market. Lastly, the Western countries and Japan exerted enormous pressure on India through private channels. Prime Minister Indira Gandhi reacted angrily to all this but was unable to defy international pressure.

Whatever the frustrations privately suffered by its nuclear establishment, India's public stance continued to occupy the moral high ground on the questions of the test ban and complete nuclear disarmament. In 1988, then Prime Minister Rajiv Gandhi made his proposal which was publicized as a bold initiative on behalf of the non-aligned countries and indeed the developing world as a whole. Annual resolutions in the UN General Assembly were also ritually tabled. In the 1989 general election the Congress Party, which had held power since 1947 except for two years, was decisively defeated and since no political party had the majority to form the government the era of coalition politics began. The short-lived coalitions under Chandra Shekhar and V. P. Singh were so preoccupied with the struggle for survival that they had no time to think about nuclear issues. In the absence of any new directives from the political leader- ship the bureaucracy simply carried on with established precedents: that is, pushing for complete nuclear disarmament and for the CTB.

NARASIMHA RAO'S GOVERNMENT AND THE CTB

P.V. Narasimha Rao's Government after the 1991 election was also a coalition, his Congress Party being the strongest partner but a little short of a majority. But for one or two crises, it remained relatively stable—stable enough for the prime minister to think about long-term policies including nuclear policy. The cold war had ended, the Soviet Union had collapsed and the USA had emerged as the dominant power in a unipolar world. India's foreign policy had to adjust quickly to this emergent reality.

While the bureaucracy had few new ideas to offer, Rao embarked on a series of new initiatives. He started to liberalize the Indian economy and took concrete steps to improve relations with China and with the USA. It was during the first three years of his premiership that he seems to have taken a fresh look at India's defence and nuclear policies. During this time Bill Clinton was elected US President and the USA, too, was rethinking its nuclear policies, clearly moving towards accepting the CTB, to which it had been opposed throughout the 1980s. Given India's consistent advocacy of the CTB, Rao decided to join the USA in co-sponsoring a resolution in the UN General Assembly to negotiate the CTB at the Conference on Disarmament (CD) in Geneva. India co-sponsored the CTB resolution in 1993 and 1994. There is no evidence that the nuclear establishment or the bomb lobby opposed this.

That lobby was taken by complete surprise, indeed shocked, when the USA and Russia both supported a test ban despite disagreements over the treaty's scope. More importantly, to the lobby's great alarm, it seemed that China, too, was moving towards accepting a test ban under certain conditions. The Indian Government realized that it could forcefully advocate a test ban only so long as there was no possibility of it becoming a reality; it could profess high principles and keep the Indian nuclear option open as a marker of protest against discriminatory global regimes. Once a non-discriminatory test ban appeared achievable, however, India's option threatened simply to disappear, for political reasons more than technical.

The fact that the 20th anniversary of the Pokhran test fell in 1994 added to the urgency of determining what a test ban would mean for India's nuclear programme. Twenty years had passed without a test. India's nuclear laboratories were presumably busy improving the 1974 design, but how were the new designs to be tested? The scientists were clearly of the opinion that testing was absolutely necessary, but no political clearance for carrying out tests could be obtained. Now that a test ban had appeared on the horizon, political clearance for a series of tests before a test ban was concluded became a matter of extreme urgency. It is difficult to know whether the Department of Atomic Energy was, in fact, in a position to carry out a series of tests even if it were directed to do so by the prime minister (who has always had the charge of that department) but given the acute anxiety expressed by retired nuclear scientists (who were obviously speaking for their colleagues still in the department) it seems that the prime minister did not approve of carrying out any tests.

For the 20th anniversary of the Pokhran test, Indian newspaper cor- respondents went round the country to get the views of both nuclear and space scientists. No scientist was prepared to speak on record; some would not even speak off the record. It was clear, however, that they were bitter and angry at the government. One of them spoke privately of the 'fear psychosis' in the Prime Minister's Office because of US pressure. They were of the unanimous view that India must not 'wilt under any sort of pressure', as one of them put it. 'The country cannot afford to allow a cap on its nuclear and missile development programmes'.

Only one retired scientist, P. K. Iyengar, who had designed the Pokhran device, said openly: 'To cap efforts in these areas is to restrain experimentation and thus cripple research and development': testing was 'a must' to improve the weapon designs.

The prime minister refused to budge. Earlier, on 13 April 1994, addressing a meeting of the army commanders, Rao had linked India's stand on the NPT or 'similar non-proliferation regimes' to Pakistan's possession of nuclear weapons. The opposition BJP reacted angrily and wrote a letter to Rao accusing him of softening India's opposition to the NPT. In his reply, Rao clarified his position: 'We are not saying that we have set our face against [the NPT] under all circumstances... Our stand is to bring [the NPT] in line with what India can accept'. Another indication that Rao was in favour of a change in India's nuclear policy was that he had changed the entire team of Ministry of External Affairs officials selected for negotiating with the USA on nuclear issues. This created a great deal of dissatisfaction within the ministry. The fact that India dropped a resolution it had earlier tabled in the UN calling for total nuclear disarmament also added fuel to the fire.

In this atmosphere, Prime Minister Rao's July 1994 visit to the USA had to be handled very carefully in the Indian media. Much was made of economic cooperation and references to discussion of nuclear matters were kept to a bare minimum. President Clinton was quoted in one report as saying that the USA wanted to know what was 'pivotal' for India's security and promised to work for that. What was pivotal, India seems to have clarified, was cooperation between China and Pakistan in defence and nuclear weapon technology. The USA then suggested that it would seek China's cooperation for achieving non- proliferation in South Asia. Only bits and pieces of what passed are available in the Indian media. It seems that the USA proposed a five- nation 'regional security dialogue' involving China, India, Pakistan, Russia and the USA. India wanted it expanded to involve Iran, Israel and Kazakhstan as well. As was to be expected nothing came of this, but India specifically rejected a role for China as a 'guarantor' of commitments undertaken by Pakistan on non-proliferation in South Asia.

Rao had noted the opposition from the nuclear and space establishments and the attempts to sabotage the changes he wanted to bring about in India's nuclear policy, but he still did not abandon his quest. It was only in January 1995 that he decided not to have India participate in the NPT Review and Extension Conference as a concession to the opposition. Even as late as February 1995, however, India's participation in that conference as an observer remained a distinct possibility. According to J. N. Dixit, who as Indian Foreign Secretary had participated in the India–USA dialogue, India had categorically ruled out signing the NPT but had nevertheless agreed to work for the CTB and the fissile material cut-off treaty (FMCT).

Perhaps because Rao had explicitly committed India to supporting the FMCT, the debate in the Indian media during the first half of 1995 was devoted to the desirability of India acceding to it. It was not an informed debate since the commentators had almost no facts about fissile material production or stockpiles in India. Much of it was devoted to the argument that, while the declared nuclear powers had huge stockpiles of fissile materials, India's stock was bound to be small and this would put India in a disadvantageous situation.

There was still little debate on the CTB. The indefinite extension of the NPT changed the atmosphere during the second half of 1995. That an overwhelming number of non-aligned states had agreed to the NPT extension came as a shock to Indian nuclear opinion makers. Their simple explanation for this was US pressure. With the NPT extension, however, opinion makers in India began to oppose all the non- proliferation regimes which India had advocated for decades and which the USA was prepared to accept after rejecting them all along. The self-congratulatory tone—at last the USA has seen the light of Indian wisdom—suddenly changed to that of hostility towards all proposals put forward by the USA, the West as a whole and Russia. The CTBT which was to follow the NPT extension became the next target.

A series of articles now began to appear in the Indian media denouncing the CTBT as a deeply flawed and discriminatory measure designed to stop India on the learning curve and to abolish India's option permanently. The authors of these articles, almost all from New Delhi and almost all in favour of India developing a fully- fledged nuclear arsenal, met in a new round of seminars organized by well-known think-tanks to reinforce each other's views and to 'educate public opinion'. These created an atmosphere in the capital in which views supporting the test ban were at best regarded as mis- guided under the influence of Western conventional wisdom or at worst as amounting to treason.

The orchestrated argument ran as follows: the CTBT, as its rolling text then stood, would not at all be 'comprehensive' since it would not shut down the nuclear weapon laboratories and the testing facilities of the nuclear weapon powers. Despite accepting zero yield, these powers, perhaps with the exception of China, would do computer simulations with the codes already obtained from their previous tests in order to come up with new designs specifically meant for use against non-nuclear weapon countries. The sub-critical tests involving fissile materials announced by the USA proved the point. Moreover, the USA had announced the setting up of the National Ignition Facility to keep itself at the cutting edge of nuclear weapon technology. It was also rumoured that the USA would not only share technology with the UK and France but also with China, thus maintaining the oligopoly of the five declared nuclear powers. As the most technologically advanced state in the developing world in nuclear matters, India must challenge this oligopoly not only on its own behalf but on behalf of those states which could not stand up to pressures from the USA.

While public opinion was being tutored in this vein, the government remained non-committal. The record of discussions and negotiations in the CD shows that the Indian delegates did not frontally challenge the CTBT as it was shaping up in Geneva. In fact, in April 1995 the Indian delegate to the CD was heard to complain that the negotiations were proceeding at too slow a pace and he wanted the nuclear weapon powers to show the political will to increase the pace.

Even as late as the end of 1995, India was moving towards joining the CTBT. This was despite the fact that articles attacking the CTBT, including those from the government-supported strategic think-tanks, had kept up a steady barrage.

Government officials were on the defensive. Still, clear directives from the highest government authority had not been sent down. The nuclear and space scientists were advising the government that signing the CTBT would mean the end of the nuclear weapon programme. Lone voices advocating that India should sign the CTBT after proposing some amendments were con- temptuously silenced by the simple expedient of questioning their patriotism.

For some time before the general election, it had become clear that Rao's Congress Party faced a rout. Perhaps as a result of so much adverse reaction both within and outside the government, Rao tried to limit his vulnerability and decided not to sponsor any resolution in the UN General Assembly urging the countries in the CD to work for a CTBT. It is thought by many observers that he wanted to dilute India's earlier commitment; by allowing the hawks to criticize the existing contents of the CTBT 'rolling text', India would seek to amend the text to make the treaty much more comprehensive.

The many amendments India sought were clearly unacceptable to the nuclear weapon powers. For example, India wanted the scope of the treaty to exclude all tests involving fissile material. Similarly, India wanted to link the CTBT to 'genuine nuclear disarmament within a time-bound framework' and for this it wanted the establishment of an Ad Hoc Committee on Nuclear Disarmament in the CD. Given the way Prime Minister Rao's mind always worked—that is to say, that problems would go away if he did nothing about them—it is entirely possible that he thought India's unacceptable additions to the treaty text would prolong the discussions in the CD well beyond the deadline or, better still, the whole process would collapse. However, while buying time, India did not reject the treaty; it adopted the moral stance of improving it. To add weight to the moral posture, Salman Haider, India's Foreign Secretary, declared in the CD on 21 March 1996: 'We do not believe that the acquisition of nuclear weapons is essential for India's security'.

A WEAK NEW GOVERNMENT

Soon after this, India entered the period of the general election, a period of great political uncertainty. In May 1996, the Rao Government was voted out of power. After an unsuccessful bid by the BJP to form a government (it lasted just 13 days), a United Front coalition of 14 parties with the Congress Party supporting it from the outside formed the government.

With this turn of events India's stance on the CTBT changed decisively almost overnight. It seems that a coalition of laboratory scientists, hard-liners in the foreign and defence ministries and hawks from the think-tanks in New Delhi quickly consolidated itself and presented the Prime Minister's Office with a unified view that India needed to stop dithering and reject the CTBT outright despite all pressures.

The weak new government, unlike its predecessor, was unable to side-step this bureaucratic-cum-strategic intellectual phalanx. It made a decision which would make it appear strong- willed. On 20 June 1996, Arundhati Ghose, India's chief delegate to the CD, declared in a hard-hitting speech that nuclear weapons were essential for India's security.

She further said that India had the sovereign right to make a decision about signing the treaty and would reject the entry-into-force clause. Even so, the issue of whether India, while not signing the CTBT, should allow the treaty to be transmitted to the UN General Assembly still remained. When the deadline approached, the position was taken to block the transmittal.

A coalition of some determined laboratory scientists and hard-liners within and outside the government (many of them retired officials) had won the day, but that coalition had no unified view about what to do next. Having saved the option, should India go ahead and test?

Opinion was divided. While this group was critical of the CTBT text as it finally emerged, no credible alternatives were suggested. The issue of the CTB became more firmly linked to a time-bound plan of complete nuclear disarmament but no concrete proposals as alternatives to the step-by-step US–Russian Strategic

Arms Reduction Talks (START) process emerged. The day had been won but the future still remained uncertain.

PROSPECTS FOR THE FUTURE

The United Front Government, having rejected the CTBT categorically, has made this the established policy of the country. It would be extremely difficult for any future government to reverse course even if it wanted to do so. With weak coalition governments, a reversal would be impossible. Yet it cannot be called a robust policy worked out in all its details.

Will a future government undertake tests and production of deliver- able nuclear weapons? The BJP's resolution states that if the security conditions so require it will deploy nuclear weapons, but it is unlikely to do so if it ever comes to power.

This is in part because it is unlikely to emerge from any election with a decisive majority; rather it will be in coalition with several other parties. Furthermore, whereas it is easy for it to appear defiant when not in power, once in power other priori- ties would take precedence—economic considerations and international repercussions, for example.

What if Pakistan tests a nuclear weapon? Domestic pressure in India then would mount to fever pitch as it did in the wake of the Chinese test of 1964. It is then possible that India would resort to a tit-for-tat test to assuage public opinion but without embarking on a fully- fledged programme of tests.

Now that opposition to the CTBT has been signed and sealed as India's firm stand—'India will not sign it; not now nor later' in the words of Ambassador Ghose—such opinion as supported the treaty in the past has now been effectively blunted. There is a long history in India of critics opposing government decisions in defence matters.

Deals to acquire aircraft-carriers, nuclear-powered submarines and deep-penetration strike aircraft, to give only a few examples, have been denounced, often by retired military officials, offering cogent arguments. Such criticism has made no difference whatsoever. The only possibility of India reversing its decision on the CTBT would arise if it became a major issue in a general election in the future.

It is very unlikely that this can happen. The other possibility, even more remote, is that a change of heart on the part of the policy makers will be brought about by intense pressures and isolation which begin to hurt beyond what proud national- ism can bear.

There have been occasions in the past when pressures have worked but the issues involved—the export of jute bags and water buffaloes to Viet Nam, for example—did not lend themselves to being exploited by opposition parties. The CTBT has now been elevated as a symbol of India's standing up to the great powers; climbing down has become all the more difficult.

The fissile material cut-off

Just as Rao's positive approach to the CTBT could have overcome the standard objections to the NPT, the FMCT could address many of India's non-proliferation concerns if India decided to participate in the negotiations and sign it.

In 1997, however, the same lobby which opposed the CTBT is opposing the FMCT as well. There is no possibility of the Indian nuclear establishment agreeing to bring existing stockpiles under the provisions of the treaty; that would completely remove the long-cherished element of ambiguity and perhaps expose the shortcomings in India's nuclear programme. A useful diversion is to link it with complete nuclear disarmament within a fixed time-frame. The debate over the CTBT has made the fixed time-frame a near-sacred principle.

India has always advocated complete nuclear disarmament and world opinion is on its side, but the insistence on a fixed time-frame is a new element in India's approach. The Rajiv Gandhi plan of 1988 mentioned a tentative date (including conclusion of the CTBT by 1994) but not a fixed time-frame as such. A cynical interpretation of why India has lately made a fixed time-frame the major issue of principle could be that it was the most effective way of opposing the CTBT. The more charitable interpretation, of course, is that India truly thinks that without a timetable there is no hope of eliminating nuclear weapons even in the distant future.

Nuclear laboratories across the world, including those in India, can- not imagine a future without nuclear weapons and in the short term, at least, they would oppose a deceleration of their work. Their great fear is that skills won the hard way would be lost. Once the goal was in sight, funding would also taper off. One established route to acquiring prestige for the nation would be closed.

Do India's political leaders want complete nuclear disarmament and that within a fixed time-frame? At present, they express it as an chapter of faith. The consequences of universal nuclear disarmament for India are far from Indian thinking. When the opinion makers take up the issue seriously, they are likely to point out that with global nuclear disarmament India would be vulnerable to conventional threats. In the case of South Asia, an expensive conventional arms race would arguably follow. Those who use complete nuclear disarmament within a short time-frame as an excuse to avoid the CTBT can be expected to change their tune when it appears achievable, as happened in the case of the CTBT.

NUCLEAR WEAPONS, ARMS CONTROL AND RELATIONS WITH PAKISTAN

The link between non-proliferation and conventional disarmament is important for addressing the issues of security for India and Pakistan. In Pakistani thinking, its nuclear capability acts as an equalizer *vis-à- vis* India's superior conventional military power. The Pakistani leaders have convinced themselves that India has stopped short of attacking the western half of Kashmir or indeed further dismembering the country because of its nuclear capability.

If for any reason India were to threaten the existence of Pakistan as a state as presently constituted, they expect to use nuclear weapons against India first. With a doctrine of this kind, which can usefully be termed 'volatility', Pakistan would not be deterred by India's nuclear capability or even overt weaponization.

The keys to Indo-Pakistani mutual security therefore lie in New Delhi and Islamabad. If a security dialogue between the two is to take place at all, India must make it known to Pakistan through all available channels that it has no intention of dismembering Pakistan. In fact, it favours a united Pakistan. It must, as it is doing at present under the United Front Government's 'Gujral Doctrine', settle the disputes over the Siachen Glacier, the Sir Creek and the Wular Barrage.

Then it must rapidly move to start a dialogue over the most important problem of all, Kashmir. The maximalist positions on Kashmir on both sides have been held for so long that they are now practically non-negotiable. Without some evidence of interest in mutual accommodation, dialogue cannot begin.

This is where the Government of Pakistan has painted itself into a tighter corner than has India. In India it is possible to propose that the line of control in Kashmir should become the international border. In Pakistan, such a proposal is not acceptable. Even so, there are signs of a change in public mood.

During the 1997 general election in Pakistan former Prime Minister Benazir Bhutto adopted a militantly anti-India platform, but her rival Mohammed Nawaz Sharif did not. Sharif won such a decisive majority that Bhutto must have wondered whether she had gone too far with her stand.

The Gujral Doctrine's emphasis on'non-reciprocity', that is to say, not seeking equal concessions from neighbouring countries and not responding to inflammatory statements from Pakistan, has enabled the two countries to begin working towards confidence-building measures, but the issue of Kashmir must wait its turn.

Once Pakistan feels secure within its borders, a security dialogue can begin. India must help Pakistan to achieve that sense of security, with some return from Pakistan in the form of cutting off the infiltration of men and *matériel* into the Kashmir Valley. India must ensure free and fair elections in Kashmir as well as a clean administration there. Then it would be easier to deal with violations of human rights by Indian troops in the valley. In short, Pakistan's sense of vulnerability *vis-à-vis* India's military superiority must be tackled if Pakistan's volatility in nuclear matters is to be limited.

Will future coalitions in India continue with the process started by the Gujral Doctrine? Only a coalition led by the BJP has the potential to alter the course, but it may not do so. Indo-Pakistani relations were at their best when the BJP leader Atal Bihari Vajpayee was Indian Minister of External Affairs in 1977–79. The BJP, when in power, cannot antagonize the 120 million Muslims in India who want good relations between India and Pakistan. It has long held virulent anti- China views but it has now accepted the series of agreements India has signed with China. It is unlikely to put back the clock in the question of relations with Pakistan.

5

The Trading of Arms from Rich Countries to Poor Countries

During the 1990s the poorest countries of the world became saturated with arms; some originated from "legal" transfers, and many formed part of the illegal trade. The arms trade destabilised already fragmented countries, making development difficult and blurring distinctions between use for military and criminal purposes. Outside governments openly or clandestinely supplied arms to factions they favoured for political reasons or for access to resources, as did some multinational companies. Many loopholes allowed weapons to enter unstable or embargoed countries—for example, ineffective or falsified end user certificates and licensed production in or brokerage through intermediate, poorly regulated countries (box). Arms brokers often supplied both sides in a conflict.

TRADE IN MAJOR CONVENTIONAL WEAPONS

In 1972, poor countries received 48% of their weapons free from the United States and the Soviet Union. By 1982 donations had declined to around 14%, but the total value of exports to non-oil producing developing countries had doubled, leading many into debt. During the 1990s the permanent members of the United Nations Security Council were the main manufacturers and exporters of major conventional weapons, delivering 65-96% of their exported arms to developing countries between 1997 and 2000. Arms were supplied to countries on both sides of the various conflicts, reducing the resources available for health and education. For example, the United Kingdom, United States, Russia, Germany, and Canada supplied both India and Pakistan with weapons despite Pakistan spending less than 1% of its gross domestic product on health. Many weapons exported to poor countries were second hand, often accompanied by trained military support; some were sold from vast stockpiles left over from the cold war.

Trade in small arms and light weapons

Although the poorest countries struggled to afford major weapons, they could buy small arms. The AK 47 rifle, for example, can be bought in Africa for a bag of maize and in Afghanistan for $10 (£6.45, €10). It needs little maintenance and with minimal training can be a deadly weapon, even when used by young children. Apart from being cheap and easy to manufacture, small weapons are also readily transported, smuggled, and hidden.

In 47 of 49 major conflicts between 1990 and 2000 small arms and light weapons were the main weapons used, causing incalculable human suffering. They continually threaten development and have been the principal weapons used in conflicts characterised by abuse of human rights. An estimated 600 million small arms and light weapons exist—one for every 10 people on earth. They are responsible for the vast majority of conflict casualties, and in 2001 they were implicated in more than 1000 deaths a day, mostly of mothers and children.

Small arms are not included in the control of major arms trading. The UN register of conventional arms is mainly concerned with the threat that major weapons pose to international or regional stability, rather than stability within countries. Indeed, the UN acknowledges that the challenge posed by small arms "involves security, humanitarian and developmental dimensions." The UN supports the need to control the proliferation of small arms but is challenged by the fact that the five permanent members of the Security Council are among the main suppliers. Despite attempts by the United States and the European Union to work together to combat the small arms trade, the United States and some members of the EU (United Kingdom, France, Germany, Italy, and Belgium) are among the main exporters. The International Action Network on Small Arms coordinates more than 340 organisations from 71 countries to prevent the proliferation and misuse of small arms and light weapons.

Illegal arms trading

Although 80-90% of the global trade in small arms is legal, trading in illegal arms (defined by the UN as exports that violate national or international law) accounts for over 50% of all weapons in circulation. As most poor countries have minimal systems to regulate the ownership of weapons, this definition applies only to arms exported to countries under mandatory arms embargoes from countries where licensing systems exist. Most illegal arms start out legally and become illegal by brokered sales, theft, and corruption, most often when non-state actors are supplied for political or economic reasons.

In the 1990s, sophisticated ploys reminiscent of other organised crimes such as drugs trafficking were used to distribute illegal weapons. For example, cargo aircraft supplying weapons flew circuitous routes, often at night using their own navigation systems, multiple landings, changes of aircraft, or falsification of aircraft registration. Pilots and planes were registered to "flags of convenience" and sometimes delivered during an "emergency landing" close to receiving factions. In Africa, where many countries have poor accountability, bureaucracy, customs procedures, and air traffic control, it was easy to complete illegal deliveries. The US Bureau of Intelligence and Research and Amnesty International reported that air charter companies from the United Kingdom and Belgium supplying arms to Rwanda, Congo, and Sierra Leone were unknown to and untouchable by law enforcers in their countries of origin.

THE HUMAN COSTS OF CONFLICT

The international arms trade is the substrate for global armed conflict, causing enormous human suffering, and mothers and children are the most vulnerable people. According to Unicef, between 1986 and 1996 two million children were killed in armed conflict, six million were seriously injured or permanently disabled, and countless others were forced to witness or take part in violence. A major proportion of victims were civilians, particularly women and children. In her report to Unicef, Graça Machel stated that "Wars have always victimised children and other non-combatants, but modern wars are exploiting, maiming and killing children more callously than ever." The indirect effects of armed conflicts cause most fatalities in mothers and children and include

- Food deprivation
- Spread of disease, in part due to disruption of public health systems
- Psychological and emotional damage (two thirds of Angolan children had witnessed murder)
- Disability
- Separation of families (in 1995, 20% of Angolan children were separated from their families)
- Loss of education
- Sexual abuse of children, including deliberate rape to drive out ethnic minorities
- Child abduction, torture, and slavery
- Child soldiers (in 1998, for example, at least 300.000 children aged under 18 were soldiers).

Another consequence of conflict is displacement. In 1997, 13.2 million people were refugees and 4.9 million were internally displaced, disproportionately more of whom were women and children than in the source population. In Rwandan refugee camps child mortality was as high as 300 per 100000 per day. Child mortality in displaced communities was more than 60% higher than among non-displaced children in the same country. In contrast, in 2001 the United States and the United Kingdom, two major arms exporters, provided haven for only 4.3% and 1.2% of the world's refugees (which totalled 12 million).

Huge differences in the health of mothers and children exist between the 10 poorest countries undergoing conflict in 2000 and the predominantly rich countries that exported arms to them (directly or indirectly). Scaling each country to a population of 50 million gives figures of 2009 children aged under 5 years dying each day and 46667 mothers dying each year during pregnancy or childbirth in the poorest country (Sierra Leone) compared with 15 children per day and 91 mothers per year in the country supplying the most arms (United States). Arms exports cannot be said to have directly caused this disparity, but to believe that they have not contributed would be unrealistic. These differences are so great that they question the humanity of arms exporting countries. Armed conflict and weapons trading may thus be seen as a form of maternal and child abuse.

BETTER REGULATION OF LEGAL MANUFACTURE AND TRADING IN ARMS

Legal trading should be a responsibility of and regulated by a newly configured United Nations that is more representative of poor nations, as well as financially less dependent on countries that manufacture arms. Legal arms should be traded only for defence (article 51 of the UN charter) and must not worsen existing conflict, cause human rights violations, or impede development.

Much more regulation of arms manufacturing companies is needed, particularly for companies that have overseas factories. The middlemen (brokers trading outside their own countries) who buy, sell, and transport arms to countries without adequate governance are most important. In parallel, tighter international regulation is needed of shipping agents and money launderers (including many reputable banks) who remain above the law by sidestepping the current weak controls. In many respects it would be better to make all brokering activities illegal (as they are with the drugs trade) and permit dealing of arms only through the UN. Brokers and company owners should be indicted for war crimes if they break international embargoes or provide arms illegally through negligence or intent. In addition, loans for the purchase of weapons by poor countries should be subject to UN approval.

The UN must do more to influence the United States, a country that exports the greatest number of weapons, refuses to accept an international criminal court, and is one of only two states refusing to ratify the UN Convention on the Rights of the Child. Regrettably, in 2001, the US undersecretary of state at the first UN conference on small arms insisted that only illegal trading should be addressed and that the United States would resist any agreement that infringed the "right to bear arms." Transparency is also important. Only seven of the world's 190 countries publish regular data on small arms exports, and only three of these provide details on the numbers and kinds of weapons involved. All weapons and ammunition should be branded to enable tracing.

Important steps forward have been taken. Attempts to develop an ethical foreign policy in the United Kingdom have resulted in annual reports of licences granted for the exports of weapons, including small arms. In 1998 an EU code of conduct on arms exports was agreed, as well as a moratorium by the Economic Community of West African States on imports, exports, and manufacture of small arms and light weapons into west Africa. An innovative proposal for controlling arms, "the international code of conduct," has come from a commission of Nobel peace laureates and is based on ethical criteria within international humanitarian law. Economic arguments in the United Kingdom have revealed the cost of the arms trade to taxpayers. The British government has also supported economic regeneration in Bulgaria and Ukraine, countries dependent on the arms industry. However, links between the trade in arms and commodities such as oil mean that for powerful arms exporting countries the resulting economic advantages in terms of all trade are complex and probably substantial. Programmes of weapons collection and destruction intended to demilitarise countries have included food, medical care, and education for individuals or communities that surrender weapons. Perhaps the country that has provided the weapons should provide the compensation.

BETTER PREVENTION OF ILLEGAL MANUFACTURE AND TRADING IN ARMS

International laws and their aggressive enforcement should stop illegal arms trading, including its support systems, such as money laundering and smuggling. An international police force (perhaps better termed an international family protection force) working closely with national police is needed to arrest and charge the hundreds of criminally active illegal arms dealers, most of whom are already known and on databases. Banks and companies supporting illegal trading should be targeted. Enhanced control of borders to detain aircraft, ships, or vehicles and arrest and charge people responsible for smuggling would have an impact. Many illegal arms dealers are based in rich, relatively well governed countries, so stopping them should be possible.

Investigations by the UN into breaches of arms embargoes often result in information about the state and individual actors involved and lead to expressions of concern but no action. No one has been convicted of violating UN arms embargoes. The UN seems to be powerless to act, and it clearly needs to find a way of mobilising states to accept an international family protection force as well as giving more power to the international criminal court. Tragically, trafficking of arms to Africa seems to be low on the world's priority list. One possible way forward could involve the UN Convention against Transnational Organized Crime, within which is a draft protocol against the illicit manufacture of and trafficking in firearms.

ARMS PRODUCTION, EXPORTS AND CONTROL IN THE ASEM PROCESS

Arms production and arms trade should be addressed within the political and security pillar of the ASEM process. Three of the EU ASEM countries are among the most prominent arms exporters - France, the UK and Germany. Of the top importers three countries are from East Asia: China, South Korea and Taiwan. Only China is itself a significant arms exporter. However, the flow of arms trade is like a river going one direction - towards Asia. Despite the fact that some recipient states embarked long ago on the creation of a domestic defence industry, they are still dependent on importing supplies.

There is an Asian as well as a European side to arms exports and production of the countries participating in the ASEM process, but this only tells a partial story. Significant differences exist both within and between regions. Europe is home to three of the ten biggest arms manufacturers worldwide. The Japanese Mitsubishi Heavy Industries with a military turnover of US$ 3.6 billion lies just behind the military industries from the US, the UK and France/Germany, making it by far the biggest arms manufacturer of Asia.

Arms production within both Europe and Asia is too diverse to be analysed as one single region. For instance, weapons production in South Korea cannot be compared with Cambodia and Greece (a top ten arms importer) and Germany are playing a very different role in the arms market. Furthermore, the provision in the Japanese constitution against arms trade is not matched in any of the EU countries. These differences indicate the need for further research in establishing the significance of the arms trade and arms production in the ASEM process and for identifying the arms trade connections between the European Union and Asia ASEM countries.

Enhanced Partnerships

In the European Commission Framework document for 'Enhanced Partnerships between Asia and Europe' the latest outline of Europe's Asia policy is given. One of the few remarks on arms trade in the document identifies arms trafficking as a common concern on the level of Ministries of Justice and Home Affairs. Arms traffickers are working across boundaries and co-operation in this field is essential to tackle the illegal flow of arms. One example from 1999 illustrates how an Israeli businessman transported 40 armoured personnel carriers from Germany to Iran. The arms followed a route through the Netherlands, Britain and Singapore before reaching Iran. The Israeli businessman was in close contact with a South Korean arms dealer known to sell arms to Iran. To tackle this kind of flows concerted action between law enforcement bodies of all involved countries is essential.

The Framework document also states that co-operation should exist "for the early and comprehensive ratification of major international Instruments such as the Comprehensive Test Ban Treaty or the Conventions on small arms and anti-personnel mines."

Regional and global security is certainly helped by an orchestrated implementation of those conventions. Landmines are a hidden killer and the removal of those weapons from the stocks of armies is essential for the security of those wanting to use the land for productive purposes such as agriculture, leisure and transport. Illegal small arms are causing death and destruction in all parts of the world and their wide distribution leads to killings by criminals, gangs and paramilitaries. The small arms convention is also addressing those used by resistance groups.

The killings by armies, democratically controlled or not, are outside this Convention and so its implementation is limited to law enforcement and control by the government. The scope of arms control is too limited when it stops at the level of law enforcement and nuclear testing. Such an approach uses a narrow concept of security - that is military security. Arms trade is a way of beefing-up allies, with consequences for regional balances of power and relations between nations and as such part of the conservative security debate. Moreover, major arms deals involving hundreds of millions or even billions of dollars of government expenditure cannot be left out of a genuine people's oriented security debate. Arms trade and acquisitions are part of such a security debate and for this reason should be part of the Framework document.

Finance Packages and Debt

When the EU adopted a strategy on Asia in 1994, it clearly identified the increase in the ambitious armament programmes in the Asian region as one of the factors "which could disrupt world equilibrium and thereby impinging on Europe's Common Foreign and Security Policy objectives." In the 2001 update of the Asia Strategy however, there is less attention to the security dimension of the relationship, with the exception of the issue of small arms trade and nuclear testing.

There can hardly be any justification for this omission. Although the impression exists that arms trade to the ASEM countries declined due to the economic crisis of 1997, this is not yet reflected in the figures given by SIPRI for 1999. Because the negotiations for arms deliveries in general take a long time it is possible that there will be a significant decrease visible in the near future. Another reason the economic crisis is not yet reflected in the figures, is that Arms companies made financial arrangements with governments and banks, such as low interest loans and favourable re-payment schedules to back up ongoing arms deals and negotiations. 'Buy now, Pay later' became the modus operandi of both arms exporters and importers. An official of the British Ministry of Defence explained it in this way: "In the United Kingdom, we view innovative financing packages as a key factor in any likely success". The Defence business was not willing to let existing deals collapse and used financial flexibility to secure additional new deals. Sales did not stop and some were merely postponed. This of course has led to further public debt. Conveniently, the international attention on the burden of debt on state budgets was put aside in order to continue arms trade.

Growing Demand

Besides, the long term effects of the crisis will be downplayed by new developments. Analysts see a growing demand for arms in South East Asia. The Malaysian Defence Minister Najib Razak told the well attended Defence Services Asia (DSA) arms fair: "With the economy of most of these countries back on track there will be a projected increase in the defence expenditure to procure platforms, weapon systems and solutions to meet national requirements." Defence companies likewise felt rewarded for participating in the DSA 2002. Malaysia alone ordered weapons valued US$ 958 million in April 2002. According to an Australian analyst, the process will go more rapidly in Southeast Asia than in the nineties: "Those that haven't started to move with new fighters, new surface combatants, new subs, are very quickly going to."

Issues raised in the nineties are very much back in the debates on arms trade in Asia. Is an arms race ongoing or not?. Do the acquisitions find their logic in modernisation, overhaul or refurbishment? Is it old shopping lists which now materialise? All these questions which had been set aside for five years are once again on the agenda.

However, there are also new issues with the turmoil in Indonesia being an important new factor. What is not yet very much back in the discussion is the ASEAN Regional Forum (ARF) or any other initiative on genuine regional security co-operation. Military exercises with the US and Australia are the most developed forms of regional military co-operation at present. The absence of a multilateral framework for regional security co-operation seriously hampers confidence among the countries in the region and arms acquisitions of one country are followed by similar acquisitions by neighbouring countries.

9/11 Becomes a New Sales Pitch

According to Malaysia's Defense Minister Razak when he defended the Malaysian arms acquisitions during the DSA arms fair "The 9/11 attack drastically changed the outlook toward national security". By invoking the 9/11 terrorist attacks, he was joining those government leaders who have used the 9/11 events to popularize a new sales pitch for arms acquisitions.

The strike on the World Trade Center and Pentagon is a weak rationale for placing submarines and fighter aircraft on the shopping list of many East and Southeast Asian countries. These are not the best weapons in the fight against terrorism.

The current weapons acquisitions are high-tech buys demonstrated during the Second Gulf War on Iraq (1990-91). Furthermore, the latest orders and wish lists follow the images of US technology shown on the Afghan battlefield: the integration of remote operation, new observation techniques, state of the art Information Technology, improved precision guided munitions, and lasers. According to an Australian expert, "we will see increasing sophistication, not only of the platforms, the ships, tanks and aircraft, but of the weapon systems that go with them."

The 9/11 attacks and the creation of US led coalition against terrorism provided the rationale for lifting arms embargoes and relaxing arms export policies on more advanced weapon systems as a reward to countries for their participation.

This applied to the Middle East, South Asia, and also in Southeast Asia e.g. Indonesia. The restrictions on military cooperation between Jakarta and Washington (developed between 1994 and 2000) have been under pressure ever since. Likewise the Philippines has received 100 million US$ in military assistance, and has allowed the intervention of US Special Forces in Mindanao.

An additional factor for further militarisation in the region is Missile proliferation and the re-emergence of the US Star Wars programme - pushing military budgets ever higher.

According to John Chipman, Director of the International Institute for Strategic Studies in London, " The nature of missile proliferation in the region holds in prospect the kind of arms race that was not seen in the first half of the 1990s"

Defence Industry in East and Southeast Asia

The economic crisis of 1997 did change the picture of the defence industry in Asia. Domestic defence industries in Southeast Asia are opening their firms to foreign investment to build equity and market links with Western nations for capital, technology and markets. Malaysia recently indicated that it wants to become a regional hub to help international defence firms to penetrate Asian markets and most of the ASEAN defence industries are eager to find a foreign partner to attract market access as well as capital. This path is also followed by South Korea. The French Thales company has a joint venture with Samsung. Taiwan wants to build the submarines offered by the US in 2001 at the China Shipbuilding Corp. as well as import the technology from abroad. All this is underlining dependence on Western funds and weapon technology, developed with large sums on Research & Development programmes (R&D) -estimated at US$ 39.3 billion in the US and at US$ 9.1 billion in Europe annually.

Singapore Technologies follows another route similar to what Western firms do - buying what it needs mainly in the US. This excludes the real state-of-the-art technology because this is prevented from foreign participation even by key allies. Of the six ASEAN countries which are producing small arms at home, only Singapore Technologies has a sound economic policy and export record. It exported ordnance, machine guns and assault rifles to a wide range of regions of tension. Other countries produce arms against higher market prices - which has more to do with national pride than with sound economics and the rule of the market.

The Chinese defence industry still produces obsolete weapon systems. It is not yet able to start the reorganisation process demanded to generate the capacity needed for the technological advanced weapon systems which the Chinese military want to possess. There has been little change in the Japanese weapons industry. However, as a result of the economic recession the Japanese car industry was opened up to foreign investment. Renault took this opportunity and its investment in Nissan resulted in the sale of the military division of Nissan Motor Corp. to Ishikawajima-Harima Heavy Industries. This reflects the imperative to keep arms production in Japanese hands.

6

Curbing the Proliferation of Small Arms and Light Weapons

Small arms control became "medium politics" on the international agenda in 1998. It was medium relative to the high politics of landmines, the issue's progenitor in many minds, but it was the subject of a feverish pace of activity compared to just one year ago. Most notable, in late October sixteen states in West Africa signed a binding agreement to ban production, import and export of small arms for a three year trial period. In addition, western hemisphere governments signed (and several ratified) a convention on illicit manufacture and transfer of firearms. Preparations for negotiation of a global protocol against firearms trafficking were begun. And, during the summer, the Canadian government proposed a treaty barring transfers of military-style small arms to insurgent forces and other non-state actors.

The European Union, OSCE, Organization of American States, Organization of African Unity, Economic Community of West African States, and the South African Development Community all took up some aspect of small arms control, and almost every part of the UN (including, increasingly, the Security Council) engaged the topic in the past year. Meanwhile, nearly a dozen governments are vying for the mantle of leadership. Most prominent have been Belgium, Canada, Japan, the Netherlands, Norway, South Africa and Switzerland—several of which hosted international governmental conferences discussing small arms control (the need for it, the feasibility of it, etc.) in 1998. And with two speeches in as many months brimming with policy proscriptions, Secretary of State Albright has recently put the United States into the running.

To varying degrees, each of these states has embraced the "Ottawa model" of government-NGO collaboration, particularly in the areas of brainstorming for policy initiativies, holding consciousness-raising seminars, and funding programs to assist reintegration of former combatants and to collect and destroy weapons. And NGOs from the north and south recently came together to launch a coordinating structure—the International Action Network on Small Arms—to rationalize and facilitate their research, advocacy and practical work.

This extraordinary explosion of activity is a result of the breadth and complexity of the "small arms problem." The issue is much broader than landmines—both in terms of the scope of the problem (as measured by the quantity of small arms in irresponsible hands or the number of civilian deaths and casualties), and in terms of factors related to the proliferation of these arms. Whereas landmines were predominately viewed as a humanitarian issue, stemming from internal conflicts (generally), many see small arms proliferation principally as a police/crime issue. To others, it is a conflict prevention/resolution issue, or a relief/development problem. Each of these frameworks suggests different remedial policies and different priorities.

In the case of mines, the biggest conceptual question was over whether to include all mines or just anti-personnel mines in the scope of control efforts. With small arms control there are many more fissures, some of which have been exploited by governments to stave off politically or economically unpalatable control measures. A principal divide is whether the main problem is existing stocks of "illicit" weaponry in circulation in zones of conflict, or whether on-going legal transfers are also of concern. If it is the former, how do you define the term, given that the licit trade and the illicit traffic in small arms are inextricably linked? Arms that are originally exported legally, but are not properly tracked or secured, often fall into illegal circulation, as theft or capture of state security forces' arms is a major source of black-market supply around the world.

While some governments and NGOs sought a big conceptual framework to tie it all together, to address all facets of the problem, a year later it is clear that there is no "holy grail." Thus, as is on going, a web of initiatives are needed to reduce the illegal use and oversupply of these weapons (not very catchy, but this phrase seems to encapsulate the overarching goal of all small arms efforts). At the same time, lest governments and NGOs burn out on "initiative fatigue," they must work together even more closely to prioritize and consolidate major areas of activity. And, since this year's focus on small arms will not be sustained indefinitely, these concerned parties must identify and press for the farthest reaching measures to reduce the dangers from small arms proliferation. This agenda includes shoring up the agreements made thus far, focusing on transparency and accountability in legal transfers, curbing the flow of arms to conflict zones, and banning weapons supply by states to insurgents.

Consolidate and Test the Achievements

The supplier governments have been quite willing to talk about "illicit" arms trafficking, by which they usually (but not always) mean stocks of weapons already in circulation outside of government control in the developing world. Evidence of this interpretation is provided by the fact that in the year and a half since the European Union adopted a program on illicit arms trafficking, several EU governments have held seminars with governments in the south to develop work plans on the demand side, but few have reformed their own national laws concerning off-shore brokering of arms deals, improved end use certification and monitoring of transfers, and increased transparency around state-sanctioned small arms exports.

Meanwhile, governments and non-governmental actors from the south tend to focus on the role and responsibility of the arms producing countries (principally, but not exclusively, located in the north) in contributing to the proliferation and misuse of military-style small arms in their regions. Field research by Human Rights Watch and the UN Commission of Inquiry have shown that newly-manufactured weapons continue to enter combat zones. The two most potentially meaningful initiatives that have come about thus far originated with governments in the south concerned about the flow of weapons into their countries. The Mexican and Colombian governments spearheaded the OAS convention on illicit firearms trafficking, and the government of Mali initiated the West African arms production and transfer moratorium.

Hopefully, both the OAS treaty and the ECOWAS initiative are prototypes for exportation to other regions, but at the present time they both remain substantially incomplete. The first order of business for concerned governments and NGOs is work to ensure the success of these two initiatives.

The ECOWAS agreement entered into force on November 1. The treaty itself is three pages long, and most of that text is "whereas" clauses, with the operational part contained in one sentence. Now remains the difficult challenge of providing some assurance that the commitment undertaken is being honored. Money is needed to facilitate demobilization and reintegration of combatants in the region, to promote sustainable development (as an alternative to armed banditry), and to facilitate gun collection and destruction programs. And, importantly, suppliers must bar their nationals from seeking to export arms to West Africa. ECOWAS members made sure to point out in the brief text of the agreement that the Wassenaar Arrangement export control forum had been briefed and its members had agreed to refrain from exporting arms to the region.

The OAS convention entered into force this autumn, with the ratification of two states. (Three have ratified it in all.) In order for other states to ratify the agreement, they will have to pass legislation defining legal and illegal arms importation and exportation, establish effective control mechanisms and a develop central contact agency on the issue. Some of this will take money. Governments must commit the necessary resources (financial and technical) to guarantee implementation of the convention and to assist states that are unable to fund implementation measures themselves. Meanwhile, the international community is apparently pressing ahead with negotiation of a global anti-firearms trafficking protocol in 1999 without first assessing how the OAS convention works. It is imperative that governments place at least equal emphasis on implementation of the extant treaty, so that lessons learned can be incorporated into the global initiative.

BROADENING THE FOCUS TO ARMED CONFLICT IN GENERAL

While a few recent wars (Bosnia, Chechnya, Turkey, Congo) have seen the use of heavy weapons, like armored personnel carriers, medium to heavy artillery, and ground attack aircraft, small arms and light weapons have been a staple of all recent armed conflicts. As stated previously, small arms and light weapons are thought to be responsible for the vast majority of war casualties around the world. Although widely assumed to be a significant factor, there has been no scientific investigation of the impact of small arms supply in terms of outbreak, sustainment or escalation of civil warfare. The dearth of data on arms transfers currently hinders the ability of researchers to conduct such studies. Relatedly, though, the 26th International Conference of the Red Cross and Red Crescent commissioned the ICRC to examine the extent to which the availability of weapons contributes to the proliferation and aggravation of violations of international humanitarian law (the laws that govern the conduct of war).

In two recent speeches —in September before a special UN Security Council session on Africa and in November at a gathering of the International Rescue Committee—Secretary of State Madeleine Albright assailed "the uncontrolled flow of arms, ammunition and explosives into tense areas of the world." Her speeches denoted a welcome broadening of US small arms policy from a previous focus on crime-related illicit firearms trafficking to a concern about weapons shipments—whether legal or not—into certain "zones of conflict."

"This dirty business," as she labeled it in her Security Council speech, "fuels conflict, fortifies extremism, and destabilizes entire regions. All of us whose nations sell such weapons, or through whose nations the traffic flows, bear some responsibility for turning a blind eye to the destruction they cause. And all of us have it in our power to do something in response."

Central Africa was the focus of the Secretary's Security Council presentation. In her November speech, Albright also pointed to recent arms purchases in Afghanistan and Angola as representative of the kinds of small arms sales that the administration finds problematic. Meanwhile, the US government (and undoubtedly others) continue to export weapons to many other combat zones. In 1997 (the most recent information available), several of the countries receiving large quantities of small arms through US surplus programs or buying weapons through commercial channels were engaged in conflict or had extremely poor records on human rights and democracy.

In Colombia more than 30,000 people have been killed in the past decade, with the bulk of these deaths attributed to right-wing paramilitaries operating with a wink and a nod from the military. Nevertheless, Colombian police and military forces received a fresh shipment of "emergency" small arms from the United States in 1997 to assist the "war on drugs." And in 1997 US companies received authorization to sell Colombian state entities over 30,000 grenades, more than one million rounds of ammunition, 7,000 M16 assault rifles, 375 submachine guns and assorted shotguns and machine guns.

In two cases the Clinton administration has announced a policy of barring sales of small arms to US friends or allies on human rights grounds. In February 1994, the State Department announced that it would deny licenses for the transfer of small or light arms and lethal crowd control items to Indonesia. Later that same year, Congress passed law codifying this ban until certain human rights conditions are met. The ban is still in place.

And, according to a July 1997 State Department report to Congress on Turkey's use of US-supplied weapons, "US policy is to restrict the sale of arms that clearly could be used to repress a civilian population, such as small arms and violent crowd-control devices." Turkey's paramilitary Jandarama and the Turkish National Police—the forces most prominently cited in the commission of gross human rights abuses in Turkey—previously purchased M16 and AR-15S assault rifles and M203 grenade launchers through State Department-licensed commercial sales. According to the same report, the State Department has no resources available to monitor the end-use of US-supplied weapons in Turkey, to ensure that they are not being used in the commission of abuses, but "mission personnel have seen some of this equipment, which is still in service." And despite the announced ban, in 1997 the State Department licensed for export nearly $5 million worth of materials for the manufacture of ammunition, hundreds of carbines, and hundreds of pistols to Turkey.

Moreover, the United States and other arms manufacturing states continue to market bombers, helicopters and other weaponry to the Turkish and (until the recent economic crisis) Indonesian armed forces. It is unclear why militaries deemed unfit to import small arms are worthy to import major platforms. By buoying warring or repressive regimes, these "big arms" transfers contribute to the quest for light weaponry by insurgents in Turkey and East Timor. If implemented aggressively, a "code of conduct" measure adopted by the 15 European Union states in May 1998 would prohibit arms transfers if (among other things) "there is a clear risk that the proposed export might be used for internal repression."

Similarly, a measure passed by Congress in November 1997 bars US military aid and arms to abusive units in foreign militaries. However, the Pentagon and State Department usually do not know which military or police units are using US-supplied arms. A necessary next step is the enactment of a "code of conduct" for all US arms exports that would establish firm human rights, democracy and non-aggression criteria in US law. Such a measure has been introduced in Congress each year since 1994. If enacted, it would help establish a more forward looking framework for US arms export policy in general, including small arms exports.

Bar Arms Supply to Non State Actors

Covert gun-running by governments to foreign insurgent groups has been a major source of small arms proliferation. Precisely because of the un-accountable nature of covert arms supply, such operations feed directly into the global black arms market. These transfers also, of course, fuel armed conflict, as they are generally intended to destabilize and topple governments.

American pipelines established to combatants in South Asia, Southern Africa and Central America during the 1980s continue to spill over today, as the weapons have been recycled to other conflicts, to bandits or to terrorists.

The classified US government operation to arm various mujahideen factions fighting in Afghanistan against Soviet invaders began in 1979. Before it ended in 1991, the CIA had shipped via Pakistan an estimated 400,000 AK-47 assault rifles; an undisclosed quantity of Stinger portable anti-aircraft missile launchers and missiles; vast quantities of Italian-made anti-personnel mines; 60,000 archaic rifles, 8,000 light machine guns and over 100,000,000 rounds of ammunition from Turkey; 40-50 Oerlikon Swiss-designed anti-aircraft guns; mortars from Egypt; Blowpipe surface-to-air missiles from Britain; and 100,000 rifles from India. The after effects of this arms supply operation can be felt not only in Afghanistan, but throughout Pakistan, into Kashmir and other parts of India.

It is the Stinger missiles that have caused successive US administrations the greatest heartburn. In her November speech, Secretary Albright said, "We have learned from bitter experience that these weapons, which will fit in a ski bag, are very difficult to control once sold. They turn civilian airliners and humanitarian relief flights into easy targets." As a result, the administration has been pressing other governments through the Wassenaar Arrangement to limit transfers of man-portable air defense missiles. While this goal is most welcome, the lesson appears to have been lost that short-term driven alliances with insurgents are unsound policy. Guerrilla forces often lack a chain of command and authority structure sufficient to ensure physical control of any weaponry—not just missiles capable of shooting passenger jets out of the sky.

Many other states reportedly are or have engaged in covert destabilization programs, including small arms supply: Uganda in southern Sudan; Sudan in northern Uganda; alleged support by Turkey for rebels in Chechnya; alleged support by Russia for

Kurdish guerrillas in Turkey; Pakistan in Kashmir; India in Sri Lanka. In many cases, these arms now pose a direct threat to the state which previously supplied them. And, while the shipments are intended to further the political and/or economic interests of the supplier state, once the conflict ends, the supplier almost never takes responsibility for either the cost of disarmament or the impact upon civil societies when disarmament fails.

At a gathering of 21 governments in Oslo on small arms last July, the Canadian foreign ministry proposed a treaty banning military-style small arms transfers by governments to insurgent forces and other non-state actors. Thus far the rough proposal has received little public support, from either governments or NGOs. Some NGOs are concerned that a convention of this type would deny arms to non-state actors opposing repressive regimes, while those regimes could legally arm themselves against their people. At a major small arms conference sponsored by the Belgian government in mid-October, the British government endorsed the proposal and expressed interest in working on the idea. Norwegian Foreign Minister Vollabaek has expressed cautious support, as well.

Developing international law barring small arms supply (usually covert) to non-state actors would be one of the most meaningful policies that concerned governments and non-governmental organizations could pursue to curb further dangerous small arms proliferation. Past (and continuing) practitioners of covert arms supply cannot be expected to endorse the proposal. But for the "group of like-minded states" and NGOs that came together first around the landmines ban treaty, and then the International Criminal Court, this would seem to be a very worthy effort to explore and further develop.

THE RUSSIAN FAR EAST, EASTERN SIBERIA

In this chapter, the problem of small arms proliferation will be examined in the region of East Siberia and the Russian Far East, including the Russian-Chinese and Russian-Korean frontiers. This area includes:

- Russian Federation: Irkutsk, Chita, Amur, Magadan, Kamchatka and Sakhalin provinces (oblasts); Krasnoyarsk, Amur and Maritim (Primorskij) territories (krais); Ethnic republics of Sakha-Yakutia and Buryatia.
- China Provinces: Heilongjiang, Jilin, Liaoning, Hebei, Beijing and Tjanjin; "Autonomous Regions"; Inner Mongolia (Nei Menggu)
- North Korea (Chongjin-Najin border area)

However, detailed coverage of political and financial aspects of the problem require some reference to the Moscow area, because major movements of small arms at the Russian-Chinese and Russian-Korean Frontiers hardly occur without decisions of major military, political, business and criminal centres of Russia, most of them in Moscow city/Moscow province area. The Tula province and Urals area of Russia (especially the two provinces of Chelyabinsk and Yekaterinburg) are also mentioned in the research as major centres of arms production of Russia. The Russian Far East, Siberia and Russian-Chinese/Russian-Korean Frontier should be regarded as an area of special concern. Small arms are proliferating there because of the weakened national systems of control on small arms production, exports and imports, particularly at extreme distances. Of major concern among neighbours is that the illicit/semi-illicit proliferation of small arms in the region may be exacerbating crime. At the same time, criminal organizations are also interested in involvement in the small arms trade.

Sources of Small Arms

China and North Korea are the countries reported to be sources of small arms proliferation in the region. In the post-Communist era, there is practically no official control over small arms production and trade. The strict ban on the owning and trade of small arms that existed before 1991 has been lifted. But even during the last decade of the Communist rule, the law banning small arms ownership was not fully enforced for all social groups. Obtaining a license to own and carry small weapons was no longer a complicated process after 1992. Now, many Russian companies and organizations have their own arsenals of small weapons without any license. Millions of private citizens of the Russian Federation are also purchasing firearms in order to protect themselves and their families from the social chaos of crime expansion in contemporary Russia.

Small Arms and the Russian Defence Industry

East Siberia and the Russian Far East have been traditionally reported as areas of increased concentration of unlicensed firearms among private citizens. Since the end of the 1970s most of the families and individuals residing in the underpopulated northern sector of the area owned from one to several rifles, revolvers, pistols or even automatic rifles. Even the Communist authorities tended to tolerate that situation keeping in mind the isolation of rural communities and individual settlements, the vital necessity of hunting and self-defence (including self-defence from wild animals), and finally restricted capability of law enforcement structures to control sparse population scattered across the vast mountainous and forested territory.

The Russian state military industry has been in crisis since the end of the Cold War. Budget cuts, in combination with gradual reduction of federal military forces, led to the degradation of its traditional internal constituency. Trying to improve their financial situation, many state enterprises are looking for new markets to sell their production. Current legal regulations make the legal, large-scale sales of Russian-made firearms to Russian consumers a difficult task, so the military industry looks to the development of small arms exports. In East Asia, Russian military industry still remains a traditional supplier of the armed forces of China, Vietnam and Cambodia. China mainly concentrates on purchasing heavy weapons, aircraft and submarines. Nevertheless, small amounts of Russian small arms are regularly purchased by China. During the last two years Russian arms dealers have been repeatedly visiting other countries of the region (among them Indonesia, Malaysia, Singapore and Thailand) trying to explore and develop new markets.

The state military industry in Russia is backed by government and parliamentary circles, making it easy for the industry to boost small arms exports to traditional partners, as well as to search for new markets. Widespread corruption and corporate protectionism in modern Russian society make it difficult to draw a distinct line between legal and illegal export of arms produced by Russian military industry (in spite of the government declarations about its "strict adherence to norms of international law"). It is also worth mentioning that human rights violations in such countries of Asia such as the PRC or Vietnam never influence the delivery of Russian arms to those countries.

All arms trading in Russia is formally controlled by the federal arms export agency, or "Rosvooruzhenije" (from the Russian: Rus[sian]/Arms). The head of Rosvooruzhenije is Yevgenij Ananev. The second main figure is Rear Admiral Oleg Belavintsev who serves as its deputy general director. Since December 1997, one of Ananev's chief advisors has been former Russian Defence Minister Pavel Grachev, who is reportedly involved in corruption scandals. (Grachev and Belavintsev are reported to be close personal friends.)

Reorganization of the Defence Industry

In February 1998, a new government commission for the financial recovery of the defence industry was formed in Moscow. On 23 February, in accordance with the resolution signed by Prime Minister Chernomyrdin, First Deputy Prime Minister Anatolij Chubais was appointed as its chairman with Deputy Prime Minister and Economics Minister Yakov Urinson appointed as deputy chairman. Chubais announced on 20 February that the government was aiming at revision of its procedure for concluding contracts with defence enterprises, as well as at reduction of the number of such enterprises receiving state orders from 1,700 to 600.

Several powerful Russian opposition leaders, holding a majority in Russian Parliament (among them Vladimir Zhirinovski), have declared the arms trade one of Russia's economic goals. They strongly believe, and try to convince the Russian public, that the arms trade is a good and reliable business which should be developed to bring cash to the country, as well as to keep military industry jobs. A number of former state enterprises in Russia specializing in small arms production (exact data not available) have sold some of their shares to private structures and citizens. As a result of this, many of them fell into the sphere of the activity of "Russian Mafia" and became sources of totally uncontrolled production and trade of small arms both for Russian and foreign markets.

The Russian Mafia

Well organized criminal groups started forming in Russia (USSR) at the end of the Civil War (1918-1922). After more than fifty years of evolution and transformation, they have managed to preserve their viability and coordination, have accumulated significant funds and have found ways to integrate themselves with the power structures of the Soviet Empire including high-ranking officials of the Communist Party of the USSR and the KGB. The processes of disintegration of the Soviet State during the period of "Perestroyka" and "Glasnost" (1986-1991) further reinforced the above-mentioned alliance between "professional mobsters" and a part of communist "Nomenclatura," thus creating a special form of organized crime which is often called "Russian Mafia." Modern structures of "Russian Mafia" operating in the sphere of arms production and sales are represented by several powerful groups consisting of criminal syndicates (sometimes called "brotherhoods") working in close cooperation with certain industrial, financial and political groups, recruiting agents in law enforcement structures and involving foreign companies and individual citizens in their network. Severe discipline, conspiracy, excellent equipment, well developed "intelligence" and "counter-intelligence" and relatively professional approach towards marketing and business — all make modern criminal groups of Russia strong and dangerous, as well as, to a greater or lesser extent, unknown and invisible to Western countries (including Canadian and American observers).

Organized criminal "syndicates" and "brotherhoods" of the Russian Federation with their headquarters in the cities of Moscow, St. Petersburg, Yekaterinburg, Chelyabinsk, Khabarovsk and Vladivostok (the latter two in the Russian Far East), were reported to be involved in small arms exports to other countries of East Asia.

By "involvement" is meant various degrees of control over the above sphere of business mainly resulting in accumulating considerable commissions from international arms deals. Smaller criminal groups operating between East Siberia and the Urals tend to control the trafficking of small arms through the provinces of Tyumen, Omsk, and Kemerovo, and through Krasnoyarsk territory, in order to obtain small commissions from the deals. The local transport police (GAI) is often involved in controlling small arms trafficking for the benefit of criminal groups.

The process of rapid decay of the Soviet Army (now Russian Federal Army) started at least at the end of the 1970s with the period of 1993-98 as its culmination. Openly corrupt top brass, an underpaid officer corps, starving soldiers, undermanned and under-equipped regiments — all these factors have resulted in massive thefts of military property, including firearms, which can be easily sold on the black market or used for private purposes such as self-defence or work in private security structures. (Many sergeants and officers combine military service with part-time or freelance work in commercial companies, often as security officers. Strictly banned until 1992, this practice is nowadays widely tolerated).

Defining the Region

The area of current research includes the territory of Transbaykal Military District embracing Chita and Irkutsk provinces and ethnic republics of Sakha-Yakutia and Buryat-Mongolia (approximately 80,000 military personnel at present) and Maritime (Primorskij) Military District embracing the provinces of Magadan, Kamchatka, and Sakhalin Island, territories of Maritim and Amur, and Chukotka (Chukchi) Autonomous District (approximately 77,000 military personnel at present).

The two Military Districts officially contain at least 60 divisions, which were originally supposed to be manned with at least 300,000 military personnel) However most of those divisions are 25 to 75% undermanned leaving thousands of small arms in stores and subject to regular misappropriation by officers, sergeants and private soldiers. The Russian Far East is also the area of Russian Pacific Fleet basing (Magadan, Petropavlovsk-Kamchatsky, Yuzhno-Sakhalinsk, Vanino, Nakhodka, Vladivostok). The above-mentioned problems of the two military districts are typical for the Pacific Fleet as well. Chinese and to some extent North Korean state-owned military industries also serve as sources of both legal and semi-illegal small arms proliferation in the area of research. In China, military industry is not controlled by organized criminal groups to the extent to which it has become in Russia (at least for the reason that in modern China there do not seem to exist well organized criminal structures similar to "Russian Mafia").73 However, corruption is well-developed in the Chinese military industry, which in combination with insufficient control over resources and production makes it possible to produce thousands of firearms for further sale, bypassing official export channels.

SMALL ARMS AND LIGHT WEAPONS: CONTROLLING THE REAL INSTRUMENTS OF WAR

One of the dominant features of the global community in the 1990s has been the violent breakdown of civil society in dozens of countries throughout the world. From the socialist states of the former Soviet bloc to Africa and Asia, we have witnessed the outbreak of ethnic, religious, racial, linguistic and other forms of communal strife and the melting away of social norms and government structures that would otherwise contain the violence. Adding to the disorder, in many instances, has been a significant upsurge in armed banditry and criminal violence.

The importance of this "failed state syndrome" during this decade can hardly be overstated. The very nature of conflict has been transformed—from traditional combat between nation-states to inter-communal conflict within states. Such strife typically involves a wide variety of actors, including governments, rebel movements, armed political militias, ethnic and religious groups, tribes and clans, expatriate and diaspora groups, criminal gangs and mercenaries. Common distinguishing characteristics of this type of intra-state conflict include multiple warring parties, blurred lines of conflict, greater involvement of civilians, and the fact that the conflict itself is not fought on traditional battlegrounds but in local communities; indeed, within society itself. Also characteristic of these conflicts is the presence among the warring parties of irregular and paramilitary forces with little or no formal military training and few compunctions about violating the rules of war. All too often, it is children and teenagers who are recruited or forced into these organizations and then made to kill, loot and rampage.

Another defining characteristic of such conflict is the fact that widespread death and suffering result not from the major conventional weapons traditionally associated with war—tanks, aircraft and warships, for example—but from small arms and light weapons. The global proliferation of assault rifles, machine guns, mortars, rocket-propelled grenades and other "man-portable" weapons has increased both the frequency and intensity of modern conflict and greatly complicated the task of restoring peace. Such weapons are readily obtainable on international markets, both legal and illicit, and are easily mastered by untrained and unprofessional soldiers, even children. Of the 49 major conflicts that have broken out since 1990, light weapons were the only arms used in 46; only one conflict (the 1991 Gulf War) was dominated by heavy weapons.

Since 1990, these conflicts have resulted in the deaths of more than 4 million people and have produced 20 million refugees and 24 million displaced persons. The resources of the international community are being overwhelmed by bitter conflicts, large-scale refugee movements and even genocide. In response to these disasters, the international community has spent tens of billions of dollars on emergency relief, refugee care and resettlement, peacekeeping, and direct military intervention. For the United Nations alone, the annual cost of humanitarian assistance and relief for war victims has increased ten-fold, from about $300 million a year in the 1980s to $3 billion a year in the mid-1990s.

In recent years, attention has come to focus on the ways in which the increased availability of low-cost small arms and light weapons contributes to the likelihood, intensity and duration of armed conflict. Although these conflicts often possess deep and complex roots, it is evident that the widespread availability of modern light weapons has emboldened belligerents to pursue their objectives on the battlefield, rather than at the bargaining table.

An analysis of contemporary warfare also reveals that such conflict overwhelmingly takes place in the world's poorest countries. In the 1990s, 30 of the 60 least-developed countries in the world have experienced conflict directly, while another 12 have had to support large refugee populations from neighboring countries in conflict. This correlation between conflict and poverty helps explain why these conflicts are generally fought with relatively inexpensive small arms and light weapons. It also explains why the victims of these conflicts are so dependent on assistance from the international community.

ADVANTAGES OF LIGHT WEAPONS

In recent conflicts, more people have been killed by small arms and light weapons than by major weapons systems. The distinguishing features of these weapons that make them so suitable to contemporary intra-state conflicts include:

Low Cost and Wide Availability. Because the production of small arms and light weapons requires little in the way of sophisticated technology, and because these weapons are manufactured for military, police and civilian use, there are plentiful suppliers around the world. In addition, the existence of many tens of millions of such weapons—whether newly produced, given away by downsizing militaries or recycled from conflict to conflict—leads to bargain-basement prices in many areas around the world.

Lethality. The increasing sophistication and lethality of rapid-fire assault rifles, automatic pistols and submachine guns and their diffusion to non-state actors has given such groups a firepower that often matches or exceeds that of national police or constabulary forces. With such weapons capable of firing up to 300 rounds a minute, a single individual can pose a tremendous threat to society. The incorporation of new technology into shoulder-fired rockets, mortars and light anti-tank weapons has only increased the firepower that warring factions bring to bear in civil conflicts.

Simplicity and Durability. Small arms are easy to use and maintain, require little maintenance or logistical support and remain operational for many years. Such weapons require little training to use effectively, which greatly increases their use in conflicts involving untrained combatants and children.

Portability and Concealability. Small arms and light weapons can be carried by an individual soldier or light vehicle, are easily transported or smuggled to areas of conflict, and can be concealed in shipments of legitimate cargo.

Military, Police and Civilian Uses. Unlike major conventional weapons, which are most often procured solely by national military forces, small arms and light weapons cross the dividing line separating military and police forces from the civilian population. Depending on the gun control laws of a particular country, citizens are permitted to own anything from pistols and sporting guns to fully automatic rifles. In many countries, moreover, there has been a dramatic increase in the number and size of private militias and security firms which, in many cases, are equipped with military-type weapons.

All of these characteristics of light weapons have made them particularly attractive to the sort of paramilitary and irregular forces that have played such a prominent role in recent conflicts. These forces have limited financial and technical means, lack professional military training, and often must operate in remote and inaccessible areas—all conditions that favor the use of small arms and light weapons. At the same time, many states have increased their purchases of these weapons for use in counterinsurgency campaigns against ethnic and political groups and to suppress domestic opposition movements.

A GLOBAL DIFFUSION OF SMALL ARMS

For many years, the global trade in major conventional weapons has been well documented. By comparison, the global trade in small arms and light weapons has proved much more difficult to track. Few national governments publish statistics on the sale or transfer of light weapons or release information about the sales activities of private companies. Moreover, much of the trade—perhaps 25 percent—is carried on through illicit and black-market channels of one sort or another.

In the absence of uniform statistics on the trade in light weapons, researchers must rely on anecdotal information and what little fragmentary data is available from government and trade sources. Fairly reliable estimates of the global trade in such weapons range from $5 billion to $7 billion a year, with some estimates running as high as $10 billion a year. And while official statistics indicate that the trade in major weapons systems has fallen sharply with the end of the Cold War, many analysts believe that global transfers of light weapons have increased during this period.

The global spread of small arms and light weapons has been facilitated by the emergence in many states, including a dozen or more developing countries, of a domestic capacity for the manufacture of such weapons. Whereas the fabrication of major weapons systems is highly concentrated, with only a dozen or so states capable of producing modern tanks, planes and warships, some 50 nations now manufacture light weapons and/or ammunition of various types. The production of modern assault rifles, for example, occurs in many of the industrialized nations as well as in Argentina, Brazil, Chile, Egypt, India, Indonesia, Iran, Iraq, Israel, Mexico, North Korea, Pakistan, Saudi Arabia, Singapore, South Africa, South Korea, Taiwan and Turkey. Many of these countries produce arms for export as well as domestic use, greatly adding to the number of sources from which a potential belligerent can obtain weapons of war.

The large number of production sites contributes not only to the expansion of national arsenals, but to the spread of arms within societies via theft, bribery and corruption. The multiplicity of trade channels leads to the diffusion of light weapons within societies—extending not only to governments and state-owned entities but also to private armies and militias, insurgent groups, criminal organizations and other non-state actors.

Accordingly, any analysis of the trade in light weapons must take into account both the sharp increase in the number of producers and suppliers and how their weapons are being transferred to an ever-expanding array of states and non-state actors in every region of the world.

The following list of legal, illegal and covert methods by which small arms and light weapons are sold, transferred and exchanged underscores the complexity of the problem:

- Grants or gifts by governments to allied governments abroad;
- Sales by governments to client governments abroad;
- Commercial sales by private firms to governments and private dealers in other countries;
- Technology transfers associated with domestic arms production in the developing nations;
- Covert transfers by governments to friendly insurgent and separatist groups in other countries;
- Gifts by governments to armed militias and paramilitary organizations linked to the ruling party or the dominant ethnic group;
- Black-market sales to the governments of "pariah" countries and to insurgent and separatist forces;
- Theft of government and privately owned arms by insurgent, criminal and separatist forces; and
- Exchanges between insurgent and criminal organizations, whether for profit or in pursuit of common political objectives.

Legal Channels. Currently, there are over 300 manufacturers of light weapons and related equipment in 50 countries around the world, a 25 percent increase in the last decade alone. Until the end of World War II, the major producers of these weapons were the industrialized nations. In recent decades, however, these established producers have been joined by China, Israel, South Africa and many developing countries. Estimates of some common models produced by these countries in the past few decades show the enormity of the problem: 5 million to 7 million Belgian FAL assault rifles produced in 15 countries; 35 million to 50 million Soviet/Russian AK assault rifles manufactured by Soviet/Russian factories and licensees; 7 million German Heckler & Koch G3 assault rifles made in 18 countries; 8 million U.S. M-16 rifles produced in seven countries; and 6 million Chinese-made AK-type assault rifles.

These numbers, as alarming as they are, do not include the millions of surplus arms that have been sold or given away as the world's major military powers have reduced their forces and/or found themselves with excess production capacity following the end of the Cold War. Because small arms and light weapons have few moving parts and are extremely durable, even weapons that are 10-to 20-years old are often fully operational and as effective as newly produced weapons. Accordingly, countries such as the United States, Russia and Germany (especially with the dismantling of the East German army) have been able to sell or transfer millions of light weapons to their allies and clients abroad.

Covert and 'Gray-Market' Channels. In addition to legal sales and military assistance programs, small arms and light weapons are disseminated through covert and "gray-market" channels (that is, channels that operate with government support even though in violation of official government policy), most often by government intelligence agencies or private companies linked to such agencies. During the Soviet occupation of Afghanistan, the CIA helped to supply some 3 million AK-47 assault rifles (mainly Chinese and Egyptian models) to rebel *mujahideen*; thousands of these weapons have since turned up in fighting in Kashmir and elsewhere in South Asia, and as far away as Southeast Asia and the Middle East. In addition, the United States and the Soviet Union supplied arms to rebel groups in Central America and sent massive amounts of weapons to various factions in Angola and Mozambique.

Since the end of the Cold War, Washington and Moscow have discontinued many of these activities. But it is widely believed that military commanders and managers of military factories in Russia and some of the other newly independent states of the former Soviet Union have engaged in large-scale covert sales of weapons to clients in neighboring states and beyond. Government officials in other states have also been accused of smuggling arms to allied groups in other countries, whether for profit or to advance particular political or religious objectives. Officials in Zaire, for instance, reportedly bought large quantities of weapons on the international market and sold them to UNITA forces in Angola for profits running into the hundreds of millions of dollars—most of which is believed to have wound up in the overseas bank accounts of former President Mobutu Seso Seko and his associates.

Another form of gray-market transfers entails the delivery of weapons from government stockpiles to political entities and ethnic militias associated with the ruling clan or party. Prior to the 1994 genocide in Rwanda, for example, the Hutu-dominated government distributed small arms and machetes to government-linked militias. Once the killing began, the Rwandan military sought to crush any organized Tutsi resistance while the militias slaughtered unarmed Tutsis and moderate Hutus. A similar pattern was evident in Haiti in the early 1990s, when the ruling military junta organized and armed the Front for the Advancement and Progress of Haiti (FRAPH) to suppress popular support for ousted President Jean-Bertrand Aristide.

Illicit and Black-Market Channels. The third major category of light weapons transfers includes illegal sales through black-market channels, the supply of arms in defiance of international embargoes and other legal sanctions, and the theft of arms from government stocks or private citizens. In recent years, there has been a striking growth in the operations of black-market dealers to satisfy the needs of non-state actors in ethnic and internal conflicts.

Because such actors are normally barred from purchases on the legal munitions market, they must acquire their weaponry from illicit sources. The growing number of UN arms embargoes has also produced an increased demand for black-market arms. Although it is impossible to estimate the value or scale of all such transactions, some estimates place 1993 black market sales to the belligerents in Bosnia alone at $2 billion or more. The black-market trade has been facilitated by the existence of vast stockpiles of surplus arms in the states of the former Soviet bloc—arms which in many cases are guarded by near-destitute soldiers and officers who are all too eager to conspire in their theft by black-market dealers or to enter the illicit trade themselves. Moreover, there are strong linkages between the illegal narcotics trade and black-market arms trafficking. These underground networks have developed sophisticated methods for the procurement, transportation and sale of small arms and light weapons, at times with the connivance of governments or corrupt public officials.

Finally, theft of weapons from military and police warehouses is a major problem in countries afflicted by civil war or insurgent violence. As civil strife spread across Albania in the spring of 1997, thousands of weapons were looted from military depots by insurgents, criminals and civilians. These weapons not only increased the levels of armed violence in Albania, but reportedly were also being smuggled across the border into the Serbian province of Kosovo, where 2 million ethnic Albanians pose an irredentist challenge to Serbian authority. In South Africa and Colombia, stolen weapons contribute to a culture of violence and criminality that undermines the stability of the state and the cohesion of society.

The Need for Policy Initiatives

Clearly, the unchecked flow of small arms and light weapons to areas of conflict represents a significant threat to world peace and security. While it cannot be said that such weapons are a *primary* cause of conflict, their worldwide availability, low cost and ease of operation make it relatively easy for potential belligerents of all kinds to initiate and sustain deadly conflict. Accordingly, policy-makers have begun to highlight the need for new international controls in this area. In a January 1998 message to the UN Conference on Disarmament, Secretary-General Kofi Annan said, "With regard to conventional weapons, there is a growing awareness among member-states of the urgent need to adopt measures to reduce the transfer of small arms and light weapons. It is now incumbent on all of us to translate this shared awareness into decisive action."

Interest in the trade in light weapons has also been spurred by a growing number of national and international non-governmental organizations (NGOs), many of which played a key role in the international campaign to ban landmines. Along with UN officials and leaders of interested governments, these groups have led the search for new policy prescriptions.

International Efforts

In line with the increased attention being focused by the international community on the dangers posed by small arms and light weapons, the United Nations has been engaged in a wide variety of activities to both publicize the problem and initiate steps toward policy controls. The two major efforts undertaken so far by the United Nations are the study conducted by the Panel of Governmental Experts on Small Arms in 1996 and 1997, which analyzed the types of weapons used in contemporary conflicts and the nature and causes of their excessive accumulation, and the parallel study of member-states' firearm regulations conducted by the UN Commission on Crime Prevention and Criminal Justice in the same two-year period.

Operationally, the United Nations has sought to monitor the effectiveness of various international embargoes on the transfer of weaponry into areas of conflict. In 1996, a UN International Commission of Inquiry on Rwanda investigated the implementation of the UN arms embargo on Rwanda, paying particular attention to specific allegations of embargo violations. In their report, members of the commission noted that " we could not fail to note the absence of an effective, proactive mechanism to monitor or implement the arms embargo the Security Council had imposed on Rwanda." Elsewhere in Africa, the United Nations has supported Mali's path-breaking efforts to collect and destroy firearms internally and to promote a regional moratorium on the trade in small arms and light weapons.

Other international organizations are also becoming involved in the light weapons issue, particularly as it relates to issues of economic and human development. The World Bank is devoting resources to issues of post-conflict reconstruction, particularly in regard to the demobilization of combatants and their reintegration into civil society. Also, the Organization for Economic Cooperation and Development (OECD), through its task force on Conflict, Peace and Development Cooperation, is putting greater emphasis on the need for "timely prevention measures" (such as limiting arms flows in areas of potential conflict) in order to forestall armed violence.

Regional Efforts

Particularly in Africa and the Americas, national governments and regional organizations are devising a variety of measures to better regulate the legal trade in light weapons and to combat illicit weapons trafficking. In November 1997, the Organization of American States (OAS) signed a convention on the illicit weapons trade that calls for standardization of national firearms regulations and increased law enforcement and customs cooperation to prevent illicit weapons flows within the Western Hemisphere. The OAS has also developed model regulations that focus on the linkages between the narcotics trade and weapons smuggling. Within the Caribbean sub-region, moreover, Jamaica has proposed that similar efforts be undertaken by the 14-member Caribbean Community.

Elsewhere, West African governments are working with the United Nations to assess the regional implications of light weapons diffusion and to craft a regional moratorium on the import, export and manufacture of such arms. In Central Africa, the United Nations has established a trust fund with which to remove small arms and light weapons from the region. Similarly, the Southern Africa Development Community has recommended the establishment of a regional database on stolen firearms and the implementation of multilateral police operations to recover such weapons.

Among European countries, there are increased pressures for controlling both legal and illegal shipments of weapons, particularly to countries experiencing civil strife and human rights abuses. In June 1997, the European Union (EU) agreed to a Programme for Preventing and Combating Illicit Trafficking in Conventional Arms. In June 1998, the EU formally adopted a "code of conduct" on arms transfers with the goal of preventing such transfers to areas of conflict and internal repression. While useful steps, both measures will require political will in constraining arms transfers and dedicated resources to help affected countries monitor arms shipments and remove excess weaponry.

National Efforts

Because so much of the light weapons trade takes place illegally, the role of national governments in tightening and enforcing export regulations will be very important. Under pressure from Mexico, the United States has cracked down on illicit gun trafficking on the U.S.-Mexican border and has agreed to stronger export controls in the context of the OAS convention signed last November. Similar efforts are underway in a number of other states, including Colombia, South Africa and EU states.

In many communities, municipal authorities and NGOs have begun grass roots campaigns to remove small arms from circulation at the local level, and to pressure their national governments to take the light weapons problem more seriously. In South Africa, such initiatives involve bringing various ethnic and tribal groups together to deal with the "culture of violence" plaguing that country. In countries like Britain and Australia that have experienced horrific massacres carried out by automatic weapons—notably the killings in Dunblane, Scotland, and Port Arthur, Tasmania, national groups have come together to lobby for more restrictive gun control laws. Elsewhere, NGOs and grass roots organizations have put the spotlight on their own governments' responsibility for supplying weapons to areas of conflict and persistent human rights abuse.

What Is to Be Done?

From all that has been learned about the international trade in small arms and light weapons, it is evident that no single set of policy initiatives will suffice to deal with this problem. Unlike the relative simplicity of the landmines issue—where the international community could focus on one particular weapon (anti-personnel landmines) and seek its elimination as a weapon of war—the effort to control the diffusion of light weapons will demand a host of initiatives, extending from the international arena to regional, national and local levels. National governments especially will have to go beyond their support for cracking down on the illegal trade in light weapons and examine their own role in the current legal weapons trade. The following initiatives represent a rough menu of the sort of steps that will be needed to subject light weapons transfers to greater international scrutiny and to reduce the flow of such munitions to areas of conflict.

Establish International Norms. The first, and perhaps most important, step is to adopt international norms against the uncontrolled and destabilizing transfer of small arms and light weapons to areas of tension and conflict. Although deference must be made to the traditional right of sovereign states to arm themselves, it must be made clear that this right has natural limits and does not extend to the acquisition of arms for the purpose of engaging in genocide or the suppression of opposition political or religious movements. It must become axiomatic, moreover, that the right to acquire arms for self-defense entails an obligation to maintain such weapons under effective government control at all times and to preclude their diversion to illicit purposes.

While it may take some time to clarify and win support for such norms, the basic groundwork has been provided by the UN Panel of Governmental Experts on Small Arms. In its 1997 report, the panel concludes: "The excessive and destabilizing accumulation and transfer of small arms and light weapons is closely related to the increased incidence of internal conflicts and high levels of crime and violence," and is, therefore, "an issue of legitimate concern for the international community." With this in mind, the report calls on UN member-states to "exercise restraint" with respect to the transfer of such weapons and to take all necessary steps to prevent the diversion of government arms supplies into illegitimate hands.

Clearly, much work is needed to strengthen these norms and to promote their acceptance by governments. As in the worldwide campaign against landmines, the media can focus public attention on the dangers posed by such weapons, especially to civilians and children. The issue is admittedly complicated by the fact that, unlike anti-personnel landmines, national governments and military and police forces can demonstrate a far greater legitimate need for light weapons for purposes of self-defense and national security. Nonetheless, the frequency with which such weapons are used against civilians and children points to a humanitarian aspect of small arms that is quite similar to that of landmines.

International norms could also be developed along the lines of the Geneva Conventions, where states-parties would be prohibited from supplying light weapons to any government, group or entity that does not have the resources to treat its wounded or those of the enemy, or has not trained its own personnel in the laws of war. In addition, public sentiment could be mobilized to support constraints on the inhumane or indiscriminate effects of light weapons, in the same way that blinding laser weapons have been banned by the recently adopted protocol to the 1980 Convention on Conventional Weapons (CCW).

Increase International Transparency. At present, efforts to monitor and control the diffusion of small arms and light weapons are hampered by a lack of detailed information on the production, sale and transfer of such munitions.

Few governments provide detailed data on imports and exports of light weapons, and the UN Conventional Arms Register covers major weapons only. To ensure effective international oversight of the legal trade in light weapons, efforts at increased transparency must be made at the national, regional and international level. National governments should be required to publish detailed annual tallies of weapons imports and exports, while regional arms registers covering light weapons should also be encouraged. Finally, at the international level, the UN arms register should be gradually extended to cover all types of munitions, including small arms and light weapons.

Enhanced international transparency is also necessary to curb the illicit trade in light weapons. In the absence of an effective transparency regime, it is relatively easy for illicit dealers to conceal their operations; as information on legal trade becomes more widely available, it will become more difficult to do this. Increased transparency will also facilitate joint efforts by law enforcement agencies to identify, track and apprehend black-market dealers.

Increase State Accountability. In the current international milieu, control over the import and export of small arms and light weapons rests with national governments; thus, efforts to better regulate the trade in such munitions will be most effective at the national level.

Increased governmental accountability is needed in two key areas: first, the establishment of effective oversight over all military-type firearms found within the national territory, so as to prevent their diversion to criminal elements and black-market dealers; and second, strict controls over the import and export of such weapons, so as to preclude their use for any purpose other than legitimate self-defense as sanctioned by the UN Charter.

Efforts to accomplish the first of these objectives should be guided by the draft proposals of the UN Commission on Crime Prevention and Criminal Justice. Particularly effective measures would include a licensing system for manufacturers and gun owners, more effective identification systems to track firearms, more effective record keeping of firearms, and safe-storage measures. An additional measure called for is the promotion of amnesty and weapons turn-in programs that encourage citizens to surrender illegal, unsafe, unwanted and excess weapons. (An Australian buy-back effort, for example, took in more than 600,000 firearms, Governments around the world should be encouraged to incorporate such measures into their national laws and regulations; those states that fail to do so should be barred from receiving arms from those states that do adopt such legislation.

Similarly, efforts to better control the import and export of small arms and light weapons should be guided by the recommendations found in the report of the UN Panel of Governmental Experts on Small Arms. These include the collection and destruction of weapons once conflict has ended; the destruction of surplus weapons no longer needed by a country's military or police forces (as opposed to selling or giving them away); and the exercise of restraint in exporting military and police weapons from one country to another.

States should also be encouraged to adopt a code of conduct for arms transfers such as those being considered at the regional

(EU) and international levels. Such codes would bar the sale or transfer of small arms and light weapons to any state that is ruled by a military dictatorship, that fails to respect the human rights of its citizens, that violates UN arms embargoes, or that cannot ensure the security of the weapons already in its possession.

Regional and International Efforts. While priority should be given to the development of effective controls at the national level, efforts should also be made to establish systems of oversight and control at the regional and international levels. Action at the regional level is particularly important because light weapons are often circulated by regional networks of illicit dealers, insurgents and permissive government agencies. Moreover, experience suggests that it may be easier to mobilize political support for control systems at the regional level than at the international level.

At the regional level, policy initiatives could include agreements for the strengthening of import and export regulations, tougher enforcement of laws against illicit trafficking and joint operations against black-market dealers. The OAS effort is one means of fostering increased cooperation between national customs services and law enforcement agencies on a regional basis. Other such efforts could be greatly facilitated by countries like the United States and Japan, which could provide the requisite technologies for computer databases of suspected illicit weapons traffickers. In southern Africa, national governments and intelligence agencies are sharing information and mounting joint operations to uncover and destroy large caches of weapons left over from previous conflicts.

The Mali moratorium on the manufacture, sale and import of small arms and light weapons is another initiative that can begin to reduce the easy availability of such weapons. As one of the more successful multilateral attempts to control the flow of light weapons both prior to and following periods of civil tension, the Mali initiative might provide a model for other regions. In West Africa, for example, the experiences of Liberia and Sierra Leone demonstrated how even relatively modest numbers of light weapons inflicted horrific casualties on civilians caught in sectarian strife.

Other regional approaches include the establishment of regional codes of conduct on arms exports similar to that of the EU. Given the particularly troublesome black-market weapons activity in Eastern Europe and the former Soviet Union, the OECD or the Organization for Security and Cooperation in Europe (OSCE) should consider adopting codes of conduct. Additionally, economic incentive plans could be devised that would facilitate the closure of excess production capacity in Eastern Europe and the former Soviet Union. For example, Western countries could buy surplus small arms and light weapons from these states and destroy them, much as the United States is purchasing excess Russian nuclear weapons material.

At the international level, emphasis should be placed on the adoption of measures needed to strengthen the implementation of weapons embargoes agreed to by the United Nations and associated bodies. While such embargoes may never be entirely leakproof, evidence has shown that even a modest number of international observers at airfields, seaports and other points of entry for weapons to an area of conflict can make a difference. When supplemented by stricter national export controls, embargoes can make it far more difficult to deliver significant quantities of modern weapons to areas of conflict.

The major arms-supplying countries should also establish a mechanism (possibly as part of the Wassenaar Arrangement for conventional arms control) for consultation on arms flows to areas of current and potential conflict, along with provisions for the imposition of a moratorium on weapons transfers to any state or region deemed to be at risk of ethnic slaughter, state failure or genocide. International inspectors should be sent to the region to ensure compliance with these measures and to suggest any other actions that might be taken to reduce the flow of arms.

Reducing Surplus Weapons. Addressing the problem of surplus weaponry generated by decades of Cold War competition is especially important because many states—particularly former Eastern bloc countries—are eager to sell arms for hard currency with few or no questions asked. Because export controls on surplus arms are generally less strict than those for newly manufactured weapons, black-market dealers find it easier to obtain and sell surplus arms than newly made weapons. The problem of surplus arms is especially acute in areas just recovering from armed conflict, where impoverished ex-combatants may try to sell their weapons for cash rather than turn them over to UN peace-keepers or other designated authorities.

Measures to reduce global stockpiles of surplus munitions—a critical component of any international effort to constrain the flow of light weapons—can take several forms. States that can afford to do so should agree to destroy the surplus arms and ammunition in their possession and to take all the necessary steps to prevent the leakage of weaponry from government depots and warehouses. An early precedent was set by the Dutch Ministry of Defense, which announced in January 1998 that it would destroy most of its surplus small arms, including 115,000 Uzi submachine guns, FAL assault rifles, Garand rifles, Browning pistols and M-1 carbines.

For their parts, the United States and Russia should agree to cooperate in locating and reclaiming (or buying back) weapons given by them to insurgent groups during the Cold War. In many regions, these weapons are now being used to fuel internal power struggles and criminal violence. Taking these weapons out of circulation would close one of the most deadly chapters of the Cold War and help promote international peace and security in the current era.

Post-Conflict Measures. A high priority should be placed on efforts to remove the large quantities of small arms and light weapons that often remain in-country once a particular conflict has ended. Too often, the availability of such weapons facilitates either a renewal of the conflict (as in Angola) or a destabilization of efforts to build a peaceful civil society (as in South Africa). The limited success of disarmament programs in countries like El Salvador, where the country suffers from an appalling rate of criminal violence despite the collection of tens of thousands of weapons, points up the complexity and difficulty of such efforts. Above all, decisions to disarm warring factions and remove light weapons from areas of conflict must be implemented uniformly and comprehensively. Moreover, in many countries around the world the possession of arms is deeply embedded in society, so that arms collection efforts may prove futile or not be politically feasible. In such cases, and more generally as well, the primary emphasis should be on economic development and social reconstruction so that ex-combatants and non-combatants have viable options in the civilian economy.

Recent initiatives on the part of the World Bank and a number of development and humanitarian NGOs to better integrate economic assistance programs with demobilization, destruction of weapons and conflict prevention strategies are a useful step in this direction.

International Capacity-Building. Ultimately, any regime to control global trafficking in small arms and light weapons will only be as effective as the weakest links in the system. As long as black-market dealers enjoy safe havens in which they can operate with impunity, it will be difficult or impossible to enforce tougher international standards on the light weapons trade. It is therefore essential that the stronger participants in the system assist the weaker elements to establish effective and reliable mechanisms for the oversight of the arms market.

As part of such efforts, technology should be developed and deployed internationally to help track the flow of small arms and light weapons, identify illicit sources of supply, and improve law enforcement and customs prosecution of illegal suppliers and traders.

In addition to developing computer databases and communications systems that can facilitate international cooperation on the light weapons trade, several other technical initiatives have been proposed for helping to increase the transparency of light weapons flows. One such initiative being developed by OAS members is more effective marking and registration of weapons, both at the point of manufacture and when such weapons are legally exported. Such marking will make it easier for law enforcement and intelligence officials to trace the supply routes of weapons originally acquired legally which then entered the black market.

Other proposals exist for the tagging of ammunition and explosives, and studies on their feasibility are being carried out by the Canadian government and the United Nations. While some of these technical solutions may prove difficult and expensive to implement, the international community has at least begun the process of thoroughly evaluating them.

An Imperative to Act

By the middle of 1998, there was increased international momentum for taking more decisive action to prevent the continuing global diffusion of small arms and light weapons. In addition to ongoing efforts on the part of the United Nations and regional organizations like the OAS, national governments—including Norway, Canada, Belgium, Mexico, Colombia, South Africa and Japan—had signalled their interest in devoting substantial political and economic resources to deal with the problem. In July 1998, the Norwegian government hosted a meeting of 21 countries, including the United States, that issued a call for stronger measures to deal with both the illicit and legal trade in light weapons.

The Clinton administration has indicated its willingness to be fully involved in international efforts to dampen the light weapons trade. In August, the administration released a list of the comprehensive initiatives the U.S. government is pursuing—through the United Nations, the OAS and at the national level—to support global efforts for combatting the threat posed by unrestrained trade in light weapons. Most of these efforts were aimed at the illicit trade in arms, though some focused on legal sales.

Clearly, the U.S. and other governments, especially those responsible for the majority of light weapons production and supply, need to do more. At the moment, most countries, including the United States, are putting greater emphasis on the illicit light weapons trade. Yet, it is the continued supply of large amounts of small arms and light weapons, through legal channels, to governments and non-state actors, that is most worrisome. All too often, supplier states continue to give away or sell at a discount hundreds of thousands of surplus light weapons that end up in the wrong hands.

In some cases, such as Somalia, these weapons are then used against U.S. peace-keeping forces that are sent to restore civil order. In other cases, such as Bosnia, Liberia and Sierra Leone, the United States and the international community will spend billions of dollars in peace-keeping and economic reconstruction when a more restrictive policy on light weapons transfers might have prevented or diminished the intensity of civil conflict in these countries.

As the international community is beginning to recognize, the humanitarian and development benefits of cutting the link between light weapons availability and civil conflict would be substantial. For the United States, the economic benefits of the light weapons trade are exceedingly minor compared to the ultimate costs of having to rescue "failed states," provide for millions of refugees, and reconstruct societies torn apart by genocide and ethnic strife. The savings inherent in preventing or greatly limiting conflict in even one Rwanda, Bosnia or Liberia would greatly outweigh the minimal political and economic benefits of being an indiscriminate light weapons supplier.

In sum, increased attention to the lethal effects of easily available small arms and light weapons on the part of humanitarian relief agencies, national governments, international organizations and the media is translating into a greater public appreciation of the need to better control the production, supply and diffusion of these weapons.

Admittedly, the problem is incredibly complex and policies to control and regulate these weapons will not come easily. Nonetheless, the scale of death and injury caused by light weapons is such that the international community must continue to search for effective means of controlling and reducing the lethal commerce of small arms and light weapons around the world.

7

Global Disarmament and Arms Control

Global, verifiable and non-discriminatory nuclear disarmament is a national security objective. India shall continue its efforts to achieve the goal of a nuclear weapon-free world at an early date. Since no-first use of nuclear weapons is India's basic commitment, every effort shall be made to persuade other States possessing nuclear weapons to join an international treaty banning first use. Having provided unqualified negative security assurances, India shall work for internationally binding unconditional negative security assurances by nuclear weapon states to non-nuclear weapon states.

Nuclear arms control measures shall be sought as part of national security policy to reduce potential threats and to protect our own capability and its effectiveness. In view of the very high destructive potential of nuclear weapons, appropriate nuclear risk reduction and confidence building measures shall be sought, negotiated and instituted.

Physics and Politics in the 1930s

In the first decades of the twentieth century, physics was revolutionized with developments in the understanding of the nature of atoms. In 1898, French physicist Pierre Curie and his Polish wife Maria Sklodowska-Curie had discovered that present in pitchblende, an ore of uranium, was a substance which emitted large amounts of radioactivity, which they named radium. This raised the hopes of both scientists and lay people that the elements around us could contain tremendous amounts of unseen energy, waiting to be tapped.

Experiments by Ernest Rutherford in 1911 indicated that the vast majority of an atom's mass was contained in a very small nucleus at its core, made up of protons, surrounded by a web of whirring electrons. In 1932, James Chadwick discovered that the nucleus contained another fundamental particle, the neutron, and in the same year John Cockcroft and Ernest Walton "split the atom" for the first time, the first occasion on which an atomic nucleus of one element had been successfully changed to a different nucleus by artificial means.

In 1934 the idea of chain reaction via neutron was proposed by Leó Szilárd, who patented the idea of the atomic bomb. The patent was transferred in secret to Britain's Royal Navy in 1936. In a very real sense, Szilárd was the father of the atomic bomb academically. In 1934, French physicists Irène and Frédéric Joliot-Curie discovered that artificial radioactivity could be induced in stable elements by bombarding them with alpha particles, and in the same year Italian physicist Enrico Fermi reported similar results when bombarding uranium with neutrons. In December 1938, the German chemists Otto Hahn and Fritz Strassmann sent a manuscript to *Naturwissenschaften* reporting they had detected the element barium after bombarding uranium with neutrons; simultaneously, they communicated these results to Lise Meitner. Meitner, and her nephew Otto Robert Frisch, correctly interpreted these results as being nuclear fission. Frisch confirmed this experimentally on 13 January 1939. Even before it was published, Meitner's and Frisch's interpretation of the work of Hahn and Strassmann crossed the Atlantic Ocean with Niels Bohr, who was to lecture at Princeton University. Isidor Isaac Rabi and Willis Lamb, two Columbia University physicists working at Princeton, heard the news and carried it back to Columbia. Rabi said he told Fermi; Fermi gave credit to Lamb. Bohr soon thereafter went from Princeton to Columbia to see Fermi. Not finding Fermi in his office, Bohr went down to the cyclotron area and found Herbert Anderson. Bohr grabbed him by the shoulder and said: "Young man, let me explain to you about something new and exciting in physics."

It was clear to a number of scientists at Columbia that they should try to detect the energy released in the nuclear fission of uranium from neutron bombardment. On 25 January 1939, an experimental team at Columbia University conducted the first nuclear fission experiment in the United States, which was done in the basement of Pupin Hall; the members of the team were Herbert L. Anderson, Eugene T. Booth, John R. Dunning, Enrico Fermi, G. Norris Glasoe, and Francis G. Slack. As the Nazi army marched into first Czechoslovakia in 1938, and then Poland in 1939, beginning World War II, many of Europe's top physicists had already begun to flee from the imminent conflict. Scientists on both sides of the conflict were well aware of the possibility of utilizing nuclear fission as a weapon, but at the time no one was quite sure how it could be done. In the early years of the Second World War, physicists abruptly stopped publishing on the topic of fission, an act of self-censorship to keep the opposing side from gaining any advantages.

From Los Alamos to Hiroshima

By the beginning of World War II, there was concern among scientists in the Allied nations that Nazi Germany might have its own project to develop fission-based weapons. Organized research first began in Britain as part of the "Tube Alloys" project, and in the United States a small amount of funding was given for research into uranium weapons starting in 1939 with the Uranium Committee under Lyman James Briggs. At the urging of British scientists, though, who had made crucial calculations indicating that a fission weapon could be completed within only a few years, by 1941 the project had been wrested into better bureaucratic hands, and in 1942 came under the auspices of a Military Policy Committee led by General Leslie Groves as the Manhattan Project.

Scientifically led by the American physicist Robert Oppenheimer, the project brought together the top scientific minds of the day (many exiles from Europe) with the production power of American industry for the goal of producing fission-based explosive devices before Germany could. Britain and the U.S. agreed to pool their resources and information for the project, but the other Allied power—the Soviet Union under Joseph Stalin—was not informed. A massive industrial and scientific undertaking, the Manhattan Project involved many of the world's great physicists in the scientific and development aspects. The United States made an unprecedented investment into wartime research for the project, which was spread across more than 30 sites in the U.S. and Canada. Scientific knowledge was centralized at a secret laboratory known as Los Alamos, previously a small ranch school near Santa Fe, New Mexico.

Uranium appears in nature primarily in two isotopes: uranium-238 and uranium-235. When the nucleus of uranium-235 absorbs a neutron, it undergoes nuclear fission, splitting into two "fission products" and releasing energy and 2.5 neutrons on average. Uranium-238, on the other hand, absorbs neutrons but does not split, effectively putting a stop to any ongoing fission reaction. It was discovered that an atomic bomb based on uranium would need to be made of almost completely pure uranium-235 (at least 80% pure), or else the presence of uranium-238 would quickly curtail the nuclear chain reaction. The team of scientists working on the Manhattan Project immediately realized that one of the largest problems they would have to solve was how to remove uranium-235 from natural uranium, which was composed of 99.3% uranium-238. Two methods were developed during the wartime project, both of which took advantage of the fact that uranium-238 has a slightly greater atomic mass than uranium-235: electromagnetic separation and gaseous diffusion—methods which separated isotopes based on their differing weights. Another secret site was erected at rural Oak Ridge, Tennessee, for the large-scale production and purification of the rare isotope. It was a massive investment: at the time, one of the Oak Ridge facilities (K-25) was the largest factory under one roof. The Oak Ridge site employed tens of thousands of employees at its peak, most of whom had no idea what they were working on. Though uranium-238 cannot be used for the initial stage of an atomic bomb, when U-238 absorbs a neutron, it transforms first into an unstable element, uranium-

239, and then decays into neptunium-239, and finally the relatively stable plutonium-239, an element which does not exist in nature. Plutonium is also fissile and can be used to create a fission reaction, and after Enrico Fermi achieved the world's first sustained and controlled nuclear chain reaction in the creation of the first "atomic pile"—a primitive nuclear reactor—in a basement at the University of Chicago, massive reactors were secretly created at what is now known as Hanford Site in the state of Washington, using the Columbia River as cooling water, to transform uranium-238 into plutonium for a bomb.

For a fission weapon to operate, there must be a critical mass—the amount needed for a self-sustaining nuclear chain reaction—of fissile material bombarded with neutrons at any one time. The simplest form of nuclear weapon is a gun-type fission weapon, where a sub-critical mass of fissile material (such as uranium-235) would be shot at another sub-critical mass of fissile material. The result would be a super-critical mass which, when bombarded with neutrons, would undergo fission at a rapid rate and create the desired explosion. The weapons envisaged in 1942 were the two gun-type weapons, Little Boy (uranium) and Thin Man (plutonium), and the Fat Man plutonium implosion bomb. In early 1943 Oppenheimer determined that two projects should proceed forwards: the "Thin Man" project (plutonium gun) and the "Fat Man" project (plutonium implosion). The plutonium gun was to receive the bulk of the research effort, as it was the project with the most uncertainty involved. It was assumed that the uranium gun-type bomb could then be adapted from it.

But in April 1944 it was found by Emilio Segrè that plutonium produced by the Hanford reactors had too high a level of background neutron radiation, and underwent spontaneous fission to a very small extent, due to the presence of impurities of the Pu-240 isotope. If such plutonium were used in a "gun assembly," the chain reaction would start in the split seconds before the critical mass was assembled, blowing the weapon apart before it would have any great effect (this is known as a fizzle). So development of Fat Man, the implosion bomb, was given high priority. Chemical explosives were used to implode a sub-critical sphere of plutonium, thus increasing its density and making it into a critical mass. The difficulties with implosion were in the problem of making the chemical explosives deliver a perfectly uniform shock wave upon the plutonium sphere— if it were even slightly asymmetric, the weapon would fizzle (which would be expensive, messy, and not a very effective military device). This problem was circumvented by the use of hydrodynamic "lenses"—explosive materials of differing densities—which would focus the blast waves inside the imploding sphere, akin to the way in which an optical lens focuses light rays.

After D-Day, General Groves had ordered a team of scientists—Project Alsos—to follow eastward-moving victorious Allied troops into Europe in order to assess the status of the German nuclear program (and to prevent the westward-moving Russians from gaining any materials or scientific manpower). It was concluded that while Nazi Germany had also had an atomic bomb program, headed by Werner Heisenberg, the government had not made a significant investment in the project, and had been nowhere near success. Historians claim to have found a rough schematic showing a Nazi nuclear bomb. Research was conducted in the German nuclear energy project. In March 1945, a Nazi scientific team was directed by the physicist Kurt Diebner to develop a primitive nuclear device in Ohrdruf, Thuringia.

By the unconditional surrender of Germany on May 8, 1945, the Manhattan Project was still months away from a working weapon. That April, after the death of American President Franklin D. Roosevelt, former Vice-President Harry S. Truman was told about the secret wartime project for the first time. Because of the difficulties in making a working plutonium bomb, it was decided that there should be a test of the weapon, and Truman wanted to know for sure if it would work before his meeting with Joseph Stalin at an upcoming conference on the future of postwar Europe. On July 16, 1945, in the desert north of Alamogordo, New Mexico, the first nuclear test took place, code-named "Trinity," using a device nicknamed "the Gadget." The test, a plutonium implosion type device, released the equivalent of 19 kilotons of TNT, far mightier than any weapon ever used before. The news of the test's success was rushed to Truman, who used it as leverage at the upcoming Potsdam Conference, held near Berlin.

After hearing arguments from scientists and military officers over the possible uses of the weapons against Japan (though some recommended using them as "demonstrations" in unpopulated areas, most recommended using them against "built up" targets, a euphemistic term for populated cities), Truman ordered the use of the weapons on Japanese cities, hoping it would send a strong message which would end in the capitulation of the Japanese leadership and avoid a lengthy invasion of the island. There were suggestions to drop the atomic bomb on Tokyo, the capital of Japan, but concerns about Tokyo's cultural heritage changed the plan. On May 10–11, 1945 The Target Committee at Los Alamos, led by J. Robert Oppenheimer, recommended Kyoto, Hiroshima, Yokohama, and the arsenal at Kokura as possible targets. On August 6, 1945, a uranium-based weapon, "Little Boy", was let loose on the Japanese city of Hiroshima. Three days later, a plutonium-based weapon, "Fat Man", was dropped onto the city of Nagasaki. The atomic bombs killed at least one hundred thousand Japanese outright, most of them civilians, with the heat, radiation, and blast effects.

Many tens of thousands would die later of radiation sickness and related cancers. Truman promised a "rain of ruin" if Japan did not surrender immediately, threatening to eliminate Japanese cities, one by one; Japan surrendered on August 15. Truman's threat was in fact a bluff, since the US had but one remaining uranium-gun type bomb completed.

SOVIET ATOMIC BOMB PROJECT

The Soviet Union was not invited to share in the new weapons developed by the United States and the other Allies. During the war, information had been pouring in from a number of volunteer spies involved with the Manhattan Project (known in Soviet cables under the code-name of *Enormoz*), and the Soviet nuclear physicist Igor Kurchatov was carefully watching the Allied weapons development. It came as no surprise to Stalin when Truman had informed him at the Potsdam conference that he had a "powerful new weapon." Truman was shocked at Stalin's lack of interest. The Soviet spies in the U.S. project were all volunteers and none were Russians.

One of the most valuable, Klaus Fuchs, was a German émigré theoretical physicist who had been a part in the early British nuclear efforts and had been part of the UK mission to Los Alamos during the war. Fuchs had been intimately involved in the development of the implosion weapon, and passed on detailed cross-sections of the "Trinity" device to his Soviet contacts. Other Los Alamos spies—none of whom knew each other—included Theodore Hall and David Greenglass. The information was kept but not acted upon, as Russia was still too busy fighting the war in Europe to devote resources to this new project.

In the years immediately after World War II, the issue of who should control atomic weapons became a major international point of contention. Many of the Los Alamos scientists who had built the bomb began to call for "international control of atomic energy," often calling for either control by transnational organizations or the purposeful distribution of weapons information to all superpowers, but due to a deep distrust of the intentions of the Soviet Union, both in postwar Europe and in general, the policy-makers of the United States worked to attempt to secure an American nuclear monopoly. A half-hearted plan for international control was proposed at the newly formed United Nations by Bernard Baruch ("The Baruch Plan"), but it was clear both to American commentators—and to the Soviets—that it was an attempt primarily to stymie Russian nuclear efforts. The Soviets vetoed the plan, effectively ending any immediate postwar negotiations on atomic energy, and made overtures towards banning the use of atomic weapons in general.

All the while, the Soviets had put their full industrial and manpower might into the development of their own atomic weapons. The initial problem for the Soviets was primarily one of resources—they had not scouted out uranium resources in the Soviet Union and the U.S. had made deals to monopolise the largest known (and high purity) reserves in the Belgian Congo. The USSR used penal labour to mine the old deposits in

Czechoslovakia—now an area under their control—and searched for other domestic deposits (which were eventually found). Two days after the bombing of Nagasaki, the U.S. government released an official technical history of the Manhattan Project, authored by Princeton physicist Henry DeWolf Smyth, known colloquially as the Smyth Report. The sanitized summary of the wartime effort focused primarily on the production facilities and scale of investment, written in part to justify the wartime expenditure to the American public.

The Soviet program, under the suspicious watch of former NKVD chief Lavrenty Beria (a participant and victor in Stalin's Great Purge of the 1930s), would use the Report as a blueprint, seeking to duplicate as much as possible the American effort. The "secret cities" used for the Soviet equivalents of Hanford and Oak Ridge literally vanished from the maps for decades to come. At the Soviet equivalent of Los Alamos, Arzamas-16, physicist Yuli Khariton led the scientific effort to develop the weapon. Beria distrusted his scientists, however, and he distrusted the carefully collected espionage information. As such, Beria assigned multiple teams of scientists to the same task without informing each team of the other's existence. If they arrived at different conclusions, Beria would bring them together for the first time and have them debate with their newfound counterparts. Beria used the espionage information as a way to double-check the progress of his scientists, and in his effort for duplication of the American project even rejected more efficient bomb designs in favour of ones which more closely mimicked the tried-and-true "Fat Man" bomb used by the U.S. against Nagasaki.

Working under a stubborn and scientifically ignorant administrator, the Soviet scientists struggled on. On August 29, 1949, the effort brought its results, when the USSR tested its first fission bomb, dubbed "Joe-1" by the U.S., years ahead of American predictions. The news of the first Soviet bomb was announced to the world first by the United States, which had detected the nuclear fallout it generated from its test site in Kazakhstan. The loss of the American monopoly on nuclear weapons marked the first tit-for-tat of the nuclear arms race. The response in the U.S. was one of apprehension, fear, and scapegoating, which would lead eventually into the Red-baiting tactics of McCarthyism. Yet recent information from unclassified Venona intercepts and the opening of the KGB archives after the fall of the Soviet Union show that the USSR had useful spies that helped their program, although none were identified by the McCarthy. Before this, though, President Truman would announce his decision to begin a crash program to develop a far more powerful weapon than those which were used against Japan: the hydrogen bomb.

The First Thermonuclear Weapons

The notion of using a fission weapon to ignite a process of nuclear fusion can be dated back to 1942. At the first major theoretical conference on the development of an atomic bomb hosted by J. Robert Oppenheimer at the University of California, Berkeley, participant Edward Teller directed the majority of the discussion towards Enrico Fermi's idea of a "Super" bomb which would utilize the same reactions which powered the Sun itself. It was thought at the time that a fission weapon would be quite simple to develop and that perhaps work on a hydrogen bomb would be possible to complete before the end of the Second World War. However, in reality the problem of a "regular" atomic bomb was large enough to preoccupy the scientists for the next few years, much less the more speculative "Super." Only Teller continued working on the project—against the will of project leaders Oppenheimer and Hans Bethe.

After the atomic bombings of Japan, many scientists at Los Alamos rebelled against the notion of creating a weapon thousands of times more powerful than the first atomic bombs. For the scientists the question was in part technical—the weapon design was still quite uncertain and unworkable—and in part moral: such a weapon, they argued, could only be used against large civilian populations, and could thus only be used as a weapon of genocide. Many scientists, such as Bethe, urged that the United States should not develop such weapons and set an example towards the Soviet Union. Promoters of the weapon, including Teller, Ernest Lawrence, and Luis Alvarez, argued that such a development was inevitable, and to deny such protection to the people of the United States—especially when the Soviet Union was likely to create such a weapon themselves—was itself an immoral and unwise act.

Oppenheimer, who was now head of the General Advisory Committee of the successor to the Manhattan Project, the Atomic Energy Commission, presided over a recommendation against the development of the weapon. The reasons were in part because the success of the technology seemed limited at the time (and not worth the investment of resources to confirm whether this was so), and because Oppenheimer believed that the atomic forces of the United States would be more effective if they consisted of many large fission weapons (of which multiple bombs could be dropped on the same targets) rather than the large and unwieldy predictions of massive super bombs, for which there were a relatively limited amounts of targets of the size to warrant such a development. Furthermore, were such weapons developed by both the U.S. and the USSR, they would be more effectively used against the U.S. than by it, as the U.S. had far more regions of dense industrial and civilian activity which would serve as ideal targets for the large weapons than the Soviet Union did.

In the end, President Truman made the final decision, looking for a proper response to the first Soviet atomic bomb test in 1949. On January 31, 1950, Truman announced a crash program to develop the hydrogen (fusion) bomb. At this point, however, the exact mechanism was still not known: the "classical" hydrogen bomb, whereby the *heat* of the fission bomb would be used to ignite the fusion material, seemed highly unworkable. However, an insight by Los Alamos mathematician Stanislaw Ulam showed that the fission bomb and the fusion fuel could be in separate parts of the bomb, and that *radiation* of the fission bomb could first work in a way to *compress* the fusion material before igniting it.

Teller pushed the notion further, and used the results of the boosted-fission "George" test (a boosted-fission device using a small amount of fusion fuel to boost the yield of a fission bomb) to confirm the fusion of heavy hydrogen elements before preparing for their first true multi-stage, Teller-Ulam hydrogen bomb test. Many scientists initially against the weapon, such as Oppenheimer and Bethe, changed their previous opinions, seeing the development as being unstoppable. The first fusion bomb was tested by the United States in *Operation Ivy* on November 1, 1952, on Elugelab Island in the Enewetak (or Eniwetok) Atoll of the Marshall Islands, code-named "Mike". "Mike" used liquid deuterium as its fusion fuel and a large fission weapon as its trigger. The device was a prototype design and not a deliverable weapon: standing over 20 ft (6 m) high and weighing at least 140,000 lb (64 t) (its refrigeration equipment added an additional 24,000 lb as well), it could not have been dropped from even the largest planes.

Its explosion yielded 10.4 megatons of energy—over 450 times the power of the bomb dropped onto Nagasaki— and obliterated Elugelab, leaving an underwater crater 6240 ft (1.9 km) wide and 164 ft (50 m) deep where the island had once been. Truman had initially tried to create a media blackout about the test—hoping it would not become an issue in the upcoming presidential election—but on January 7, 1953, Truman announced the development of the hydrogen bomb to the world as hints and speculations of it were already beginning to emerge in the press. Not to be outdone, the Soviet Union exploded its first thermonuclear device, designed by the physicist Andrei Sakharov, on August 12, 1953, labeled "Joe-4" by the West. This created concern within the U.S. government and military, because, unlike "Mike," the Soviet device was a deliverable weapon, which the U.S. did not yet have. This first device though was arguably not a "true" hydrogen bomb, and could only reach explosive yields in the hundreds of kilotons (never reaching the megaton range of a "staged" weapon). Still, it was a powerful propaganda tool for the Soviet Union, and the technical differences were fairly oblique to the American public and politicians.

Following the "Mike" blast by less than a year, "Joe-4" seemed to validate claims that the bombs were inevitable and vindicate those who had supported the development of the fusion program. Coming during the height of McCarthyism, the effect was most pronounced by the security hearings in early 1954 which revoked former Los Alamos director Robert Oppenheimer of his security clearance, on the grounds that he was unreliable, had not supported the American hydrogen bomb program, and had made long-standing, left-wing ties in the 1930s.

Edward Teller participated in the hearing as the only major scientist to testify against Oppenheimer, a role which resulted in his virtual expulsion from the physics community. On February 28, 1954, the U.S. detonated its first deliverable thermonuclear weapon (which used isotopes of lithium as its fusion fuel), known as the "Shrimp" device of the "Castle Bravo" test, at Bikini Atoll, Marshall Islands. The device yielded 15 megatons of energy, over twice its expected yield, and became the worst radiological disaster in U.S. history. The combination of the unexpectedly large blast and poor weather conditions caused a cloud of radioactive nuclear fallout to contaminate over 7,000 square miles, including Marshall Island natives and the crew of a Japanese fishing boat, as a snow-like mist. The contaminated islands were evacuated (and are still uninhabitable), but the natives received enough of a radioactive dose that they suffered far elevated levels of cancer and birth defects in the years to come.

The crew of the Japanese fishing boat, *Lucky Dragon 5*, returned to port suffering from radiation sickness and skin burns. Their cargo, many tons of contaminated fish, managed to enter into the market before the cause of their illness was determined. When a crew member died from the sickness and the full results of the contamination were made public by the U.S., Japanese concerns were reignited about the hazards of radiation and resulted in a boycott on eating fish (a main staple of the island country) for some weeks.

The hydrogen bomb age had a profound effect on the thoughts of nuclear war in the popular and military mind. With only fission bombs, nuclear war could be considered something which could easily be "limited." Dropped by planes and only able to destroy the most built up areas of major cities, it was possible to consider fission bombs simply a technological extension of previous wartime bombing (such as the extensive firebombing which took place against Japan and Germany during World War II), and claims that such weapons could lead to worldwide death or harm were easily brushed aside as grave exaggeration. Even the decades before the development of fission weapons there had been speculation about the possibility for human beings to end all life on the planet by either accident or purposeful maliciousness, but technology had never allowed for such a capacity. The far greater power of hydrogen bombs made this seem ever closer.

The "Castle Bravo" incident itself raised a number of questions about the survivability of a nuclear war. Government scientists in both the U.S. and the USSR had insisted that fusion weapons, unlike fission weapons, were "cleaner" as fusion reactions did not result in the dangerously radioactive by-products as did fission reactions. While technically true, this hid a more gruesome point: the last stage of a multi-staged hydrogen bomb often used the neutrons produced by the fusion reactions to induce fissioning in a jacket of natural uranium, and provided around half of the yield of the device itself. This fission stage made fusion weapons considerably more "dirty" than they were made out to be, a fact made evident by the towering cloud of deadly fallout which followed the "Bravo" test. When the Soviet Union tested its first megaton device in 1955, the possibility of a limited nuclear war seemed even more remote in the public and political mind: even if a city or country was not the direct target of a nuclear attack, the clouds of fallout and harmful fission products would disperse along with normal weather patterns and embed themselves in the soil and water of non-targeted areas of the planet as well. Speculation began to look towards what would happen as the fallout and dust created by a full-scale nuclear exchange would affect the world as a whole, rather than just the cities and countries which had been directly involved. In this way, the fate of the world was now tied to the fate of the bomb-wielding superpowers.

THE GLOBAL THREAT OF SMALL ARMS AND LIGHT WEAPONS — A PRIMER

What are light weapons?

Broadly speaking, the term refers to any weapon that can be carried by one or two people. Examples range from military-style guns—pistols, carbines, assault rifles, and light machine guns—to grenade launchers, mortars, mobile anti-tank guns and rocket launchers, and shoulder-fired anti-aircraft missile launchers. Munitions used with these weapons (such as bullets, grenades and missiles), landmines, and explosives are also encompassed by the term.

Why the focus on these weapons now?

With the end of the cold war, increased attention is being paid today to the devastation wrought by armed conflict around the world. Previously referred to by official Washington as "low intensity conflicts," these wars have resulted in the death of well over one million people this decade. The vast majority of these casualties—as many as 90 percent—are civilian victims of indiscriminate warfare.

The International Committee of the Red Cross has determined that small arms are the principal cause of death in conflicts. In fact, these arms are thought to be responsible for 90 percent of recent war casualties. Small/light arms are cheap and portable, and are used by all combatants—state militaries, militias, and insurgents. It is the prevalence—that is, the widespread proliferation—of these arms, combined with their indiscriminate use, that renders them responsible for so much of the killing.

In addition, small and light arms are used in crime and terrorist acts around the world.

Who's impacted by the spread of these arms?

Civilians—- Millions of people are caught in the crossfire of warfare or become victims of armed crime. Many are women and children.

Children—- The light weight and small size of these weapons has made it possible [easy] for children to be recruited or compelled to become soldiers. Child soldiers were particularly exploited in recent wars in Liberia and the Sudan.

Political dissidents, union organizers, land rights activists, journalists, etc.—- Small arms are the principal tool of intimidation used by repressive police and military forces. The massacre in

Chiapas last December of 45 unarmed civilians, carried out by government-affiliated paramilitary forces with high-powered AK-47 assault rifles, is one of countless examples.

Foreign relief and development workers—- Armed conflict often creates the humanitarian emergencies that relief workers are called in to alleviate. In addition, aid workers are increasingly coming under fire—being killed, kidnapped, or threatened.

International peacekeeping troops—- The United Nations found that small arms and light weapons pose the principal threat to international troops seeking to establish or maintain peace among combatants.

Local and foreign businesspeople—- Wealthy businesspeople are often kidnapped or extorted with these arms. More generally, the widespread diffusion of weapons undermines economic development and often results in the total collapse of a functioning economy.

Tourists and the tourism industry—- Armed violence has a devastating impact on local tourism, which is the largest industry in the world today and the leading source of revenue for many countries. In several recent cases, such as the massacre of 66 people at Luxor, Egypt last November, tourists are particularly targeted.

Does this proliferation constitute a national security threat?

In recent years the White House and Pentagon have identified international crime (including drug trafficking), terrorism and internal and regional conflict as major security threats. Speaking before the UN General Assembly in 1995, President Clinton highlighted these threats and urged states to work with the United States "to shut down the grey markets that outfit terrorists and criminals with firearms." In addition, as U.S. troops are increasingly participating in peacekeeping operations they are coming under direct threat or fire from these arms.

How many of these weapons are out there?

Estimates range from 100 to 500 million military style weapons in circulation, in addition to hundreds of millions more designed for police or civilian use. The wide range points to the lack of available data: Small arms and light weapons are rarely reported in official statistics on the arms trade, are impossible to quantify independently, and are often manufactured and transferred covertly.

Where are these guns coming from?

More than 70 states produce various light weapons and ammunition. Direct sales from weapons manufacturers to foreign governments or private entities are a principal source of supply. Such sales are usually regulated (that is, licensed for export) by national governments. In 1996, for instance, the U.S. State Departments licensed over $470 million of light military weapons for export. The Commerce Department, which has jurisdiction over industry-direct sales of shotguns and police equipment, approved an additional $57 million of exports. While these amounts are small in the context of the overall arms trade (estimated at some $30 billion annually), at $100-300 per gun these figures represent enormous quantities of weapons.

Cold war-era surplus stocks are a second major source of light weapons supply today. In the past few years the U.S. military has given away or sold at discount vast quantities of excess assault rifles, carbines, caliber pistols, machine guns and grenade launchers. Germany, the Netherlands, the former Soviet republics and several Eastern European countries have been unloading surplus guns on the world market.

Covert gun-running by governments to foreign governments or—more often—insurgent groups is a third source of small/light arms proliferation. Such policies are frought with danger, as evidenced by the disastrous legacy of weapons shipped by the Soviet Union and United States to combatants in Afghanistan, Angola and Central America. These weapons outlived the original purpose for which they were shipped and have since been recycled to other conflicts or to bandits.

The black market is another major channel of supply, where private dealers knowingly violate the arms sales laws and policies of the source, transit or recipient state for commercial gain.

Are most of the weapons of concern obtained legally or illegally?

There is a thriving global black market in small/light weapons. These arms are particularly attractive to smugglers, as they are cheap, and easily concealed and transported. The secretive nature of arms smuggling makes it impossible to know with any certainty the magnitude of the traffic, but some have estimated that it accounts for as much as half of all light weapons transfers. Moreover, illegally-acquired arms contribute disproportionately to the violent conflict and crime plaguing much of the world, since they constitute the principal source of supply for insurgents, governments under embargo, and criminals. Human Rights Watch found, for instance, that illegal gunrunning to both sides of the conflict in Burundi has fueled tensions and made possible the commission of serious human rights abuses.

The licit and illicit traffic in small arms are closely intertwined. Arms that are originally exported legally, but are not properly tracked or secured, often fall into illegal circulation. In 1994, for instance, foreign governments reported 6,238 unlawfully acquired U.S.-origin firearms to the Bureau of Alcohol, Tobacco and Firearms. Over half—3,376—were discovered in Mexico. In 1996, the BATF received approximately 30,000 requests to trace weapons used in crimes.

Theft or capture of state security forces' arms are a major source of black market supply around the world. In one frightening example, the General Accounting Office has reported that U.S. military forces cannot account for 40 "Stinger" shoulder-launched anti-aircraft missiles shipped to the Middle East during the Persian Gulf war. These weapons are ideal for terrorists.

The domestic U.S. gun market is another principal source of black market guns. For several years, the Mexican government, in particular, has pointed out that drug cartels (and other criminals) are getting many of their arms north of the border. Underscoring the point, several recent high-profile assassinations in Mexico were carried out with guns purchased illegally in the United States.

Finally, cold war "covert" arms supply by the U.S. and Soviet Union, particularly during the 1980s, is a principal source of the light arms in unlawful possession around the world today. The two countries donated huge quantities of rifles, machine guns, mortars and other weapons to insurgents or government allies in Afghanistan, Angola and Nicaragua. Because these weapons were transferred in a secretive and unacountable manner, they are particularly prone to fall into the black market. Many of these arms remain in active service today, contributing to a legacy of insecurity and violence in southern Asia, southern and central Africa and Central America.

What controls on light weapons flows are already in place?

Traditional arms control arrangements, such as the U.N. Register of Conventional Weapons and the "Wassenaar Arrangement," pay scant attention to light weapons. During 1997, however, governments and international organizations made progress in clamping down on illicit weapons trafficking.

Last November, the United States and 27 other governments from the hemisphere signed a Mexican-backed convention, negotiated through the Organization of American States, against illicit manufacture and trafficking of firearms, ammunition and related materials. The treaty requires states to strengthen border controls, mark firearms and share information on weapons producers, dealers, importers and exporters. The 15 members of the European Union, meanwhile, made a political commitment to prevent illicit trafficking in conventional weapons in June 1997, and the "Group of 8" industrialized nations (which includes Russia) is considering the adoption of an international agreement along the lines of the OAS convention.

The United Nations has also been at the forefront of efforts to restrain the spread of light weapons, from both a conflict prevention and crime prevention perspective. In 1995, a panel of governmental experts investigated the proliferation of small/light arms and recommended increased information sharing, stronger laws and regulations, improved security for surplus weapons storage, and the destruction of weaponry within the mandate of

UN peacekeeping operations. The panel also called for an international conference on illicit weapons trafficking. The UN's Economic and Social Council has also been evaluating ways to combat crime by cracking down on the illegal trade in firearms.

In addition to these regional or international agreements, most governments have national policies in place to regulate imports and exports of light weapons. In the United States, for example, the Bureau of Alcohol, Tobacco and Firearms deals with the import of firearms, while the State, Commerce and Defense Departments have jurisdiction over arms exports from the United States.

Won't a focus on weapons deflect attention away from efforts to deal with the root cause of conflict and crime? The vast supply of small and light military style arms, while perhaps not *causing* conflicts, encourages the resort to warfare (as opposed to other means of conflict resolution or state formation), thus creating more demand. In addition, the easy availability of arms lengthens the duration and lethality of wars, not only causing immense casualties but also creating massive refugee flows. Even when conflicts are ended, they leave a legacy of an armed and insecure society, which undermines the consolidation of peace and the re-establishment of governance and economic activity, contributing directly to the principle root causes of conflict and crime.

Is the issue really one of a global gun ban? A ban on small arms and light weapons is unrealistic, given the widespread acceptance of their legitimacy in the hands of militaries and some police forces. The focus of efforts should be to end the indiscriminate use and curb the oversupply of these weapons, with the aim of reducing the damage and suffering they cause.

Is it really possible to limit the oversupply of these weapons? As a first step, governments and advocates must learn more about the scale of the problem. At present, data is non-existent, and there is no formal information collection mechanism. One approach might be to expand the UN Register of Conventional Arms to include all light weapons and small arms transfers. Improved national transparency and oversight of light weapons would also contribute toward stronger controls.

Controls on the illicit trade in light weapons are possible and palatable for governments. The OAS Convention is hopefully only the first of these initiatives. There is considerable scope for national, regional and international controls in the form of tighter national law enforcement and customs policies, and multilateral conventions that require governments to increase cooperation and information sharing, strengthen existing legislation and implement new controls. These include marking of small arms and ammunition, the development of national registries of gun ownership and transfer, and the establishment of stricter verification mechanisms on the final destination of weapons transfers.

Much like the war on drugs, government rhetoric in favor of eradicating illicit weapons trafficking has developed much more rapidly than the practical measures that will actually impact the trade. It is vital that governments translate these policies into action, and commit the necessary resources to guarantee their implementation. At the same time, proposals for curbing the illicit trade only address one element of light weapons proliferation. Governments should not be allowed to use illicit controls as a smokescreen to divert attention away from the violence and suffering caused by legally traded guns.

Codes of conduct on arms transfers can help ensure that legally traded weapons do not fall into the hands of those who abuse human rights and threaten peace and stability. In the past, supplier nations have been too quick to sell weapons to anyone who would buy them, and as a result, have armed abusive regimes and provided weaponry for repression. Codes of conduct which would prevent future transfers of military equipment to such regimes are gaining ground in the U.S. Congress, the European Union and within the international community.

If the harmful impact of light weapons proliferation is viewed as a violation of humanitarian law, there is some scope for an international convention to curb their misuse. A convention could focus on the excessively harmful and injurious results of the wrongful of use of small arms and light weapons, and commit governments to, among other things, collects and destroy weapons, ensure safe storage, restrain transfers and prohibit exports to countries which do not agree to the provisions of the treaty. There are a number of other practical options for control. Limiting ammunition production and transfers holds promise as a means of reducing violence, while the post-conflict destruction of surplus weaponry would prevent arms from being recycled to other wars and to criminals. In El Salvador, where tens of thousands of weapons are in circulation, the homicide rate has increased by 36 percent since the end of the civil war. Similarly, in South Africa, the easy availability of weapons from across the border in Mozambique and Angola has led to a dramatic increase in armed crime.

Certain types of light weapons may lend themselves to an outright ban, such as landmines, blinding laser weapons and other hi-tech arms. In fact, it may be possible to enact prohibitions on some of these before they reach full development and manufacture. Similarly, norms or bans on civilian possession of military-style weapons would reduce the capacity for violence around the world.

Many of these measures would be rendered ineffectual without tighter domestic laws on gun purchase and ownership. Countries with lax domestic gun laws create a permissive environment for illegal transfers and the misuse of small arms and light weapons, and undermine global initiatives at control. It is crucial that international agreements require states to establish stricter gun laws.

PROLIFERATION OF SMALL ARMS AND LIGHT WEAPONS

The end of the Cold War removed constraints inherent to superpower rivalry, and contributed to an outbreak of inter-state and intra-state wars and conflicts, often of a religious or ethnic character and often involving unusual violence and cruelty. In addition, some of the proxy wars fuelled during the Cold War decades within states remained unresolved. These wars and conflicts were fought not only by regular armies, but also by militias and armed civilians, in support of the regular forces. They had to be armed and in the process this led to an excessive and uncontrolled proliferation of small arms and light weapons

(SALW). The decade of the 90s particularly saw expanding civil wars, in former Yugoslavia, mass starvation in Somalia and so forth, arising out of civil wars enlarging into ethnic cleansing. To control the increasing incidents of regional and inter-state conflicts, Boutros Boutros Ghali, the new Secretary-General of the United Nations at the time, came up with an 'Agenda for Peace' in June 1992, stressing a central role that ought to be played by the UN, and reviewed the various methods for a more effective role of the Security Council in preventing, controlling or resolving disputes through preventive diplomacy, peace-keeping, peace-making and peace-related efforts, as well as for arms control and disarmament. By 1993, the 'Agenda for Peace' was already under criticism for UN's ineffectiveness, given that fratricide grew into ethnic cleansing in Yugoslavia, the peace mission to Somalia failed miserably, there was a political standoff in Haiti, and civil chaos surfaced in Zaire and Tajikistan.

At that point, SALW were considered responsible for deaths and violence in most conflicts and for the collapse of state institutions, especially the police and judiciary, with resulting paralysis of governance, a breakdown of law and order, and general anarchic conditions of banditry and chaos. The SALW used in these conflicts and civil wars were mainly acquired during the Cold War. However, after the Cold War, the SALW used in these conflicts were proliferated through arms black markets, private production, and smuggling. As a result, the full extent of the destabilising consequences of an excessive accumulation, proliferation, transfer and use of small arms and light weapons began to be felt as a major global threat. It led to the re-evaluations of security in international forums such as the UN.

In 1995, in a position paper, entitled 'Supplement to Agenda for Peace' the UN Secretary-General noted that while there were some agreed upon global norms and standards against weapons of mass destruction, there were no such norms or standards that could be used against the excessive and destabilising accumulation of small arms and light weapons. It was then realised that uncontrolled proliferation of small arms and light weapons posed, and continues to pose, a major non-traditional threat to international as well as regional peace and security. The 1995, General Assembly resolution 50/70B first raised the issue of proliferation of SALW. In this resolution, the UNGA, by reaffirming the role of the UN in the field of disarmament stated its realisation regarding SALW in the following words.

'That arms obtained through the illicit arms trade are most likely to be used for violent purposes and that even small arms when so obtained, directly or indirectly, by terrorist groups, drug traffickers or underground organisations can pose a danger to regional and international security, and certainly to the security and political stability of the countries affected.' As a result, the UN Secretary-General established a panel Group of Governmental Experts on Small Arms to report on types of SALW, nature and causes of their proliferation, and the ways and means to prevent and reduce the excessive and destabilising accumulation and transfer of small arms and light weapons, as they cause or exacerbate conflict. At that time many prevailing conflicts inflicted heavy causalities on the people involved, and the victims were mostly women and children. It was estimated that, by 1996, over 35 million people in 23 countries throughout the world were at risk of facing civil strife, either owing to ongoing humanitarian crises, or as a result of a slow recovery from past ones.

The Group of Governmental Experts on Small Arms held a number of different regional and international workshops and finally presented its consolidated report in 1997 on types of SALW, nature and causes of their proliferation, and recommendations to control and prevent their proliferation. In this report, Bangladesh, Sri Lanka, Nepal, Pakistan and India shared the growing concern over the trans-boundary movement of illicit and covert arms trade from Afghanistan, and emphasised on the need for a worldwide campaign to raise global consciousness of the consequences of the inflow to, and outflow of, weapons from Afghanistan. The 1997 report by Governmental Experts on Small Arms acted as a catalyst and placed the issue of SALW on the international agenda. On December 9, 1997, the UNGA endorsed all issues raised by the report in its resolution 52/38J. In 1998, the UNGA established another Group of Governmental Experts on Small Arms to assist the UN Secretary-General to prepare a report on the progress made in the implementation of the recommendations of the 1997 report and further actions recommended to be taken. On August 19, 1999 the UN Secretary-General presented the report of Group of Governmental Experts on Small Arms to the UNGA, in preventing and reducing the excessive and destabilising accumulation of small arms and light weapons. As a result of these efforts the UNGA decided to convene an international conference on the illicit arms trade in all its aspects no later than 2001.

In October 2000, the UN Secretary-General Kofi Annan, in his Millennium Report, 'We the People', presented to the UNGA, attached a special concern to the problems associated with proliferation of SALW. Significantly, Annan described small arms as 'weapons of mass destruction' because the death toll from small arms dwarfed that of all other weapons systems, and in most years greatly exceeded the toll of the atomic bombs that had devastated Hiroshima and Nagasaki. Annan further said that

'The proliferation of small arms, and munitions and explosives has also aggravated the violence associated with terrorism and organised crime. Even in societies not beset by civil war, the easy availability of small arms has in many cases contributed to violence and political instability. These, in turn, have damaged development prospects and imperilled human security in every way. Small arms proliferation is not merely a security issue; it is also an issue of human rights and of development. The proliferation of small arms sustains and exacerbates armed conflicts. It endangers peacekeepers and humanitarian workers. It undermines respect for International Humanitarian Law (IHL). It threatens legitimate but weak governments and it benefits terrorists as well as the perpetrators of organised crime.'

In his Millennium Report, Annan urged the Member States to participate fully in the UN Conference on Small Arms in order to take serious actions to curtail the illicit trade in small arms. From July 9-20, 2001, the UN Conference on the Illicit Trade in Small Arms and Light Weapons in All Its Aspects took place at New York.

In order to combat and eradicate the illicit trade in SALW, the States adopted a wide range of political undertakings at the national, regional and global levels. The significant step was the adoption of the Programme of Action (PoA) with consensus by the Member States. The PoA mainly covers the areas of legislation, destruction of weapons that were confiscated, seized, or collected, as well as international cooperation and assistance to strengthen the ability of States in identifying and tracing illicit arms and light weapons. Finally, the Member States agreed to hold a review conference in 2006, as well as biennial meetings along the way. These meetings would allow NGOs and governments to keep the momentum moving forward on the small arms issue under the PoA framework.

On December 23, 2003, the UNGA passed resolution 58/241 and established an open-ended working group to negotiate an international instrument to enable States to identify and trace, in a timely and reliable manner, illicit small arms and light weapons. The working group is making its every effort to ensure that a positive outcome would be achieved.

In February 2005, the United Nations Secretary-General presented its report of 'Small Arms' to the UNSC and recommended that the UNSC and the UNGA should establish a committee to look into how the two organs could work together in the areas of illicit SALW brokering.

The UNSC declaring its primary responsibility for maintaining international peace and security, also appealed to the arms-exporting countries 'to exercise the highest responsibility in small arms and light weapons transactions' in accordance with international law.

Currently, more than 640 million items of SALW are in circulation around the world. Around 59% of it are owned or controlled by civilians while the rest are owned by governments, armed forces, police, insurgents and other non-state forces. The annual trade in small arms is about $40 billion. Two-thirds of global arms deliveries go to the developing countries. Small arms are produced by more than 1,000 companies in at least 98 countries, with about 7 million new arms produced annually. Since 1990, more than four million people have been killed, the majority of them were civilians (90%) of whom an overwhelming 80% were women and children. According to a recent report from the UN, 'two million children have been killed in the last ten years in conflicts where small arms have been used; five million have been disabled, and twelve million left homeless.' A 'small arm' thus exists for every twelve persons in the world.

The same is the case with South Asia where proliferation of SALW is very high. In South Asia the proliferation of SALW is linked to insurgencies, ethnic and sectarian violence, organised crimes, political movements and private militias, terrorist activities, inter-state wars, guerrilla warfare and many other violence-related activities. Proliferation of SALW is not only threatening human security, but also impacting on the societal peace, livelihood and economic development of the countries and the communities of the region. It is not an easy task to control the menace of SALW so as to end human misery and sufferings in South Asia.

Since the introduction of the PoA, Pakistan, India, Sri Lanka, and Bangladesh have implemented PoA and submitted their respective national reports on voluntary basis. These reports deal with legal, administrative and procedural measures to combat proliferation of SALW. Despite these measures, the menace of small arms is still prevailing in their respective societies. There is a need to identify weaknesses and problems in these measures to devise a coherent regional approach to address the problems of SALW. There is a growing need that South Asian states should proactively participate in the first UN review conference in 2006 to curb proliferation of SALW, since South Asia itself has such a proliferation of SALW. A coherent regional approach would contribute towards strengthening an international mechanism to curb the proliferation of SALW in all its aspects, because a regional approach is an effective mechanism to curb proliferation of SALW which is a trans-border phenomenon.

8

Transparency in the Legal Small Arms Trade and Control

In the past few years governments and civil society have devoted increasing levels of attention to the long-neglected humanitarian danger posed by the proliferation and misuse of military style small arms around the world. To date, however, concerned parties have not come to broad agreement as to the main problem.

Is the major threat posed by existing stocks of "illicit" weaponry in circulation in zones of conflict? Or are on-going legal transfers also of concern? If it is the former, how does one define the term, given that the licit trade and the illicit traffic in small arms are inextricably linked? For example, arms that are originally exported legally, but are not properly tracked or secured, often fall into illegal circulation, as theft or capture of state security forces' weapons is a major source of black-market supply around the world. And what about legally transferred weapons that are used in an illegal manner (e.g., by repressive government forces to carry out human rights abuses)?

Currently there is very little hard data available about the principal sources of small arms supply and trafficking. As a result, the relative importance of the legal versus the illegal trade in arming combatants and criminals around the globe is unknown. In the absence of basic information about the magnitude and destinations of state-sanctioned small arms supply, well-intentioned policymakers might be prioritizing complicated and perhaps costly policy options related to the illicit trade that would have less impact than would relatively simple and straightforward measures relating to accountability in the legal trade.

One of the most important initiatives that governments concerned about the humanitarian and criminal impact of small arms proliferation could undertake is to provide greater transparency around the small arms exports they are authorizing.

Approximately seventy states produce small arms and/or ammunition. Some small arms production enterprises are state-owned (usually military armories), and some are privately-owned companies. Researching what the major small arms producing states manufacture is not difficult; there are several standard sources of information. Determining production quantities (or output) is much more difficult, and knowing where weapons are being exported is nearly impossible. The standard sources of data on the international arms trade—SIPRI, the UN Register of conventional Arms, World Military Expenditures and Arms Transfers—do not include information on small arms shipments. Few governments provide information to their public or parliaments on major weapons exports they have approved (like tanks and jets), and even fewer provide information on this low-end sector of the trade.

The US government is the most notable exception to the prevailing pattern of secrecy. Since 1996, except for covert arms supply operations, the United States openly reports in a disaggregated manner its small arms shipments and export license approvals. The Canadian government provides less detailed, but fairly specific information about its small arms exports, and the Netherlands, Norway and Sweden provide aggregated data on their exports, as well.

Fuller information about the magnitude and destination of current and future small arms shipments is a necessary prerequisite for development of sound policy recommendations. Transparency would also facilitate and improve the ability of governments to ensure end-use verification of weapons exports they are authorizing. If such information were made public, increased transparency would allow the non-governmental community, as well as national legislatures, to play an important role in aiding governments' efforts to curb diversion of these arms by providing oversight through research, questioning and reporting.

Such information is also important to aid and relief workers, who might be working in a region where a sudden influx of guns has occurred or is anticipated. Transparency around planned arms shipments (that is, timely information exchange about license approvals granted) could prove to be an early warning indicator of pending violence and instability. While individual states might not be granting unusually large numbers of export licenses to a particular destination, when placed side by side with other suppliers' export approvals, disturbing trends might become apparent.

Greater governmental transparency would also help evaluate the real impact of small arms on people and societies. Although widely assumed to be a significant factor, there has been no scientific investigation of the impact of small arms supply in terms of outbreak, sustainment or escalation of civil warfare. The dearth of data on arms transfers currently hinders the ability of researchers to conduct such studies.

On a more positive note, increased openness about weapons shipments could serve as a confidence-building measure among forces within a state, or states in a region, potentially heading off some purchases spurred on by "fear of the unknown." Finally, such information would greatly facilitate disarmament, whether through peacekeeping or other initiatives, by providing some baseline information about arms supply in the state or region.

Increased transparency is possible at the global, regional and national levels. The United Nations and regional security organizations can help facilitate the former two, but such initiatives are, of course, predicated on a willingness by governments to engage in greater openness. Policy analysts continually promote expansion of the UN Register of Conventional Arms to include small arms and light weapons as a desirable goal, but an expert panel reviewing the Register in 1997 decided against doing so, largely because the rationale for the Register is to indicate destabilizing build-ups of major weapons systems.

Meanwhile, with no elaboration, US Secretary of State Albright called in September 1998 for the creation of an "international center" for exchange of information on small arms transfers. There has been no further elaboration of this idea. The already extant Wassenaar Arrangement might prove a particularly suitable forum for regular (perhaps quarterly) information exchange by its members on potential small arms shipments licensed for export— if traditional resistance in this regard by some members can be overcome.

The research community could help lay out a realistic template for governmental transparency, identifying and rebutting obstacles to openness. What must be revealed by exporters (and importers)? What would be nice to know, but could be omitted in an effort to protect business confidentiality? Given the difficulty of persuading all countries (most importantly, supplier countries) to participate in a transparency regime, what would the value be of partial participation in such an effort?

Concerned states need not wait for some complicated global agreement. They can and should become transparent unilaterally, as did the United States and Canada. Small arms are not strategic weapons. Openness about production and shipment of such weapons will not jeopardize national security, although it might compromise business interests of a firm trying to make a sale, if the buyer wants the deal to remain cloaked in secrecy. But the need on the part of the buyer for secrecy should be examined, and the business interests of the arms firm must be weighed against other interests of the exporting state.

IMPACT OF GLOBALIZATION ON MILITARY EXPENDITURE AND ARMS TRANSFERS

Although the term 'globalization' did not appear until recently, the notion of globalization has existed for a long time. The concept is being used for a wide variety of phenomena and trends and the descriptions of current trends in globalization and the conclusions as regards its impact differ accordingly. There exists not one discourse of globalization but several. In a recent survey of the debate and the literature, five major discourses on globalization are identified, basically falling into the areas of economics, sociology, political science, culture and ecology. All these aspects of globalization, together with the globalization of technology, have an impact of the trends and patterns in military expenditure and arms transfers, directly or indirectly by their impact on the causes of military expenditure, arms production and arms transfers.

The process of globalization has gone through several phases during which the various aspects have assumed different importance. During the cold war period, the political aspects were predominant. The impact of this phase of globalization on trends and pattern of military expenditures and arms transfers was significant and is well documented. During the subsequent, current, phase of globalization, the politico-military dynamic of the cold war has been overtaken by a mainly financial phase. It began in the second half of the 1980s, with the enormous expansion of trading in foreign currency after the breakdown in the 1970s of the international Bretton Woods currency system, and has resulted in the abolishing of state controls of capital markets and opening up of new financial world markets, in privatizations of public enterprises and services, in a break-up of national champion monopolies, and in a general encouragement of global competition. Simultaneously with the globalization of financial and economic activities, the end of the cold war has meant a deglobalization of political action.

These factors, around the existence of which there is fairly broad consensus, have an impact on military expenditure and arms transfers in several ways, perhaps primarily through its effect on the arms industry. While the military sector has been the sector most resistant to privatization, commercialization and reduced political control, all these trends are currently affecting the production, procurement and international transfers of arms. The arms industry is increasingly being privatized and commercialized. The European arms industry is going through a process of internationalization, until now relatively limited and primarily through cross-border joint ventures, but more recently (during 1999) also through cross-border mergers of arms producing companies. European companies are also acquiring armsproducing companies in other continents, recent examples include Australia, South Africa and South Korea, while transatlantic military-industrial links are still rare in spite of the lively debate on both sides of the Atlantic about their potential.

The increasing privatization, commercialization, competition and internationalization of arms production, have resulted in an increased pressure from the arms industry to export their excess supply of weapons, and thus to increased commercialization also of the arms trade, in which marketing and generous sales terms play an increasing role. At the same time, increased internationalization means reduced possibilities for national governments to implement national arms export regulations, since companies can choose to export their products from a business unit in another country with more liberal export regulations. For this reason, national export laws are becoming increasingly irrelevant. This points to the need for common or international export rules.

However, globalization may render also international control more difficult. The globalization of technology in general, and in the context of a gradual closing of the gap between military and civil technology, will make it increasingly difficult to control the international transfer of militarily relevant technologies in the future. The challenge is to achieve international limitations in the transfer of military technology without resorting to controls which will inhibit international transfers of all types of advanced technology, that is, also civil technologies which would benefit economic growth in the recipient countries.

A relatively new development is the impact of globalization on armed conflict and the financing of these. The fragmentation and decentralization of the state has produced a new type of wars and with it increasingly financing of wars outside traditional government defence budgets. As described by Mary Kaldor, these new wars take place in the context of extreme globalization, under which territorially-based production has more or less collapsed and production continues only of a few valuable commodities (diamonds, emeralds, drugs), which provide a source of income for whoever can provide 'protection'. These wars are fought by various types of fighting units, public and private, state and non-state, including regular armed forces or remnants thereof, paramilitary groups, self-defence units, foreign mercenaries, and regular foreign troops, usually under international auspices. During these conditions governments, like privatized military groups, need alternative sources of funding for their military activities, many of which involve criminal activities. These fall into the following categories: 1) 'Asset transfer', i.e. the redistribution of existing assets to benefit the fighting units (such as loot, robbery, hostage-taking, and deriving profits from control over market prices); 2) 'war taxes' or 'protection' money from the production of primary commodities and various forms of illegal trading; and 3) external assistance, in particular for imports, such as (a) remittances from abroad to individual families, b) direct assistance from the Diaspora living abroad; (c) assistance from foreign governments; and 4) humanitarian assistance diverted by governments and warring factions for their own use. For countries involved in such new wars, data on government military expenditure are irrelevant for measuring military expenditure. What is more important is that the set of social relationships which are formed by these systems for financing wars constitute strongly resisting factors for the ending of war.

Privatization of security is an increasing trend also in countries which are not involved in regular armed conflict but where there is a demand for more security services than the government can offer. There is an emerging group of private security companies whose main task is the provision of security in many Third World countries, especially in Africa. The demand for private security services has emerged from a combination of factors, including from western governments seeking to reduce defence budgets, African governments in search of security, international mining corporations and rebel movements. They provide a variety of services, ranging from guarding installations, protecting convoys, supporting humanitarian assistance operations to performing reconnaissance and intelligence services, providing logistical and transport support, military training, strategic planning, and engaging in combat. These companies have developed to fill the need for security in the current context of conflict in Africa, in weak states with limited government legitimacy and with limited economic resources, and in which the international community is increasingly reluctant to intervene.

THE ROLE OF NUCLEAR WEAPONS

So far, the improvement of Sino-Indian relations has not explicitly addressed the nuclear issue. The issue has special characteristics in the Sino-Indian context. China is a nuclear weapon state, while India has demonstrated its nuclear capability but refuses to produce nuclear weapons. Since China has undertaken not to use or threaten to use nuclear weapons first, there is not necessarily any more for them to talk about.

Increasing international efforts on nuclear arms control have coincided with the improvement of Sino-Indian relations, but both sides have good reason not to raise any issue which might be unnecessarily divisive. The nuclear issue is sensitive for both states, even if that sensitivity has little to do with their relationship to one another, and even if the topic were on the bilateral agenda there would not be much space in which to manoeuvre. In any case, the nuclear issue is not central to Sino-Indian relations. Neither country has accorded the issue a high priority in their meetings.

On both sides changes in their security situations have made domestic politics a more important factor in the nuclear weapon pro- grammes. Since the nuclear issue is not yet a topic of public debate in China, its role in domestic politics remains largely one of state élites expressing the strength of the government and the skills of its scientists. In India, domestic politics has an important influence over nuclear decision making, as demonstrated by the polarization of the debate over the test ban in late 1995 and 1996.23 In the 1996 general election all parties, despite their differences on other issues, closed ranks on the nuclear issue. It is becoming harder for the Indian Government to participate in any nuclear arms control initiative, if it ever wanted to.

Have nuclear weapons ever been significant in Sino-Indian relations? China appears relatively unconcerned about India's nuclear enterprise. It has never seen India alone as a nuclear threat, although in the 1960s and 1970s it worried about India as a component of Indo- US or Indo-Soviet collusion to encircle China.

China started its nuclear weapon programme in the 1950s mainly to break the nuclear monopoly of the imperialist powers and to acquire a nuclear deterrent to nuclear blackmail from the USA and the USSR. During the Korean War and the 1958 Taiwan Strait crisis, the USA threatened to use nuclear weapons against China. Later, China began to consider the Soviet Union as the main nuclear threat. China has missiles that can strike India, but has never developed a missile specifically to target at India. In the era of military reform, China is still working on three new strategic nuclear missiles. The range of these missile is 8000–12 000 km. They are obviously not developed with India in mind.

In the era of economic reform and since Deng's assertion that major war could be avoided, and especially given the increasing demand for nuclear energy, China's nuclear programme has paid more attention to the energy industry. As a result of the previous strategy of 'primacy of the military objective', while the nuclear weapon programme achieved remarkable progress, China's civilian nuclear industry remained underdeveloped. This strategy has now been replaced by 'military–civilian integration'. Although China has not stopped the qualitative upgrading of its small nuclear arsenal, the speed of development is slowing down. Of the 45 nuclear tests China conducted in 32 years before halting them in 1996, only 20 took place during the 18 years since economic reform began in 1978.

On balance, however, China would rather not have another nuclear weapon state on its border. The effect on the security environment of nuclear proliferation has not escaped military attention altogether in China. This concern was reflected in China's insistence that India and 43 other countries ratify the CTBT before it can enter into force.

Nevertheless, the Chinese ambassador to India, Pei Yuanying, has remarked, 'Unlike the Americans, we will not pressurize India to sign [the NPT] or the CTBT. We respected India's independence in the matter'.

There are at least three reasons why China is indifferent to nuclear developments in India. First, even if relations soured, conventional weapons better serve the cause of security given the limited nature of the disagreements between China and India. In any case, China perceives the probability of war with India to be small. Finally, it might be inferred (as one Indian observer has noted) that China continues to enjoy an advantage in nuclear capability over India, both in warheads and in delivery systems. On this view, as long as the heartland of China is beyond the range of Indian nuclear delivery systems and a large part of India is within range of Chinese aircraft carrying nuclear weapons, deterrence will allow China to rest easy.

India has shown more concern about China's nuclear build-up. Some Indian observers are quick to point out that the whole of India is within the range of Chinese missiles. Some Indians further suspect that China has based nuclear weapons in Tibet and dumped nuclear waste on the plateau. A final concern is Sino-Pakistani missile cooperation, which poses a threat to Indian security and the balance of power in South Asia.

A closer look at the history of the relationship suggests that India never really took the supposed nuclear threat from China seriously. China's first nuclear explosion in 1964 was soon forgotten, and India waited a full decade before carrying out its own test, which could have been achieved much sooner. Even after the Pokhran explosion in 1974, for 20 years India has not tried to race to catch up and has been content with its 'option' policy. The policy is based on the claim that it has the capability to manufacture nuclear weapons but would deploy them only in dire circumstances. This is consistent with an 'existential' philosophy of nuclear deterrence. Although there are those who would have India weaponize its nuclear capability in order to cope with those of its neighbours, particularly Pakistan, this has not happened. During these 20 years there has not been a single Chinese attempt at the nuclear blackmail of India. The historical experience of living with the Chinese bomb has helped to reduce the fear of

Chinese nuclear might, although those concerns have not entirely disappeared, at least at the level of public rhetoric.

In recent years India has worked more assiduously on missiles, stimulated mainly by the nuclear weapon programme in Pakistan. India is clearly concerned more with Pakistan than with China, although the nuclear weapon programme has always been justified with reference to China's. India has emphasized short-range missiles, which can cover the main cities in Pakistan. The Agni intermediate- range missile could reach some Chinese cities in the south-west part of China, but has progressed slowly and been put aside.

More notably, China and India have begun to cooperate on civil nuclear technology. On 5 January 1995, India's Department of Atomic Energy announced that a supply of enriched uranium had arrived that day from China at its nuclear fuel complex in Hyderabad. The uranium will be mixed with domestically produced plutonium oxide and used to fuel the Tarapur nuclear power plant near Bombay.

There is a contradiction in Indian statements respecting the Chinese nuclear capability. The supposed Chinese nuclear threat has not been mentioned in the Ministry of Defence annual report between 1985/86 and the controversy over the CTBT in 1996. The Indian Ministry of External Affairs links its arms control policy with China's pro- gramme, and the Ministry of Defence has again begun to cite the China threat. Does the linkage mean that India is simply using China as an excuse? At the very least, that linkage has helped to ease inter- national pressure on some of India's less popular policies, since a concern with China is seen by many observers as legitimate.

APPROACHES TO ARMS CONTROL

China and India have idiosyncratic approaches to the nuclear arms control regime rooted in their defence policy cultures. The similarities and differences in their approaches, beginning with an examination of their aims and means and then assessing where there is potential for competition and cooperation.

Aims and means

In the 1960s and 1970s China criticized arms control and disarmament on the grounds that they formed a regime controlled by the super- powers. It claimed that the primary goal was to prevent other countries from getting nuclear weapons so that the superpowers could maintain their nuclear monopoly. Since then China's nuclear arms control policy has been in a process of change, although the overall principles and goals have remained the same. In the words of Foreign Minister Li Huaqiu, the change is 'from idealism to realism; from a completely Chinese way of doing things towards gradual application of international practices and ways of doing things; and from criticism to joint cooperation'.

China has been actively involved in different arms control forums. By participating in the negotiations rather than condemning them, it is able to prevent the creation of obligations that would threaten its security interests, deal with problems that cannot otherwise be solved, and show its willingness to accept responsibility befitting its inter- national role. In multilateral forums China has made important contributions. After belatedly signing the NPT and taking an ambiguous position in favour of 'smooth extension', it agreed to the indefinite extension of the treaty. It showed flexibility in the CTBT talks, giving up its earlier positions on permitted activities, peaceful nuclear explosions, verification and on-site inspections. China was among the first signatories in September 1996.

China's new approach to arms control policy encompasses both long-range goals and short-term pragmatism. The long-range goal is the total elimination of nuclear weapons, but China accepts that the realization of this goal will require a protracted process, during which it can accept interim arrangements. As a participant in these arrangements, China established its practical aims. First among these is reducing the number of nuclear weapons held by the nuclear weapon states, including itself, a process in which the superpowers should take the lead. Since Russia and the USA still have the largest nuclear arsenals in the world, they are expected to reduce their weapons first. Specifically, Russia and the USA should reduce their arsenals to a level comparable with the holdings of the other nuclear weapon states. China also seeks to prevent nuclear proliferation, especially in neighbouring countries, and to remove the threat of nuclear blackmail. In particular, China has consistently called for the nuclear weapon states to reach an agreement under which they would not use or threaten to use nuclear weapons first against each other and would not use or threaten to use their nuclear weapons against non-nuclear weapon states at all.

In contrast, India has been active in arms control and disarmament since Independence. It was the first country to propose a test ban treaty and a cut-off on the production of materials for nuclear weapons. It signed the PTBT soon after it was concluded in 1963. In the mid-1960s, however, its retreat from its earlier enthusiasm for arms control began. It criticized the discriminatory nature of the NPT and refused to sign it.

Since the end of the cold war, India has had to adjust to the new world order, especially in its relationship with Russia. Thus far, however, there has not been a radical modification of India's nuclear policy. India remains one of the few countries outside the inter- national non-proliferation regime. If anything, India's opposition to arms control as practised in existing forums has strengthened, and some observers seem to be encouraging India to test and deploy nuclear weapons simply to flout the emergent nuclear order. Even so, like China, India continues to hold fast to the ideal of eliminating nuclear weapons completely.

If China and India share some goals, there might be as many similarities as differences in their approaches. With their relations improving, the similarities could lead to greater cooperation.

To summarize the similarities, both resist Western hegemony and its embodiment in nuclear weapons. For almost two decades China also criticized the NPT as discriminatory, and it has been subject to US sanctions. Both countries are concerned that inspection regimes will cause problems for their sovereignty and security. Finally, both sup- port the elimination of nuclear weapons as a final goal and a no-first- use pledge by the nuclear weapon and nuclear weapon-capable powers.

Nevertheless, there remain differences. China has shown its flexibility and taken a practical approach to nuclear arms control, while India emphasizes principle and long-term goals. China has actively participated in the arms control regimes while India is still reluctant to get involved. China now accepts that arms control can serve its security interests, while India apparently sees arms control as a threat to its security. China prefers gradual disarmament, while India insists on disarmament within a specific time-frame.

Competition or cooperation?

The existence of similarities despite important differences suggests scope for developing a common approach where their interests are shared. China—as a permanent member of the UN Security Council and an unambiguous nuclear weapon state—is in a better position to take up these challenges, but India can also play a role.

Criticizing contemporary power politics is a staple topic during meetings between their leaders. During his 1994 trip to New Delhi, Li Peng said that if China and India support each other politically they could be a great force in the world arena. The same year, when US Defense Secretary William Perry said that prevention of the nuclear arms race in South Asia was an issue on which China and the USA could cooperate, China did not take up the offer, preferring to respect India's independent policy.

Nevertheless, China's new flexibility has done more to complicate Indian policy than to simplify it. India is more isolated as a result of China's tactical abandonment of some shared principles. This isolation can only increase if India continues to avoid the non-proliferation regime—and even more so if it exercises its nuclear option and weaponizes.

IMPLICATIONS FOR THE FUTURE OF NUCLEAR ARMS CONTROL

For the foreseeable future, nuclear arms control will not be an important topic in the improving relations between China and India. So far, there are few indications that either Beijing or New

Delhi seeks to discuss the nuclear issue. At the regional level, China has clearly supported Sri Lanka's proposal to make the Indian Ocean a Zone of Peace but has been reluctant to enter a regional dialogue on nuclear non-proliferation. Recently it has shown a more positive attitude and may get involved if a basis for discussion is accepted by the other parties. Given recent progress in Sino-Indian relations, China may be more cautious about its role in Pakistan's nuclear programme, perhaps pressing for inspections by the IAEA.

Finally, at the global level, India is only likely to play a more positive role if it can be convinced that nuclear arms control reinforces its security interests and accepts that it need not weaponize its nuclear capability. China, as India's largest neighbour and a nuclear weapon state, can contribute on both scores. Still, India's choice between the alternatives of nuclear arms control and nuclear armament will not ultimately be the result of a threat from China, or even of relations with Pakistan, but of considerations of international power and influence. An arrangement beyond Sino-Indian bilateral relations is necessary to the Indian role in the post-cold war nuclear order.

9

Nuclear Arms Race

The nuclear arms race was a competition for supremacy in nuclear warfare between the United States, the Soviet Union, and their respective allies during the Cold War. During the Cold War, in addition to the American and Soviet nuclear stockpiles, other countries also developed nuclear weapons, though none engaged in warhead production on nearly the same scale as the two superpowers.

WORLD WAR II

The first nuclear weapon was created by the American Manhattan Project during the Second World War and was developed to be used against the Axis powers. Scientists of the Soviet Union, then an ally of the United States, were aware of the potential of nuclear weapons and had also been conducting research in the field.

The Soviet Union was not officially informed of the American experiments until Stalin was briefed at the Potsdam Conference on July 24, 1945. The Americans did not trust the Soviets enough to keep the information safe from German spies but also distrusted the Soviets and their intentions generally, despite their wartime military alliance. Even during the war several government and military figures in the USA saw the USSR as a potential enemy in the future.

Despite their official ignorance, the Soviets were well aware of the program due to a ring of spies operating within the American nuclear program. The atomic spies (including Klaus Fuchs and Theodore Hall) kept Stalin well informed of American progress. When U.S. President Harry S. Truman informed Stalin of the weapons, he was surprised at how calmly Stalin reacted to the news and thought that Stalin had not understood what he had been told. In fact Stalin had long been aware of the program. The program was top classified meaning even Truman did not know about it or the weapons until he became president.

In August 1945, atomic bombs were dropped on Truman's orders on designated Japanese cities. The first bomb was dropped on Hiroshima, and later another bomb was dropped on Nagasaki by the B-29 bombers *Enola Gay* and *Bock's Car* respectively.

Early Cold War

In the years immediately after the Second World War, the United States had monopoly on specific knowledge of and raw materials for nuclear weaponry. Initially, it was thought that uranium was rare in the world, but this turned out to be wrong. American leaders hoped that their exclusivity would be enough to draw concessions from the Soviet Union, this proved ineffective. Behind the scenes, the Soviet regime was working on building their own atomic weapons. During the war Soviet efforts had been limited due to a lack of uranium, but new supplies in Eastern Europe were found and provided a steady supply while the Soviets developed a domestic source. While American experts had predicted that the USSR would not have nuclear weapons until the mid-1950s, the first Soviet bomb was detonated on August 29 of 1949, shocking the entire world. The bomb, named "Joe One" by the West, was more or less a copy of the bomb the United States had dropped on Japan, "Fat Man".

Governments spent massive amounts to increase the quality and quantity of their nuclear arsenal. Both nations quickly began working on the hydrogen bombs and the United States detonated their first of these on November 1, 1952. Again, the Soviets surprised the Americans by exploding a deployable thermonuclear device next August, though it was not a real multi-stage hydrogen bomb, which followed in 1955.

The most important development in terms of delivery in the 1950s was the introduction of intercontinental ballistic missiles, ICBMs. Missiles had long been regarded the ideal platform for nuclear weapons, and were potentially a more effective delivery system than strategic bombers, which was the primary delivery method at the beginning of the Cold War. On October 4, 1957, the Soviet Union showed the world that they had missiles able to reach any part of the world when they launched the Sputnik. The United States launched their own satellite on the 31 October 1959. The Space Race showcased technology critical to the delivery of nuclear weapons, the ICBM boosters, while maintaining the appearance of being for science and exploration.

This period also saw some of the first attempts to defend against nuclear weapons. Both superpowers built large radar arrays to detect incoming bombers and missiles. Fighters to use against bombers and anti-ballistic missiles to use against ICBMs were also developed. Large underground bunkers were constructed to save the leaders, and citizens were told to build fallout shelters and taught how to react to a nuclear attack. These measurements were called civil defense.

Mutual Assured Destruction (MAD)

None of these defensive measures were secure, and in the 1950s both the United States and Soviet Union had nuclear power to obliterate the other side. Both sides developed a capability to launch a devastating attack even after sustaining a full assault from the other side (especially by means of submarines), called a second strike. This policy was part of what became known as Mutual Assured Destruction: both sides knew that any attack upon the other would be devastating to themselves, thus in theory refraining them from attacking the other.

Both Soviet and American experts hoped to use nuclear weapons for extracting concessions from the other, or from other powers such as China, but the risk connected with using these weapons was so grave that they refrained from what John Foster Dulles referred to as brinkmanship. While some, like General Douglas MacArthur, argued nuclear weapons should be used during the Korean War, both Truman and Eisenhower opposed. Both sides were unaware of the capacity of the enemy's arsenal of nuclear weapons. The Americans suffered from a lack of confidence, and in the 1950s they believed in a non-existing bomber gap. Aerial photography later revealed that the Soviets had been playing a sort of Potemkin village game with their bombers in their military parades, flying them in large circles, making it appear they had far more than they truly did. The 1960 American presidential election saw accusations of a wholly spurious missile gap between the Soviets and the Americans. On the contrary, the Soviet government exaggerated the power of Soviet weapons to the leadership and Nikita Khrushchev.

An additional controversy formed in the United States during the early 1960s concerned whether or not it was certain if their weapons would work if the need should occur. All of the individual components of nuclear missiles had been tested separately (warheads, navigation systems, rockets), but it had been infeasible to test them all combined. Critics charged that it was not really known how a warhead would react to the gravity forces and temperature differences encountered in the upper atmosphere and outer space, and Kennedy was unwilling to run a test of an ICBM with a live warhead. The closest thing to an actual test was 1962's Operation Frigate Bird, in which the submarine USS *Ethan Allen* launched a Polaris A1 missile over 1,000 miles to the nuclear test site at Christmas Island. It was challenged by, among others, Curtis LeMay, who put missile accuracy into doubt to encourage the development of new bombers. Other critics pointed out that it was a single test which could be an anomaly; that it was a lower-altitude SLBM and therefore was subject to different conditions than an ICBM; and that significant modifications had been made to its warhead before testing.

Initial nuclear proliferation

In addition to the United States and the Soviet Union, three other nations, the United Kingdom, People's Republic of China, and France also developed far smaller nuclear stockpiles. In 1952, the United Kingdom became the third nation to possess nuclear weapons when it detonated an atomic bomb in Operation Hurricane in Australia on October 3, 1952. During the Cold War, British nuclear deterrence came from submarines and nuclear-armed aircraft. The Resolution class ballistic missile submarines armed with the American-built Polaris missile provided the sea deterrent, while aircraft such as the Avro Vulcan, SEPECAT Jaguar, Panavia Tornado and several other Royal Air Force strike aircraft carrying WE.177 gravity bomb provided the air deterrent.

France became the fourth nation to possess nuclear weapons on February 13, 1960, when the atomic bomb Gerboise Bleue was detonated in Algeria, then still a French colony [Formally a part of the Metropolitan France.] During the Cold War, the French nuclear deterrent was centered around the Force de frappe, a nuclear triad consisting of Dassault Mirage IV bombers carrying such nuclear weapons as the AN-22 gravity bomb and the ASMP stand-off attack missile, Pluton and Hades ballistic missiles, and the Redoutable class submarine armed with strategic nuclear missiles.

The People's Republic of China became the fifth nuclear power on October 16, 1964, when it detonated a uranium-235 bomb in a test codenamed 596. Due to Soviet/Chinese tensions, the Chinese might have used nuclear weapons against either the United States or the Soviet Union in the event of a nuclear war between the United States and the Soviet Union. During the Cold War, the Chinese nuclear deterrent consisted of gravity bombs carried aboard H-6 bomber aircraft, missile systems such as the DF-2, DF-3, and DF-4, and in the later stages of the Cold War, the Type 092 ballistic missile submarine.

Richard Nixon's Program of Détente

Economic problems caused by the arms race in both powers, combined with China's new role and the ability to verify disarmament led to a number of arms control agreements beginning in the 1970s. This period known as détente allowed both states to reduce their spending on weapons systems. SALT I and SALT II limited the size of the states arsenals. Bans on nuclear testing, anti-ballistic missile systems, and weapons in space all attempted to limit the expansion of the arms race through the Partial Test Ban Treaty.

These treaties were only partially successful. Both states continued building massive numbers of nuclear weapons, and new technologies such as *multiple independently targetable reentry vehicles* (also known as MIRVs) limited the effectiveness of the treaties. Both superpowers retained the ability to destroy each other many times over.

Reagan and the Strategic Defense Initiative

Towards the end of Jimmy Carter's presidency, and continued strongly through the subsequent presidency of Ronald Reagan, the United States rejected disarmament and tried to restart the arms race through the production of new weapons and anti-weapons systems. The central part of this strategy was the Strategic Defense Initiative, a space based anti-ballistic missile system derided as "Star Wars" by its critics. During the second part of 1980s, the Soviet economy was teetering towards collapse and was unable to match American arms spending. Numerous negotiations by Mikhail Gorbachev attempted to come to agreements on reducing nuclear stockpiles, but the most radical were rejected by Reagan as they would also prohibit his SDI program.

Post–Cold War

With the end of the Cold War the United States, and especially Russia, cut down on nuclear weapons spending. Fewer new systems were developed and both arsenals have shrunk. But both countries still maintain stocks of nuclear missiles numbering in the thousands. In the USA, stockpile stewardship programs have taken over the role of maintaining the aging arsenal.

After the Cold War ended, a large amount of resources and money which was once spent on developing nuclear weapons in USSR was then spent on repairing the environmental damage produced by the nuclear arms race, and almost all former production sites are now major cleanup sites. In the USA, the plutonium production facility at Hanford, Washington and the plutonium pit fabrication facility at Rocky Flats, Colorado are among the most polluted sites. United States policy and strategy regarding nuclear proliferation was outlined in 1995 in the document "Essentials of Post–Cold War Deterrence".

Despite efforts made in cleaning up uranium sites, significant problems stemming from the legacy of uranium development still exist today on the Navajo Nation in the states of Utah, Colorado, New Mexico, and Arizona. Hundreds of abandoned mines have not been cleaned up and present environmental and health risks in many Navajo communities.

India and Pakistan

The South-Asian states of India and Pakistan have also engaged in a nuclear arms race. India detonated what it called a "peaceful nuclear device" in 1974 ("Smiling Buddha") much to the surprise and alarm of the world who had been giving India nuclear technology for civilian, energy producing and peaceful purposes. The test generated great concern in Pakistan, which feared that it would be at the mercy of its long-time arch rival and quickly responded by pursuing its own nuclear weapons program. In the last few decades of the 20th century, Pakistan and India began to develop nuclear-capable rockets, and Pakistan had its own covert bomb program with Chinese proliferation which extended over many years since the first Indian weapon was detonated. In 1998 India, under Atal Bihari Vajpayee government, test detonated 5 more nuclear weapons. While the international response to the detonation was muted, domestic pressure within Pakistan began to build steam and Prime Minister Mian Muhammad Nawaz Sharif ordered the test, detonated 6 nuclear war weapons in a tit-for-tat fashion and to act as a deterrent.

NUCLEAR ARMS RACE AND MILITARY DEVELOPMENT

India's defeat in war in 1962 was quickly followed by another uncomfortable military development for India, China's explosion of a nuclear device in 1964. This may have been carried out by Beijing primarily with the US and perhaps the Soviet Union in mind. However, one side effect was that India was now faced not only with a territorial foe, but also a nuclear foe, an uncomfortable power imbalance from India's point of view.

There may have been some limited moves toward reducing Sino-Indian hostilities following Rajiv Gandhi's trip to China in 1988, but relations still remained quite cool in the 1990s. Underlying perceptions of mistrust were very clear on India's side, as well as a sense of having been overtaken in the global pecking order and estimation. China was firmly in Indian sights in the late 1990s, as someone to be strategically matched, something of an ongoing quest. At the time, 1997, Mohan felt that given "the national determination in India to liberate itself from the current second class status in world affairs ... New Delhi will find it impossible to give up its search for global status similar to that of China"; in which "New Delhi is most unlikely give up its determination to acquire a functional nuclear deterrent against Beijing ... India will remain committed to building a small but functional deterrent against China." China's installation of CSS-5s medium range missiles in Tibet, with a range of about 1,333 miles, was highlighted in the Indian media during 1997 as targeting India.

Raja Mohan's 1997 predictions were quickly met, as India moved in 1998 toward transforming its implicit 1974 nuclear capability into an explicit realized capacity. The Prime Minister Atal Bihari Vajpayee was blunt concerning China factors behind the Pokhran-II tests by India:

> We have an overt nuclear weapons state [China] on our borders, a state that committed armed aggression against India in 1962. Although our relations with that country have improved in the last decade or so, an atmosphere of distrust persists, mainly due to the unresolved border problem. To add to the distrust, that country has materially helped another neighbour of ours [Pakistan] to become a covert nuclear weapons state.

Vajpayee may not have intended this letter to the US president to be publicized; but the sentiments were clear enough, objectively and subjectively. Indian commentators like General Amarjit Kalkat, who had commanded the Indian peace keeping forces in Sri Lanka in 1987, were also clear at the time where the message of India's nuclear explosions was aimed. It was not a local regional demonstration against Pakistan. Instead, Kalkat argued that: What strikes me as being particularly significant is their effect on India-China relations. These will be put on an even footing ... The tests are really an attempt to correct the current military and technological imbalance vis--vis China, which is already in the threshold of being a world super power ... Countries tend to respect equals and nuclear parity does help provide the level playing field needed to build such an equalitarian relationship. China has been a nuclear power for long, but India was not till it showed its capability this week.

Similar logic was apparent with India's successful testing of an Agni-II medium range (2,500-3,000 kilometers/1,550-1,860 miles) missile in 1999. Dinkar Shukla at the Government of India's Press Information Bureau asserted that "Pokhran-II and Agni-II are a symbol of a resurgent India," in which "the Pakistani threat is only a marginal factor in New Delhi's security calculus. Agni is at the heart of deterrence in the larger context of the Sino-Indian equation." Such considerations were why Chellaney argued in 2000 that "a major motivation for India's 1998 nuclear tests was the growing military asymmetry with China."

IR theory enters the picture with regard to China's differing responses in 1962 and 1998. Whereas China took military action against India in 1962, it initially responded fairly mildly to India's nuclear explosion in 1998. Lei Guang argues that different perceptions were in play.

In 1962, China could feel that its identity was at stake through India refusing to negotiate over what China considered was an unequal treaty imposed on it in earlier times of weakness. Guang argues that "given the centrality of territory to the Chinese national identity, what constituted the border between China and its neighbour was no longer simply a matter of administrative marking." Instead, there was a threefold challenge to China, to its perceived territory, sovereignty and legitimacy. Consequently, this "triple assault on China's fundamental identity as a nation-state contributed to its final decision to resort to violence in 1962." Such consideration are rightly seen by Guang as an example of IR constructivism.

Conversely, China took a more subdued and restrained approach to India's nuclear testing in 1998. Guang explains this difference by arguing that China's core identity was not particularly threatened by this event; India's nuclear explosion "did not constitute a frontal attack on the PRC's identity in 1998. On the contrary, it testified to China's nuclear power and affirmed its position as a major power in the region." This did not mean that China was not concerned about India's nuclear explosion. What it did mean was that China responded in different ways and at a different pitch than in 1962. As Guang argues, "a main thrust of the Chinese reaction to India's nuclear tests in 1998 was geopolitical in nature. Unlike in 1962, what was at stake for China in 1998 was its national security, not its fundamental identity as a modern nation-state." Its power advantages enabled a cooler calculated restraint in 1998.

Nuclear rivalry continues to affect Sino-Indian relations. A nuclear arms race, and its "nuclear security dilemma" dynamics, adds a competitive spiral element to their relationship. Even as the dust from India's Pokhran-II tests was settling, further deployment of Chinese missiles was causing alarm in India, Chellaney pointing out in 2000 that "India's largest neighbor [China] is conducting the biggest expansion of missile capabilities anywhere in the world. The first of these new missiles, the Dongfeng (DF) 31, last tested in July 1999, can reach every corner of India but little of U.S. territory." Chellaney's own sense of the political context of China's nuclear program was stark, "India's existing modest deterrent capabilities will be gravely undermined as China builds up its nuclear and missile armories. The Sino-Indian asymmetry will increase ... India will have every incentive to acquire similar assets that play a primary role in power-projection strategies." An offensive weapons spiral was in the offing from both sides. Whilst welcoming US attempts to develop a AMD (Anti-Missile Defence) system, Chellaney acknowledged and concluded that "nevertheless, the likely response of those states whose security will be directly affected, particularly China, will significantly affect India's interests. This is what India has to worry about"; even though "in due course, the action-reaction cycle triggered by missile defenses could drive India closer to the United States." Strategic alignment between India and the US is Beijing's nightmare.

In terms of power projection, China's control of Tibet has seen its installation of various medium and intermediate range missile systems. These missile systems are irrelevant to curbing domestic discontent inside Tibet, but do literally and strategically point outside Tibet toward India, its capital Delhi and other major Indian cities. Indian analysts are acutely aware of these implications. For Mahapatra, this military buildup in Tibet is "not only aimed at overwhelming India militarily, but to enable Chinese coercive diplomacy in respect of the border dispute."

Asymmetrics is in play. Installation of intermediate and medium range ballistic missiles enables China to immediately and easily threaten India; whereas the main centers of China, Beijing, Shanghai, Guangzhou remained far away from India. Back in 1999, Kanwal was lamenting that "realistic deterrence against China can only be achieved by developing a demonstrated capability to target major Chinese cities such as Beijing and Shanghai with nuclear weapons."

However, India's successful testing of the Agni-III intermediate range ballistic missile in 2007 and 2008, with a range of 3,500 kilometers (2,170 miles), for the first time brings many of China's main cities within range of India's nuclear strike capability. The Agni-I short range ballistic missile is clearly oriented towards Pakistan, Agni-III is equally clearly oriented towards China, "China-specific" in Pandit's eyes. India's nuclear mobility is strengthened by the submarine based Sagarika ballistic missile launches carried out in 2008. India is set to test its augmented Agni-III+/IV missile system, with a range of 5,000 kilometers (3,110 miles) in early 2009, enabling India to target all of China for the first time. From China's point of view, this increases its nuclear encirclement, in part from India, in part from India in conjunction with the United States.

Of course, India's and China's modernization and expansion of their nuclear and missile capability is not necessarily just aimed at each other. India has its ongoing concerns with Pakistan, China has its own set of concerns with the United States. Nevertheless, India and China also feed off each other's nuclear programs.

The final twist in the nuclear relationship is India's drive to establish an effective anti-ballistic MDS (Missile Defence System), in part through collaboration with the United States, but in part under its own efforts. Following successful interceptor missile tests in 2006 and 2007, India claims to have developed an ABM (Anti-Ballistic Missile) capacity, with operational deployment scheduled by 2011. Classic security dilemma dynamics operate here. As admitted by Mohanty, "China would watch India's growing missile defence capability very carefully ... there is hardly any doubt that both China and Pakistan would most likely try to strengthen their missile strike capabilities to maintain the strategic deterrence." From India's point of view, China's close nuclear links with Pakistan remains a further exacerbating and exasperating factor in Sino-Indian relations, and is part of their respective encirclement and alignment scenarios to which we now turn.

10

Nation-State System in Arms Control and Disarmament

ARMS CONTROL

Arms control is a term for international restrictions upon the development, production, stockpiling, proliferation and usage of small arms,conventional weapons, and weapons of mass destruction. Arms control is typically exercised through the use of diplomacy which seeks to impose such limitations upon consenting participants through international treaties and agreements, although it may also comprise efforts by a nation or group of nations to enforce limitations upon a non-consenting country.

Enactment

Arms control treaties and agreements are often seen as a way to avoid costly arms races which could prove counter-productive to national aims and future peace. Some are used as ways to stop the spread of certain military technologies (such as nuclear weaponry or missile technology) in return for assurances to potential developers that they will not be victims of those technologies.

Additionally, some arms control agreements are entered to limit the damage done by warfare, especially to civilians and the environment, which is seen as bad for all participants regardless of who wins a war.

While arms control treaties are seen by many peace proponents as a key tool against war, by the participants, they are often seen as simply ways to limit the high costs of the development and building of weapons, and even reduce the costs associated with war itself. Arms control can even be a way of maintaining the viability of military action by limiting those weapons that would make war so costly and destructive as to make it no longer a viable tool for national policy.

Enforcement

Enforcement of arms control agreements has proven difficult over time. Most agreements rely on the continued desire of the participants to abide by the terms to remain effective. Usually, when a nation no longer desires to abide by the terms, they usually will seek to either covertly circumvent the terms or to simply end their participation in the treaty. This was seen in Washington Naval Treaty (and the subsequent London Naval Treaty), where most participants sought to work around the limitations, some more legitimately than others. The United States developed better technology to get better performance from their ships while still working within the weight limits, the United Kingdom exploited a loop-hole in the terms, the Italians misrepresented the weight of their vessels, and when up against the limits, Japan simply left the treaty. The nations which violated the terms of the treaty did not suffer great consequences for their actions. Within little more than a decade, the treaty was abandoned. The Geneva Protocol has lasted longer and been more successful at being respected, but still nations have violated it at will when they have felt the need. Enforcement has been haphazard, with measures more a matter of politics than adherence to the terms. This meant sanctions and other measures tended to be advocated against violators primarily by their natural political enemies, while violations have been ignored or given only token measures by their political allies.

More recent arms control treaties have included more stringent terms on enforcement of violations as well as verification. This last has been a major obstacle to effective enforcement, as violators often attempt to covertly circumvent the terms of the agreements. Verification is the process of determining whether or not a nation is complying with the terms of an agreement, and involves a combination of release of such information by participants as well as some way to allow participants to examine each other to verify that information. This often involves as much negotiation as the limits themselves, and in some cases questions of verification have led to the breakdown of treaty negotiations (for example, verification was cited as a major concern by opponents of the Comprehensive Test Ban Treaty, ultimately not ratified by the United States).

Nations may remain in a treaty while seeking to break the limits of that treaty as opposed to simply withdrawing from it. This is for two major reasons. To openly defy an agreement, even if one withdraws from it, often is seen in a bad light politically and can carry diplomatic repercussions. Additionally, if one remains in an agreement, competitors who are also participatory may be held to the limitations of the terms, while withdrawal releases your opponents to make the same developments you are making, limiting the advantage of that development.

THEORY OF ARMS CONTROL

Scholars and practitioners such as John Steinbruner, Jonathan Dean or Stuart Croft worked extensively on the theoretical backing of arms control. Arms control is meant to break the security dilemma. It aims at mutual security between partners and overall stability (be it in a crisis situation, a grand-strategy, or stability to put an end to an arms race). Other than stability, arms control comes with cost reduction and damage limitation. It is different from disarmament since the maintenance of stability might allow for mutually controlled armament and does not take a peace-without-weapons-stance. Nevertheless, arms control is a defensive strategy in principle, since transparency, equality, and stability do not fit into an offensive strategy.

History

Pre-19th century

One of the first recorded attempts in arms control was a set of rules laid down in ancient Greece by the Amphictyonic Leagues.

Rulings specified how war could be waged, and breaches of this could be punished by fines or by war.

There were few recorded attempts to control arms during the period between this and the rise of the Roman Catholic Church. The church used its position as a trans-national organization to limit the means of warfare. The 989 Peace of God (extended in 1033) ruling protected noncombatants, agrarian and economic facilities, and the property of the church from war. The 1027 Truce of God also tried to prevent violence between Christians. The Second Lateran Council in 1139 prohibited the use of crossbows against other Christians, although it did not prevent its use against non-Christians.

The development of firearms led to an increase in the devastation of war. The brutality of wars during this period led to efforts to formalize the rules of war, with humane treatment for prisoners of war or wounded, as well as rules to protect non-combatants and the pillaging of their property. However during the period until the beginning of the 19th century few formal arms control agreements were recorded, except theoretical proposals and those imposed on defeated armies.

One treaty which was concluded was the Strasbourg Agreement of 1675. This is the first international agreement limiting the use ofchemical weapons, in this case, poison bullets. The treaty was signed between France and The Holy Roman Empire

19th century

The 1817 Rush–Bagot Treaty between the United States and the United Kingdom was the first arms control treaty of what can be considered the modern industrial era, leading to the demilitarization of the Great Lakes and Lake Champlain region of North America. This was followed by the 1871 Treaty of Washington which led to total demilitarisation.

The industrial revolution led to the increasing mechanisation of warfare, as well as rapid advances in the development of firearms; the increased potential of devastation (which was later seen in the battlefields of World War I) led to Tsar Nicholas II of Russia calling together the leaders of 26 nations for the First Hague Conference in 1899. The Conference led to the signing of the Hague Convention of 1899 that led to rules of declaring and conducting warfare as well as the use of modern weaponry, and also led to the setting up of the Permanent Court of Arbitration.

20th century to 1945

A Second Hague Conference was called in 1907 leading to additions and amendments to the original 1899 agreement. A Third Hague Conference was called for 1915, but this was abandoned due to the First World War.

After the World War I, the League of Nations was set up which attempted to limit and reduce arms. However the enforcement of this policy was not effective. Various naval conferences such as the Washington Naval Conference were held during the period between the First and Second World Wars to limit the number and size of major warships of the five great naval powers.

The 1925 Geneva Conference led to the banning of chemical weapons (as toxic gases) during war as part of the Geneva Protocol. The 1928Kellogg-Briand Pact, whilst ineffective, attempted for "providing for the renunciation of war as an instrument of national policy".

Since 1945

After World War II, the United Nations was set up as a body to promote world peace. The United States proposed the Baruch Plan in 1946 as a way to impose stringent international control over the nuclear fuel cycle and thereby avert a global nuclear arms race, but the Soviet Union rejected the proposal and negotiations failed. Following President Eisenhower's 1953 Atoms for Peace speech to the UN General Assembly, the International Atomic Energy Agency was set up in 1957 to promote peaceful uses of nuclear technology and apply safeguards against the diversion of nuclear material from peaceful uses to nuclear weapons. The 1968 Nuclear Non-Proliferation Treaty was signed to prevent further spread of nuclear weapons technology to countries outside the five that already possessed them: the United States, the Soviet

Union, the United Kingdom, France and China. The Strategic Arms Limitation Talks (SALT) between the United States and Soviet Union in the late 1960s/early 1970s led to further weapons control agreements. The SALT I talks led to the Anti-Ballistic Missile Treaty and an *Interim Strategic Arms Limitation Agreement*, both in 1972. The SALT II talks started in 1972 leading to agreement in 1979. Due to the Soviet Union's invasion ofAfghanistan the United States never ratified the treaty, however the agreement was honoured by both sides.

The Intermediate-Range Nuclear Forces Treaty was signed between the United States and Soviet Union in 1987 and ratified in 1988, leading to an agreement to destroy all missiles with ranges from 500 to 5,500 kilometers.

The 1993 Chemical Weapons Convention was signed banning the manufacture and use of chemical weapons.

The Strategic Arms Reduction Treaties were signed, as START I and START II, by the US and Soviet Union, further restricting weapons. This was further moved on by the Treaty on Strategic Offensive Reductions, which was in turn superseded by the New START Treaty.

The Comprehensive Test Ban Treaty was signed in 1996 banning all nuclear explosions in all environments, for military or civilian purposes, but it has not entered into force due to the non-ratification of eight specific states.

In 1998 the United Nations founded the United Nations Office for Disarmament Affairs UNODA. Its goal is to promote nuclear disarmament and non-proliferation and the strengthening of the disarmament regimes in respect to other weapons of mass destruction, chemical and biological weapons. It also promotes disarmament efforts in the area of conventional weapons, especially landmines and small arms, which are often the weapons of choice in contemporary conflicts.

In addition to treaties focused primarily on stopping the proliferation of nuclear weapons, there has been a recent movement to regulate the sale and trading of conventional weapons. As of December 2014, the United Nations is preparing for entry into force of the Arms Trade Treaty, which has been ratified by 55 nations.

ARMS CONTROL AND DISARMAMENT

Arms control and disarmament sit at the intersection of foreign and defense policy. With the possible exception of policies governing decisions to use force or to form or break defense alliances, arms control and disarmament pol-icy has the greatest potential to further or damage a state's national interest. As a result, sovereign states will not will-ingly cede control over arms control policy to outside forces unless the specific topic on the agenda is one in which they do not have a direct stake.

Given the compelling national interests at stake, it would be expected that the United Nations and its affiliated international organizations would be expected to play at most tangential roles in arms control and disarmament. This was certainly the case during the Cold War, when the United States and the Soviet Union addressed the most important arms control issues on a bilateral basis. The problem is that the United Nations and other international institutions have ambitions that far outstrip this appropriate and modest role. On this basis, they organize their insti-tutions to address matters of arms control by raising the pursuit of irresponsibility to an art form.

In this context, the U.N. and its affiliated international organizations seek to expand both their bureaucratic structures and their claims to authority. Yet the U.N. as an international organization has no direct stake in the sub-stantive outcome of any arms control or disarmament issue, only the purely procedural accomplishment of concluding agreements. The people who serve in the U.N. and its affiliated international organizations are not held accountable for protecting the lives and well-being of the people who may be made vulnerable by poorly conceived or biased arms control agreements and implementing measures. U.N. officials are not elected and claim no constituencies other than their colleagues and the nongovernmental organizations (NGOs) with which they work closely. These NGOs frequently see arms control and disarmament measures as ends in themselves and regard the national security interests of particular nations as only tangential concerns. Unsurprisingly, the U.N. disarmament and arms control structures tend toward far-flung and overlapping institutions that diffuse responsibility and accountability rather than a tight structure focused on outcomes and effectiveness.

In some cases, U.N. elites also seek governing authority without accountability to those whom they would govern. In arms control and disarmament policy, these elites disparage the concept of the national interest and see their neutrality as proof of their moral superiority. In reality, this neutrality is the height of irresponsibility because these elites maintain no direct obligation to provide security to the people over whom they claim authority to set policies that directly affect their safety. In short, these elites seek to destroy the nation-state system without offering a viable substitute that can assume responsibility for and ensure the security of peoples in nations around the world. If this international elite realizes these purposes, there will be catastrophic results.

To put the United Nations and its affiliated international organizations in their appropriately modest roles of creating and implementing arms control and disarmament agreements, it is necessary to examine the various component institutions of the U.N.:

1. The Security Council
2. The First Committee on Disarmament and International Security of the General Assembly
3. The Department for Disarmament Affairs (DDA) under the Secretariat
4. The Conference on Disarmament
5. The International Atomic Energy Agency (IAEA), the most important U.N.-affiliated international organization with arms control responsibilities
6. The myriad NGOs involved in arms control at the U.N.

This chapter examines each of these component institutions, recommends appropriate reforms, and suggests alternative venues that could prove more effective. The recommendations are designed to narrow the scope of U.N. involvement in arms control and disarmament, in accordance with the more direct interests and responsibilities of sovereign member states to provide security to their people. The recommendations are also designed to increase the level of responsibility that U.N. institutions and alternative institutions must bear in the narrow areas where they have appropriate roles to play.

The U.N. Security Council

The U.N. Security Council is the United Nations' foremost institution for keeping the peace and responding to threats to peace and security at the international level. As a result, the Security Council generally addresses arms control and disarmament matters in the context of both immediate and projected threats to international peace and security. This was the case, for example, when the Security Council adopted a series of resolutions after the first Gulf War that, among other things, imposed restrictions on Iraq's nuclear, biological, and chemical weapons programs and its ballistic missile program.

The Security Council consists of fifteen members, including five permanent members (China, France, Russia, the United Kingdom, and the United States). The permanent members have the power to exercise a veto on substantive matters. The ten nonpermanent Security Council members are elected for two-year terms by the U.N. General Assembly.

This organizational structure represents both the central strength and weakness of the Security Council. On one hand, veto power allows the United States and other permanent members to prevent the Security Council from taking action that is deemed unwise or unjust. On the other hand, the veto power undermines timely and aggressive action by the Security Council when it is called for and frequently results in a lowest-common-denominator approach to drafting resolutions that address important and pressing security issues.

For example, the United States has frequently exercised its veto when other Security Council members have offered resolutions that unjustly criticize Israel or that would undermine Israel's security. It is easy to underestimate how much the adoption of such resolutions would undermine stability in the Middle East by isolating Israel and effectively encourage attacks on it. If not for the United States' vetoes, the Security Council—supposedly the United Nations' foremost institution for preserving peace and security—would have been encouraging aggression.

Conversely, the Security Council's tendency to adopt a lowest-common-denominator approach to important arms control problems has produced quite weak resolutions on Iranian and North Korean nuclear weapons pro-grams. Former U.S. permanent representative to the United Nations John Bolton has described the Security Council's process of drafting these resolutions as one in which even France and the United Kingdom—allies of the United States—work to water down sanctions resolutions that respond to Iran's and North Korea's provocative behaviour and enormously destabilizing weapons activities. The behaviour of China and Russia, in threatening and casting vetoes, is even worse. In this process, adoption of any resolution, no matter how weak, is perceived as a success. In the meantime, Iran has ignored Security Council demands to cease uranium enrichment activities and North Korea continues to pursue nuclear weapons, conducting explosive tests in October 2006 and May 2009.

The Insidious Assumption of Moral Equivalency

The source of the problem in the Security Council's process for drafting resolutions on arms control and disarmament is the assumption of moral equivalency between regimes. For example, the process too easily treats the structures and purposes of the regimes in Iran, Israel, and North Korea as morally equivalent. From this point of view, a particular kind of weapon in Israeli hands is the same as one in Iranian or North Korean hands. The result is a process that fails to differentiate between weapons programs that truly threaten international peace and security and those that would bolster peace and security.

Regrettably, no approach to institutional reform under the U.N. Charter is guaranteed to overcome this assumption of moral equivalency in U.N. bodies, including in the Security Council. The best the United States can do is to pursue an agenda that distinguishes among regimes, even in the Security Council. The United States should under-take a long-term and determined effort in the General Assembly to identify regimes that pose such immediate threats to liberty that they should be ineligible to serve on Security Council.

For example, Iran launched a bid for a nonpermanent Security Council seat starting in 2009. Iran is actively seeking nuclear weapons in defiance of international treaties and Security Council resolutions. Iran's president has threatened to attack and destroy Israel, a U.N. member state. Because nonpermanent seats are allocated geographically, the United States needs to work with Asian countries to defeat Iran's bid by promoting a more desirable Asian candidate, such as Japan. If the United States can successfully reduce support for unacceptable candidates, this effort will not only improve the quality of members on the Security Council, but also counterbalance the assumption of moral equivalency in Security Council deliberations.

If U.S. efforts to exclude those regimes most opposed to liberty from the Security Council do not progress in the General Assembly, the United States should pursue a different approach.

It should seek to create a competitor to the United Nations that consists of a coalition of nations committed to global freedom and security. This Global Freedom Coalition should undertake similar responsibilities as the Security Council in maintaining world peace and security, including arms control and disarmament matters. Unlike the Security Council, it would not involve an international bureaucracy. Rather, the coalition would be based on the nation-state system, and its member states would contribute their own resources to coalition activities. Generally, the Global Freedom Coalition would serve as a balancer in international affairs. Its arms control initiatives would support this balancing role and be pursued on a selective basis. Accordingly, its arms control initiatives would support the balance and not become ends in them-selves.

As long as the Security Council remains a viable institution such that the United States determines to have value or influence over matters critical to its national interests, the United States should remain an active participant, if only to veto actions inimical to its interests, the interests of its allies, or the cause of liberty.

Undermining the Right of National Self-Defense

The Security Council and other U.N. institutions and affiliated organizations compound problems when they seek to operate outside the nation-state system. This is most dangerous when the Security Council seeks to ignore both the letter and the spirit of Article 51 of the U.N. Charter by undermining the inherent right of states to individual and collective self-defense. Article 51 states:

Nothing in the present Charter shall impair the inherent right of individual or collective self-defence if an armed attack occurs against a Member of the United Nations, until the Security Council has taken measures necessary to maintain international peace and security. Measures taken by Members in the exercise of this right of self-defence shall be immediately reported to the Security Council and shall not in any way affect the authority and responsibility of the Security Council under the present Charter to take at any time such action as it deems necessary in order to maintain or restore international peace and security.

The most alarming attacks on state sovereignty by Security Council members occurred in 2002 and 2003 during deliberations in advance of allied military actions against Iraq. In large measure, these deliberations were over how to respond to Iraq's unwillingness to comply with earlier Security Council resolutions requiring its disarmament in certain categories of weapons. For example, France and Germany asserted that the United States and its coalition partners could not take military action against Iraq unless specifically authorized by the Security Council.

Insofar as the United States and its coalition partners deemed Iraq a threat and considered the use of military force an exercise of their right to self-defense, the French and German position represented a de facto attempt to amend Article 51. The French and German argument claims that Article 51 does not recognize the inherent right of all states to defend themselves, but refers to a privilege that may be extended to states only by the Security

Council—despite the clear language of Article 51 to the contrary. France and Germany, therefore, were effectively trying to use Security Council deliberations to amend the U.N. Charter by means other than those established by the Charter itself. Further, France attempted to use its veto to force this outcome. Its action was the international equivalent of Congress's attempting to repeal the First Amendment to the U.S. Constitution by simply enacting a statute. It utterly lacked legitimacy.

Bolstering the proposition that self-defense is a right and not a privilege should foreclose opportunities to repeat this abuse. The United States should make every effort to persuade the Security Council to adopt a resolution that affirms Article 51. Such a resolution should explicitly state that the Security Council recognizes the inherent right of all states to defend themselves and shall take no action that would subordinate that right to other specific Security Council actions. The language should clearly recognize that no state requires prior approval from the Security Council to engage in defensive actions, including the use of force. For its part, the United States should issue a unilateral statement of policy that it will not accept any U.N. Security Council action or withholding of action that in any way would impede both its right and ability to provide for its own defense and/or the defense of its allies.

Sadly, although its record in addressing arms control and disarmament matters is decidedly mixed, the Security Council represents the high-water mark of effectiveness of the U.N.'s component institutions. Its limited effectiveness stems from its semblance of a hierarchical structure (represented by the permanent members and their individual veto power) that has a small number of members, including at least some that have a sense of responsibility for the dangers and opportunities that arms control and disarmament efforts pose to international security.

Nevertheless, whether the Security Council in its current form furthers or undermines U.S. interests in arms control and disarmament is at best an open question. The question can be restated simply as: Can the United States use its veto in the Security Council to further its interests more effectively than the other permanent members can use their vetoes to thwart U.S. interests? If the United States can openly and honestly conclude that it can, then it should seek to preserve the Security Council in its current form. If the United States concludes the opposite, it should seek to create an alternative institution and use it in lieu of the Security Council to achieved desired multi-lateral outcomes in arms control.

The General Assembly and Its First Committee

The U.N. General Assembly consists of all member states and operates under one country, one vote rules. Article 11 of the U.N. Charter states:

The General Assembly may consider the general principles of co-operation in the maintenance of international peace and security, including the principles governing disarmament and the regulation of armaments, and may make recommendations with regard to such principles to the Members or to the Security Council or to both.

Clearly, the Charter envisions that the General Assembly should serve a supportive rather than a leading role in disarmament and arms control matters.

This makes eminent sense considering the General Assembly's nonhierarchical structure. Yet as with other matters, the members' direct responsibility for the results of arms control and disarmament is inversely proportional to the power that they seek to exert. Under these circumstances, the General Assembly is prone to adopting resolutions that essentially criticize the few members that have a direct stake in arms control and disarmament matters and a sense of responsibility for the consequences of their actions. For these benighted few among the member states, the adage "no good deed goes unpunished" has become a way of life in the U.N.

Under these circumstances, the assumption of moral equivalency is even more strongly entrenched in the General Assembly. At times, the General Assembly even turns the concept of moral judgment on its head by focusing its criticism on member states that take responsibility for their actions within the body. Its propensity to approve resolutions criticizing Israel and its silence on Syria's clandestine nuclear reactor program are cases in point.

The First Committee of the General Assembly suffers from the same defects. The only difference is that the First Committee focuses narrowly on arms control, disarmament, and international security. Its primary work is to assist in drafting resolutions for consideration by the General Assembly. It also issues reports and records.

Counterproductive Procedures

The General Assembly's procedures encourage countries with limited interests in specific arms control and disarmament initiatives to involve themselves in these matters. Too many resolutions on arms control and disarmament issues brought before the General Assembly are sponsored by nations with only a distant or tangential interest in the subjects. Many are introduced on behalf of the Non-Aligned Movement (NAM). The result is resolutions that tend to point out and complain about problems, but offer only abstract and/or impractical solutions.

For example, Indonesia sponsored a draft resolution in 2007 on the relationship between disarmament and development on behalf of the Non-Aligned Movement. This resolution would take a portion of the resources made available by the implementation of arms control agreements and divert them to economic and social development, thereby reducing resources for arms control (in which Indonesia has little stake) in favor of development (in which Indonesia is strongly interested). Because countries with little direct stake in arms control dominate the General Assembly, its resolutions make virtually no direct contributions to solving problems related to the threats posed by dubious countries that possess or are seeking to acquire certain kinds of weapons.

This unduly broad involvement in arms control and disarmament could be corrected by implementing the voluntary funding mechanism that Ambassador Bolton recommends in the foreword to this book. Participation in the execution of General Assembly resolutions on arms control and disarmament and other matters should be limited to those countries that are willing to play a direct role by contributing resources to the effort. The text of the resolutions themselves should be limited to instructions to the U.N. Secretariat's Department of Disarmament Affairs to provide clerical and organizational support to the countries (sponsors) directly involved in resolving the relevant matter.

For example, if outside monitors were needed to confirm that a country is divesting itself of certain classes of weapons, this approach would permit only member states that are willing to contribute resources to the monitoring system and monitoring activities to sponsor the resolution. Further, this kind of resolution should have a sunset clause that would terminate U.N. involvement in the activity if the specific pledges of resources by sponsoring countries did not materialize or if the prescribed monitoring activity had been concluded. This way the resolutions would clearly identify the problem to be solved, avoid an unfunded mandate that would likely be financed by all member states through the U.N. regular budget, and provide a more direct path to the practical resolution of the problem. It would also ensure that those countries most directly involved would guide the process.

The First Committee's Excessively Broad Roles and Functions

It is appropriate for the First Committee to assist in drafting General Assembly resolutions in a manner consistent with the process described above. However, it is not appropriate for the First Committee to issue reports on the general subjects of arms control and disarmament. Such reports have too often consisted of simple hectoring statements and are largely criticisms of the United States, such as the committee's November 2007 report *General and Complete Disarmament*.

Instead, the First Committee should be a small group. This means the First Committee and by extension all the main committees should no longer be committees of the whole. Limiting membership of the First Committee will require the General Assembly to adopt an implementing resolution under Article 22 of the Charter, which instructs the General Assembly to "establish such subsidiary organs as it deems necessary for the performance of its functions." The smaller First Committee should focus on working with the sponsoring states to draft resolutions. As described earlier, these resolutions should generally consist of establishing mandates to the Secretariat's Department of Disarmament Affairs to provide clerical and logistical support to the sponsoring countries involved in the activities established by the resolutions. They should also catalogue the specific contributions that the involved (sponsoring) countries have pledged to the activity. Effectively, the First Committee should become a drafting board for resolutions to be presented to the General Assembly. The other existing roles and functions of the First Committee, including the drafting of reports, should be eliminated.

The Secretariat and the Department for Disarmament Affairs

The U.N. Secretariat performs the executive functions of the organization. Its management duties cover the full range of U.N. activities, including those related to arms control and disarmament. At the heart of the Secretariat is its staff: 36,579 (excluding more than 200 on special leave without pay or seconded to other organizations) were under contract as of June 30, 2007. Of this total, 30,745 were employed on contracts of one year or more. Slightly less than one-third (11,253 people) were employed at U.N. headquarters in Geneva, Nairobi, New York, and Vienna. A U.N. budget document indicates that 9,993 "established and temporary posts" in New York were pro-posed for the 2008–2009 biennium.

Secretariat operations, led by the secretary-general, and its staff are funded out of the U.N. regular budget and through extrabudgetary resources. The personnel are identified as international civil servants and are answerable only to the United Nations for their activities. In fact, they take an oath that precludes them from seeking or receiving instructions from member governments.

The secretary-general's direct line of authority on arms control and disarmament proceeds through the Department for Disarmament Affairs. Its breadth of activities cuts across the full range of arms control and disarmament matters, including such detached subjects as gender and disarmament. By outward appearances, DDA staff spends the majority of its time advocating disarmament.

In 2007, secretary-general Ban Ki-moon understandably proposed rolling the DDA into the Department of Political Affairs, its companion institution inside Secretariat. The proposal drew criticism from both the Non-Aligned Movement and NGOs that advocate arms control. Shortly thereafter, the secretary-general dropped his proposal. As in many other instances, the permanent U.N. bureaucracy demonstrated considerable skill in the art of institutional survival. Whether or not DDA should be a separate department under the secretary-general, how-ever, is less important than operating a responsible and effective institution for addressing arms control and disarmament matters.

Lack of Accountability to Member Governments

The offices and personnel of the U.N. Secretariat are not accountable to the member governments. The fact that Secretariat personnel, including those in the DDA, are accountable only to the U.N. is tantamount to saying that they are accountable to nobody. This is the chief problem with Secretariat, both generally and specifically in the DDA. The current system is wrong to separate the Secretariat from member states. In fact, the entire U.N. structure should serve the members.

Once again, a system of voluntary contributions from member governments to support U.N. activities would effectively correct the lack of accountability. It would build on the process of adopting resolutions. The resolutions, which would be sponsored by the members committed to participating in the activity established by the resolution, would establish the task for the Secretariat. A task-oriented Secretariat would be manned by officials from the participating governments, who would maintain their positions as officials of their sponsoring governments. Inherent in this approach is elimination of the oath currently administered to Secretariat personnel and their designation as international civil servants. Under this arrangement, seconded staff from participating governments would enjoy the privileges and immunities as U.N. staff, but strictly in the context of the missions assigned to them by the cooperating member states. Furnishing manpower for these pur-poses would constitute a voluntary in-kind contribution to the U.N. and its value would be counted toward the member governments' overall contributions to the activity established by resolution, whether that resolution is a Security Council resolution or a General Assembly resolution. Other contributions, of course, could be purely financial.

For example, in a monitoring activity, the participating countries would provide the resources to establish the appropriate task force within the DDA. In the greater scheme of things, the DDA would henceforth consist of a variety of ad hoc task forces. All personnel participating in the task force would remain employees of their sponsoring governments, cooperating with one another under the terms of the relevant resolution. Financial and material resources would be contributed by the participating countries and would be managed and consumed by the task force. Given the task-oriented structure of the system and the required sunset clause in the authorizing resolution, the task force would be dissolved upon completion of the assigned task or its failure to complete the task by the established deadline. The sponsoring governments would then assign their personnel to new positions on other U.N. activities or national activities. The task forces would continue only if reauthorized under a new resolution. This system would make the Secretariat and its activities accountable to the member states and restore the concept of state sovereignty to its proper place in the Secretariat.

The U.N. Conference on Disarmament

The United Nations touts the U.N. Conference on Disarmament as "the single multilateral disarmament negotiating forum of the international community." It has sixty-five member states and is located in Geneva, Switzerland. The Conference on Disarmament provides an annual report to the General Assembly. Its 2007 annual report listed the following items on its agenda in 2007:

1. Cessation of the nuclear arms race and nuclear disarmament.
2. Prevention of nuclear war, including all related matters.

3. Prevention of an arms race in outer space.
4. Effective international arrangements to assure non-nuclear-weapon States against the use or threat of use of nuclear weapons.
5. New types of weapons of mass destruction and new systems of such weapons; radiological weapons.
6. Comprehensive programme of disarmament.
7. Transparency in armaments.
8. Consideration and adoption of the annual report and any other report, as appropriate, to the General Assembly of the United Nations.

The Conference on Disarmament operates by consensus. While it has not produced a major arms control treaty in recent years, earlier efforts by it and its institutional predecessors have produced:

- The Convention on the Prohibition of the Development, Production and Stockpiling of Bacteriological (Biological) and Toxin Weapons and on Their Destruction of 1972 (Biological Weapons Convention)
- The Convention on the Prohibition of the Development, Production, Stockpiling and Use of Chemical Weapons and on Their Destruction of 1993
- The Comprehensive Nuclear Test Ban Treaty (CTBT) of 1996

All three treaties are fatally flawed to the point that they cannot accomplish their purposes because some countries refused to join the regimes or because compelling evidence exists that countries that joined are prepared to or are currently violating their obligations under these treaties. For these reasons, the U.S. Senate soundly rejected the Comprehensive Nuclear Test Ban Treaty on October 13, 1999. In this instance, the Conference on Disarmament was the primary contributor to this outcome because it unwisely overreached by negotiating a "zero-yield" test ban, ignoring the fact that a zero-yield ban is not verifiable.

An ongoing example of overreaching is the Chinese and Russian proposal for a treaty on the "prevention of an arms race in outer space" (PAROS). In May 2008, the Chinese and Russians issued a joint statement in Beijing reiterating their support for such a treaty. In this case, the treaty will attempt to ban something (i.e., space weapons) that experience demonstrates cannot be defined. For example, the Soviet Union sought to define the U.S. space shuttle as a weapon during the Cold War.

It is far from clear why the broader U.N. system would want to have a single multilateral negotiating forum on arms control and disarmament. The varying agendas of the sixty-five participants have undermined any sense of coherence and purpose. Its unwieldy structure has also exposed it to pressure from outside NGOs that advocate an unrealistic disarmament agenda. For example, numerous NGOs pressed for adoption of the unverifiable and unenforceable CTBT.

Given the flawed products that the conference has produced, its susceptibility to pressure from NGOs, and its lack of productivity in recent years, the U.N. should abolish the Conference on Disarmament, as proposed by the United States Institute of Peace's Task Force on the United Nations. The task force also recommended that the Security Council establish ad hoc negotiating bodies of manageable sizes to take on narrowly defined tasks.

The ad hoc approach recommended by the task force is the correct approach, except that the Security Council is not needed to establish these groups. Instead, the nations that are interested and willing to undertake such a narrowly defined arms control and disarmament negotiating task should form the groups themselves. If at an appropriate point the ad hoc group feels that it would benefit from Security Council support, it should appeal to the Security Council.

The Proliferation Security Initiative (PSI) is an example of a successful ad hoc arrangement. President George W. Bush proposed the establishment of the PSI at the G-8 summit in Poland on May 31, 2003. The PSI's governing principles were adopted at a meeting in Paris on September 4, 2003. The PSI established a means for participating states to cooperate in interdicting transshipments of weapons of mass destruction. Its strength is that, unlike U.N. bodies, it remains an activity and not an international organization. This permits it to harness the power of sovereign states and their institutions to achieve specific security, arms control, and nonproliferation goals. While PSI is not a U.N. initiative—nor should it be—it is an existing and ongoing example of how a more flexible arrangement can be very successful where more traditional efforts have failed. Indeed, it is an excellent reason not to rely solely on the U.N. in pursuing arms control and disarmament efforts.

If the treaty under negotiation is designed to involve only the participating states in the negotiations, then the treaty should specifically identify these states as parties to the treaty. If the treaty under negotiation is designed to appeal to a broader group of nations, then the treaty should establish accession arrangements that provide due regard for state sovereignty. Under no circumstances should any arms control or disarmament treaty drafted by a group include provisions that could be binding on any state that has not signed and ratified it.

The IAEA and Other U.N.-Affiliated Institutions

The U.N. includes not only the institutions within its structure, but also affiliated institutions that perform specific tasks, including a number of institutions that deal with arms control and disarmament issues. Among the most prominent is the International Atomic Energy Agency (IAEA). While each of the affiliated institutions has unique characteristics, their institutional structures are similar enough that the IAEA's structure can serve as a model for needed institutional reforms in this broader group of affiliated institutions.

The IAEA consists of three bodies: the General Conference, the Board of Governors, and the staff. The General Conference consists of all the participating states. Typically, the General Conference meets annually and approves the budget and other matters brought before it by the Board of Governors. The Board of Governors is the IAEA's policymaking body and consists of thirty-five member states, which are elected by the General Conference. The outgoing board designates the new members for election based on each state's advancement in atomic energy technology and geographic distribution. The Board of Governors typically meets five times a year. It also selects the IAEA's director general. The director general leads the IAEA staff, which currently consists of 2,200 individuals from ninety countries. The staff is organized to perform work in three general areas: improving the safety and security at nuclear facilities, advancing nuclear science and technology for peaceful purposes, and applying safeguards and verification measures to ensure that peaceful nuclear programs are not diverted to weapons purposes. The safeguards and verification measures bring the IAEA into the field of arms control and disarmament.

Many other international institutions associated with the United Nations, including those with arms control and disarmament responsibilities, have similar structures. Generally, they consist of a general assembly of all the member states, a board with a smaller number of member states, and a staff that is led by an executive official. As such, these organizations possess both the strengths and weakness of the IAEA.

The IAEA's Unduly Broad Mandate

The IAEA is charged with simultaneously expanding access to advanced nuclear technology and preventing the spread of nuclear weapons; this dual function creates a tension between these responsibilities because expanding nuclear technology can easily increase the risk of nuclear weapons proliferation. When U.N.-affiliated organizations have broad areas of responsibility, these kinds of tensions are all but certain to arise.

In the IAEA, this tension can jeopardize international security. The 1968 Treaty on the Non-Proliferation of Nuclear Weapons (NPT) assigns the IAEA the responsibility to detect diversions of nuclear facilities and materials to weapons purposes. Effectively, this function is designed as a verification measure to ensure that nonnuclear-weapon states fulfill their treaty obligation of not pursuing nuclear weapons. Even though the risks to peace and security posed by diversion far outweigh the benefits of expanding nuclear technology, the IAEA's responsibility to safeguard against nuclear diversion is forced to compete against its responsibility to expand access to nuclear science and technology. Because these competing priorities are treated as equals, they can cause the organization to undermine its various efforts in either direction. In short, its unwieldy mandate has produced an unwieldy organization.

The answer to the IAEA's unduly broad mandate is to prioritize its competing responsibilities. Because its safe-guard responsibilities are far more important than its responsibilities to expand access to nuclear technology and facilities, the IAEA Board of Governors should focus funding and staff on the safeguard mission and limit the scope of the assistance programs. It should make this prioritization explicit in its funding decisions, and its instructions to the staff to remove all doubt inside the organization about how it functions and where it should focus its attention. Preventing the diversion of nuclear material and facilities must come first.

Other U.N.-affiliated organizations with unduly broad mandates should also be forced to prioritize among their competing responsibilities.

The Director General's Involvement in Diplomatic and Political Matters

The director general's position is intended to be nonpolitical. He is to supervise the staff in fulfilling its bureaucratic functions. Dr. Mohamed ElBaradei, the current IAEA director general, has certainly exceeded his mandate by involving himself in diplomatic and political matters related to Iran's nuclear program. Reports indicate that he has specifically demanded that the United States offer economic and security concessions to Iran. In outward appearances, he behaves like a mediator, not an executive agent.

The IAEA Board of Governors needs to rein in the director general, specifically warning him against involving himself in diplomatic and political affairs. It should reaffirm that his mandate is to put in place safeguards to detect attempts by nonnuclear-weapon states (e.g., Iran) to divert nuclear materials and facilities to weapons purposes. It should prohibit him from undertaking any negotiations on the substance of any suspect nuclear program. Rather, his interactions with any nonnuclear-weapon state, including suspect states, should focus on putting the necessary safe-guards in place and reporting to the board if a state is limiting a safeguard system in any way.

Other U.N.-affiliated institutions with executive branches that inappropriately engage in diplomatic and political functions should take similar steps to rein in such behaviour.

The IAEA's Monopolistic Behaviour

The IAEA staff essentially considers itself the sole authority for designing and managing the safeguard system referred to in the NPT. Like all monopolies, it has become complacent and self-indulgent regarding its responsibilities. The discoveries of Iraq's clandestine nuclear facilities after the first Gulf War revealed that the IAEA staff was reluctant to challenge Iraq on the accuracy of its list of declared facilities prior to the conflict. Prior to the second Gulf War, the IAEA staff's assessment regarding the lack of an Iraqi nuclear weapons program proved more accurate. However, it is entirely possible that its accuracy in this case was more the result of its traditional complacency than of a careful assessment of Iraq's program.

The argument demonstrating IAEA complacency is bolstered by its staff's failure to discover an illicit shipment of nuclear-related equipment to Libya. This discovery was a contributing factor in Libya's decision to declare and dismantle its nuclear weapons program in December 2003. In the aftermath of the Libyan declaration, the IAEA director general acknowledged that the IAEA would need to "kick start the process of verification."

The answer to the IAEA staff's monopolistic behaviour is for prominent states to break the monopoly. The United States should lead an effort by interested states to create a competing international institution to perform the safe-guard mission. They can do this in two ways. First, the participating states can agree to undertake safeguard measures among themselves. These measures should be stricter than the IAEA's safeguards and should be conducted in addition to IAEA measures. They should be performed by national inspection teams on a reciprocal basis. Second, those states involved in negotiations to ensure nonproliferation goals regarding suspect states (e.g., the six-party talks on North Korea) should not simply allow the IAEA to manage the safeguard and verification systems resulting from any agreement. Instead, they should insist on conducting safeguard and verification activities that augment IAEA measures. These inspections should also be performed by national teams.

These two steps would fill the gaps in the safeguard system created by the IAEA's complacency and self-indulgence and they would force the IAEA to compete in performing safeguard functions or risk becoming irrelevant.

As needed, other U.N.-affiliated organizations that are involved in arms control and disarmament matters should likewise be forced to compete with other safeguard, verification, and inspection regimes.

Nongovernmental Organizations

A wide variety of nongovernmental organizations participate in U.N. arms control and disarmament efforts. Many are nothing more than arms control and disarmament advocacy groups. Such NGOs have little interest in protecting member states' inherent right of individual and collective self-defense as stated in Article 51. They are interested in elevating the cause of arms control and disarmament as an end unto itself, rather than as a means to enhance national security or international peace and stability. This even includes pressuring the U.N. on internal organizational decisions that could be perceived as downgrading the value of arms control and disarmament in purely abstract terms. As noted, some NGOs challenged the U.N. secretary-general's proposal to fold the Department for Disarmament Affairs into the Department for Political Affairs in the U.N. Secretariat. The secretary-general abandoned his proposal shortly thereafter.

NGOs are too closely involved in the internal procedures of the U.N. This incident suggests that the NGOs are directly participating in the decision-making process in the U.N. structure, as opposed to performing an educational or advocacy function from outside the organization. To the extent that such participation leads the U.N. Secretariat to take one action instead of another, it undermines the U.N.'s primary purpose, which is to serve and be responsible to the member states. Indeed, some elements of the U.N. structure appear to answer more to the NGOs than to the member states.

In arms control, this shift started with the Ottawa Process, which produced a treaty banning antipersonnel land mines. In the Ottawa Process, the NGOs assumed roles functionally equivalent to the diplomatic representatives of states, although in collaboration with approving state delegations. Further, these NGOs did not even bother to claim that they represented a broad cross section of public opinion on the issue of banning antipersonnel land mines. They were explicitly advocates of a complete ban.

The latest cause of the arms control and disarmament advocacy groups is to establish a treaty banning cluster munitions. Regardless of this proposal's merit or lack of merit, the conference convened in Dublin on May 19, 2008, reveals how NGOs are beginning to dominate the arms control process at the United Nations. First, the Dublin conference permitted a sponsorship arrangement in which the U.N. Development Program covered the participation costs of some states. Many U.N. member states are pressed for funding and find it difficult to attend the multitude of U.N. meetings, conferences, and summits held every year. They frequently do not send representatives to events that they consider irrelevant or of limited interest. This is and should be their prerogative and serves as an important filter to limit attendance to those countries that highly value the particular conference. By funding attendance at these conferences, the U.N. discourages countries from appropriately weighing their priorities when deciding which conferences are most important to their governments and citizens and therefore justify the expense of attending. Instead, the U.N. is substituting nonnational priorities.

Second, the conference listed 259 individuals on the official list of delegates as NGO representatives. These NGO representatives were provided direct access to the conference proceedings. This is the equivalent of the U.S. House of Representatives granting floor privileges to lobbyists. It mocks the role and stature of government representation in U.N. activities.

Worse, the NGO representatives were not broadly based. Judging from the names of their organizations, nearly all 259 were arms control advocates and almost certainly committed to adopting a ban on cluster munitions. None appeared to represent organizations concerned about the ability of national militaries to fulfill their assigned missions.

The first step to restoring an appropriate relationship between internal U.N. bodies and NGOs is to restore the sovereign state to its preeminent position in the U.N. If the U.N. insists that member states take direct responsibility for their actions in the various U.N. processes, the NGOs will be forced to advocate their positions at the domestic level. This will limit their efforts to circumvent the member states to push their own agendas supranationally within the U.N. structure.

The second step is to implement a voluntary contribution mechanism. If U.N. positions are filled only by employees of the member states at their own expense, the NGOs will be effectively barred from assuming roles that should belong to the participating governments.

The third step is to limit arms control negotiating groups to those states with a direct interest in the outcome. The NGOs have worked their way into inappropriate positions within U.N. arms control and disarmament institutions through states that have no interest in the outcome. If these disinterested states are excluded from a particular negotiating structure, the NGOs will not have the political space to involve themselves directly in the process.

The final step is for the U.N. to bar member states from granting proxies to NGOs to assume their responsibilities in U.N. activities. This step will eliminate the mechanism that the NGOs have used to assume inappropriate responsibilities, such as happened at the cluster munitions conference in Dublin.

The U.N. Charter

Given the myriad structural shortcomings of the greater U.N. system in relation to arms control and disarmament issues, it is reasonable to ask whether adopting a new U.N. Charter would be the best way of reforming the entire system. If the changes to the U.N. system proposed in this chapter are not adopted, then the alternative of a new U.N. Charter should be examined. Too much has gone wrong with the U.N. in the field of arms control and disarmament since its creation in 1945 to let the problems continue to fester. Further, there is growing pressure to increase the size of the Security Council. The United States, in principle, supports expanding the Security Council to include Japan.

The wisdom of expanding the Security Council is questionable. Even a modest expansion would make the council more unwieldy, contribute to gridlock, and dilute U.S. influence in the council. Expansion would inevitably make the council less able to respond to crises and less supportive of the United States on many key issues. Ambas-sador Bolton said,

I felt strongly that any increase in the Council's overall size should be minimal, since it was hard enough to get any real work done with fifteen members, and each new addition increased that difficulty not just arithmetically but probably geometrically. The United States was certainly the most concerned about maintaining the Council's (limited) effectiveness as a decision-making body. Many aspirants for permanent membership never considered the consequences of expanding the body to twenty-four or twenty-five members, so eager were they to get a chair around that horse-shoe table, regardless of what would follow. I must confess, from time to time I had an "Atlas Shrugged" moment, concluding that we should just let the Council expansion happen, and, as we predicted, watch the whole thing slide into a ditch. But then, my sense of responsibility would assert itself, and I would revert to diligent defender of the Council's effectiveness. Regardless of the consequences, there is considerable interest in expanding the council. Expanding the Security Council would require revising the Charter, thus the United States must be prepared to undertake a revision in the Charter in any event.

However, amending or revising the U.N. Charter is not easy. The Charter amendment process is appropriately challenging. It is not the sort of document that should be tampered with frequently or for insignificant reasons, nor should a few countries have the power to change a treaty affecting all nations. Yet this also means that amending the Charter to address the organization's weaknesses will be difficult. In particular, it would be extraordinarily difficult for the United States to gain support from two-thirds of the General Assembly for any proposal limiting the U.N.'s role, revising U.N. staffing and funding procedures, or limiting participation in activities long considered the province of all U.N. member states to only those states with a direct interest. Nevertheless, considering the options for revising the Charter is necessary because the organization is seeking to override state sovereignty in a way that threat-ens liberty worldwide.

Given the difficult process of revising the U.N. Charter and the likelihood that other nations would use the opportunity to propose amendments inimitable to U.S. interests, the United States should be very wary of support-ing a process to revise the Charter and should regard any such effort as a long-term enterprise. It would require a consistent vision, patience, and determination—qualities not usually associated with the U.S. State Department, which would likely oversee the negotiations.

The United States will come under enormous pressure to adopt the product of a Charter amendment pro-cess, even if it is clearly inconsistent with U.S. interests. Therefore, the United States must be certain and clear about what it wants to obtain through a revision in the U.N. Charter and publicly state that goal. Clarity of pur-pose and a public statement of intent will provide a basis for U.S. leaders in Congress and the executive branch and for the public to judge whether the revision process is running in the wrong direction and would make the U.N. even less effective, or if it would expand U.N. authority in a manner that threatens state sovereignty and the cause of liberty. Knowing that the result will be held to a public metric of what constitutes a desirable out-come will stiffen U.S. resolve when other governments and NGOs pressure the United States to accept a deleterious outcome.

The two options for amending or revising the U.N. Charter. Under the first option, the General Assembly can adopt an amendment by a two-thirds vote of its members. The amendment would enter into force when two-thirds of the members, including all five permanent members of the Security Council, have ratified it. Under the second option, two-thirds of the members of the General Assembly and any nine members of the Security Council can vote to convene a charter review conference. The conference may recommend alterations in the Charter by a two-thirds vote. The alterations would enter into force when two-thirds of all members, including all the permanent members of the Security Council, have ratified them.

The United States should view an effort to revise the U.N. Charter as a long-term enterprise and should prepare to opt for the latter option if the revision process is being initiated. With this approach, the United States would signal to other members of the General Assembly its willingness to support a resolution calling for the convening of a review conference. This approach would allow initiation of the Charter revision process, which otherwise could be blocked at the outset by a recalcitrant permanent member of the Security Council.

However, entering into a Charter amendment process is far more likely to yield an unsatisfactory result. Indeed, a two-thirds majority of the member states is far more likely to expand U.N. authority in ways that would replicate or exacerbate the organization's current flaws than to restrict the U.N.'s role and make it more focused on and accountable to member states.

Moreover, if an effort to revise the Charter, whether initiated to expand the membership of the Security Council or for some other reason, were moving in the wrong direction, the United States would have little choice but to abandon the U.N. altogether. Once such misdirected amendments were submitted for ratification, many member states would eagerly press forward to ratify them, either because they would support increasing the U.N.'s authority and power or because they would face little consequence from such an expansion of power. Pressure on the permanent members of the Security Council to ratify such amendments would mount and ultimately prevail. At that point, the reform process would clearly have arrived at a dead end, and U.S. interests would be far better served by ending U.S. participation in the U.N. than by continuing to participate, with the notable exception of maintaining its presence on the Security Council to veto objectionable resolutions. While reaching such a dead end in the U.N. reform process is not inevitable, the United States cannot just hope for the best. The United States will need to take steps in the interim to reserve its options. Simply leaving the U.N. would not be wise. While a number of national interests are not served by working through multilateral institutions, some indisputably are best served by working through that framework. The United States will need to move to an alternative institution. It can do this by taking concrete steps to build such an institution. Kim Holmes, vice president of The Heritage Foundation, has proposed creating a Global Freedom Coalition. While it need not be created as an explicit alternative to the U.N., a Global Freedom Coalition could evolve into that if circumstances warrant.

The Way Forward

The United Nations system has assumed a large and influential role in international efforts on arms control and disarmament. While the U.N. and some of its affiliated bodies certainly have roles to play in this arena, the United States should undertake an effort to revise and reform the U.N.'s arms control and disarmament infrastructure to make it smaller and more focused and to eliminate the processes and traditions that have proven counterproductive.

PRESERVING AND PROTECTING THE PRIMACY OF NATIONAL SOVEREIGNTY

The slow, incremental expansion of U.N. authority, power, and influence in a host of international areas is infringing on the authority and sovereignty of nation-states. This is unjustified and inappropriate because the nation-state is the sole means through which the rights and privileges of individuals can be protected and preserved. While numerous governments abuse their power by failing to promote the best interests of their citizens or even by oppressing them, no viable or superior alternative exists to a representative government with ample checks to prevent abuse. Certainly, subordinating national governments to a largely unaccountable international bureaucracy is not a recipe for success. The United States should:

- Press the Security Council to adopt a resolution that unequivocally affirms every state's right to self-defense
- Seek to make the offices of the U.N. Secretariat accountable to the member states through the system of voluntary contributions and by requiring all personnel participating in U.N. activities to remain the employees of their sponsoring states
- Block NGOs from directly participating in U.N. activities by forcing them to work through the governments of member states to further their positions

Promoting the Values of Liberty in the U.N. and Elsewhere

The presence of despotic nations on key U.N. bodies, including the U.N. Security Council, can dramatically undermine the bodies' effectiveness. The United States should use its influence to impede those member states most opposed to liberty from election to the Security Council, or at the very least, seeking to bar member states currently under Security Council sanctions from sitting on the Security Council. The United States should also use its influence to convince regional groups to support good candidates for the Security Council, rather than spoilers such as Iran and Venezuela. If these efforts fail to improve the composition of the Security Council, the United States should seek to create a competitor institution to the United Nations composed solely of members committed to liberty. This alternative institution should include a body that has responsibilities similar to the Security Council's mandate to maintain world peace and security, including arms control and disarmament matters.

Overhauling the International Arms Control and Disarmament System

The current system for dealing with disarmament and arms control issues has fallen increasingly under the U.N.'s purview. This shift away from a state-based system is undesirable and counterproductive because it gives undue influence to those who are not responsible for and are not accountable to the people who may be made vulnerable by poorly conceived or biased arms control agreements and implementing measures. The United States should seek to implement a series of changes to return the focus of international arms control and disarmament efforts to states that have a direct, vested interest in negotiating realistic, effective, and verifiable agreements. Specifically, the United States should seek to:

- Narrow participation in the General Assembly's First Committee on Disarmament and International Security to a smaller number of key countries central to the discussion, and narrow the committee's jurisdiction to assisting in drafting resolutions that recommend arms control measures for member states to consider, individually or in the General Assembly
- Reform the funding mechanism by shifting from assessed budgetary support to a voluntary contribution funding mechanism focused on executing specific General Assembly resolutions on arms control
- Review and reform the international organizations focused on arms control and disarmament. Specifically, the United States should seek to abolish the U.N. Conference on Disarmament, clarify the mandate of the IAEA to emphasize its safeguard responsibilities over its mandate to access to nuclear technology, prohibit the IAEA director general from engaging in political and diplomatic activities, and establish alternative forums to compete with the IAEA and break its monopoly on nuclear safeguards
- Promote alternative institutions and options in arms control and disarmament. The Proliferation Security Initiative is a sound, successful example of how a non-U.N. effort can enhance arms control and disarmament efforts. The PSI option should be explored and replicated where appropriate.

Refusing to Sign or Ratify Arms Control Treaties That Would Undermine U.S. Interests

Recent arms control and disarmament treaties emanating from the U.N. system have proven greatly flawed. The Biological

Weapons Convention and the Comprehensive Nuclear Test Ban Treaty are flawed to the extent that they are unable to accomplish their purpose. Yet the United States participated in formulating these agreements and even signed them. To avoid this in the future, U.S. negotiators should be instructed to demand that:

- Arms control treaties include provisions that further a relevant military or security goal outlined by U.S. strategy. For example, an arms control treaty could ease the burden on the U.S. military by eliminating targets that are difficult to hold at risk.
- The United States will not be bound in any way by a treaty that it does not sign and ratify or that fails to enter into force for other reasons.

The United States should clearly state that failure to accommodate these principles in the treaty will lead the United States to refuse to sign future agreements, precipitate a decision to "unsign" existing agreements, and even lead the United States to consider withdrawing from current agreements to which it is a party.

11

Negotiation of Arms Control Treaties

It is fitting in this centenary year of the First Hague International Peace Conference of 1899 to reflect on the influence of humanitarian principles on the negotiation of multilateral arms-control treaties. Two of the three themes of the 1899 conference were the *laws of war* (or international humanitarian law) and *arms control and disarmament* . There is no question that part of the motivation in 1899, and indeed at the Second Hague International Peace Conference of 1907, in considering these two themes was humanitarian concern to alleviate the suffering of victims of armed conflict. After 100 years of international law-making in both fields, 1999 is an opportune anniversary to evaluate the extent to which humanitarian principles have continued to impact upon efforts to regulate the effects of particular weapons.

In 1899, Czar Nicholas II was concerned about technological advances in weaponry and saw an international peace conference as a way of promoting a general limitation on armaments. Even 100 years ago, the Czar's initiative was possibly prompted as much for strategic security reasons as for humanitarian ones. However, he did suggest that an International Peace Conference focusing on armaments and on the laws of war was an appropriate way to implement the general prohibition on "the employment of arms which uselessly aggravate the sufferings of disabled men, or render their death inevitable", articulated in the preamble to the St Petersburg Declaration 30 years before. The States participating at the 1899 Conference refused to commit themselves to a general limitation of armaments but did agree to several specific instruments prohibiting the use of, for example, projectiles for the diffusion of asphyxiating or deleterious gases and expanding— or "dum-dum" — bullets.

Developments in the international legal regulation of weapons subsequent to 1899 focused on consequences for combatants — at least until 1945. In World War II, with its new technological developments in weapons, the international community witnessed the relative proportions of military to civilian casualties in armed conflict beginning to reflect dramatic increases in the incidence of civilian casualties. The so-called principle of "distinction" — prohibiting, *inter alia* , the deployment of weapons which are incapable of discriminating between military and civilian targets and the deployment of weapons in a discriminatory manner — was developed to increase protection for civilians.

Few would suggest that humanitarian principles determine the outcome in multilateral arms-control negotiations. The purpose of this chapter is to examine the extent to which humanitarian principles have influenced negotiations. We commence with an analysis of the various objectives of arms-control agreements and then attempt to answer our principal query with a series of case studies on specific multilateral agreements in the latter part of the 20th century. The particular role of the International Committee of the Red Cross (ICRC) in promoting and encouraging the development of arms-control treaties is also discussed.

THE REGULATION OF WEAPONS THROUGH ARMS-CONTROL REGIMES

Unfortunately, any objective analysis of the last 100 years must lead to the conclusion that the general humanitarian principles prohibiting the deployment of weapons which exert their effects indiscriminately or cause superfluous injury or unnecessary suffering have had very limited success. Jozef Goldblat, the noted arms-control expert, has suggested that " ll laws of war suffer from one common weakness: the rules of conduct established for belligerents in time of peace may not resist the pressure of military expedience generated in the course of hostilities, and the attempts to 'humanise' war may sometimes prove futile. The danger that the weapons prohibited may, under certain circumstances, be resorted to — as has occurred on several occasions — will not disappear as long as these weapons remain in the arsenals of States. Hence the intrinsic link between the development of the humanitarian laws of war and progress in the field of disarmament."

Indeed, one could argue that if the principle of distinction or the prohibition on the use of weapons which cause superfluous injury or unnecessary suffering had been respected by all belligerents, disarmament and arms-control treaties would be less necessary.

Disarmament is the traditional term for the elimination, as well as the limitation or reduction (through negotiation of an international agreement) of the means by which nations wage war. The term *arms control* was coined in the 1950s to denote an international agreement to limit the arms race, in particular the nuclear arms race between the USA and the Soviet Union, following recognition that general and complete nuclear disarmament would not be readily achieved.

Arms control originally was meant to denote internationally agreed rules limiting the arms competition rather than reversing it; it had a connotation distinct from the reduction or elimination of armaments (i.e. disarmament).

Indeed, the term "arms control" was not popular with a number of supporters of disarmament. Subsequently, however, the meaning of the term has become significantly broadened, and is now commonly used to denote international agreements which are intended to:

- freeze, limit or abolish specific categories of weapons;
- prevent certain military activities;
- regulate the deployment of forces;
- proscribe the transfers of militarily important items;
- reduce the risk of an accidental war;
- constrain or prohibit the use of certain arms in war; or

- build up confidence among States through greater openness in the military field, and thereby produce an international climate conducive to disarmament.

It is in this broad sense that the term "arms control" will be used throughout this chapter. It should be noted that, with this definition, arms control includes the complete prohibition of possession of a category of weapons (that is, disarmament has come to be regarded as a subset of arms control). Likewise, various international agreements (for example, the 1925 Geneva Protocol which were originally regarded as being international humanitarian law agreements, also fall within the arms-control rubric.

As far as its basic purpose is concerned, arms control serves four objectives:

- reducing the likelihood of war, especially by trying to impose limits on the evolution and proliferation of weapons that may destabilize strategic relationships and thus create incentives for preventive attacks;
- reducing suffering and damage in the event of war;
- reducing the expenditure on armaments and saving resources; and
- contributing to conflict management by providing a framework for negotiation between opposing sides, by reducing suspicion and by generally contributing to an atmosphere conducive to relaxation of tensions.

Traditional arms control and disarmament has for the most part concentrated on containing the threat caused by nuclear, chemical and biological weapons. However, within the broad definition already referred to, arms control includes the 1980 Convention on Prohibitions or Restrictions on the Use of Certain Conventional Weapons Which May be Deemed to be Excessively Injurious or to Have Indiscriminate Effects which covers a number of specific conventional weapons, as well as the recently concluded 1997 Convention on the Prohibition of the Use, Stockpiling, Production and Transfer of Anti-Personnel Mines and on Their Destruction. More recently, international attention has been drawn to the dangers of unregulated trade in conventional weapons, although current responses to these dangers are limited to a voluntary register of the transfer of certain conventional weapons. We turn now to a series of case studies on specific weapons categories.

SPECIFIC WEAPONS

Chemical Weapons

The First Hague Peace Conference in 1899 prohibited the use of "asphyxiating or deleterious gases", a ban bolstered by prohibitions on the use of "poisons or poisoned weapons" at the Second Hague Conference in 1907. These agreements failed to prevent the extensive use of chemical weapons in World War I, during which approximately 125,000 tonnes of toxic chemicals resulted in 1,300,000 casualties, more than 100,000 of them fatal – a major human tragedy. In an appeal to the belligerents on 6 February 1918, the ICRC stated that:

"We wish today to take a stand against a barbaric innovation... This innovation is the use of asphyxiating and poisonous gas, which will it seems increase to an extent so far undreamed of... We protest with all the force at our command against such warfare which can only be called criminal."

In the immediate aftermath of World War I, chemical weapons were described as "a fundamentally cruel method of carrying on war" and "criminal" and their deployment against non-combatants was described as "barbarous and inexcusable". In 1920, there were preliminary discussions within the League of Nations on the feasibility of developing a chemical disarmament treaty, which was strongly supported by the ICRC. However, on the issue of verifying "non-production" of chemical weapons by the chemical industry, it was concluded that "it would be useless to seek to restrict the use of gases in wartime by prohibiting or limiting their manufacture in peacetime". So diplomats settled for an easier option based on the principles of international humanitarian law. The International Conference on the control of the international trade in arms, munitions, and implements of war convened in Geneva in 1925 under the auspices of the Council of the League of Nations and adopted the text of the Protocol for the Prohibition of the Use in War of Asphyxiating, Poisonous or Other Gases, and of Bacteriological Methods of Warfare. Under the terms of the Protocol, the States Parties "so far as they are not already Parties to Treaties prohibiting such use" were prohibited from the use in war of "asphyxiating, poisonous or other gases, all analogous liquids, materials or devices ... [and] bacteriological [weapons]".

The 1925 Geneva Protocol, like most of its contemporary multilateral instruments, represented a mixed achievement. The instrument did represent a collective response to the horrors of the use of chemical weapons in World War I and was intended to achieve more than its predecessors in relation to that particular category of weapons. However, the Protocol also suffered from some major limitations which rendered it, in effect, no more than a prohibition on the first use of chemical weapons.

Even at the time of agreement there was a view that the 1925 Geneva Protocol was inadequate because a mere declaration of determination not to have recourse to the prohibited means of warfare might not stand the strain of actual hostilities, and also that the envisaged convention on the reduction and limitation of armaments should include more stringent measures. In 1926, a disarmament conference was organized by the League of Nations and held several sessions between 1926 and 1930 but was unable to even commence serious negotiation of a chemical disarmament treaty.

Chemical weapons have been used at various times since World War I despite the existence of the 1925 Geneva Protocol. The most blatant recent example of this was in the 1980s by Iraq against Iranian soldiers and against Kurds in northern Iraqi villages. Although visual images of Kurdish inhabitants of Halabja, lying dead in the streets of that otherwise non descript village, provoked humanitarian outrage and did contribute to the momentum for serious negotiations to ban chemical weapons, it is also the case that in the years since World War I the military utility of chemical weapons has diminished. States have developed effective protective equipment against chemical attack and other weapons have been developed which are less dependent upon favourable climatic conditions such as wind speed and direction, and the absence of rain. Most States have reached the conclusion that chemical weapons are not indispensable to their strategic military capabilities. Further, the Iraqi use of chemical weapons against unprotected civilians demonstrated the dangers posed by proliferation of chemical weapons. This combination of diminished strategic value and the potential proliferation threat has facilitated a greater level of multilateral agreement than had been possible hitherto.

An additional factor complemented the confluence of circumstances facilitating the conclusion of a comprehensive treaty ban on chemical weapons. In 1987, the Soviet Union (with the advent of *glasnost* and *perestroika*) accepted the concept of challenge inspection for verification of compliance with a chemical weapons convention, admitted possessing chemical weapons, and hosted an international meeting of arms-control negotiators at one of its chemical weapons facilities. All of these developments would have been inconceivable prior to the improvement in East-West relations in the mid-1980s.

Negotiation of the Chemical Weapons Convention CWC) commenced in 1969 in Geneva and was not concluded until 1992. Although this 23-year process was a slow and tortuous one, it was ultimately rewarding. Unlike the 1925 Geneva Protocol, the CWC requires the complete elimination of chemical weapons (within 10 years of entry into force) and has introduced a verification regime which will ensure compliance by the States Parties, but which will not hinder the development of peaceful chemical industry. Verification under the CWC includes compulsory national declarations about relevant industrial and military activities, and a regime of routine inspections of declared industrial and military facilities. A particularly important feature is the provision for a "challenge inspection" whereby a State party can request an inspection of any site in another State party at short notice.

The CWC entered into force on 29 April 1997. There are currently 121 States Parties and an additional 48 States signatories. Perhaps most importantly, the States Parties include both the USA and the Russian Federation — the two largest possessors of chemical weapons — the major chemical producing and exporting States of Western Europe and some of the major developing States with chemical production capability. Several key Middle Eastern States have still refused to participate in the Convention but an increasing number of States are choosing to do so. The Organisation for the Prohibition of Chemical Weapons (OPCW), which has been established in The Hague to administer the CWC, is responsible for the verification regime. There are now more than 200 inspectors employed by the OPCW and they have already undertaken many of the inspection tasks outlined in the verification regimes to ensure compliance with CWC obligations by the States Parties.

At the time the Convention was opened for signature and again, at the first Conference of States Parties after the Convention had entered into force, many representatives of States and of international organizations acknowledged the significance of the multilateral achievement to ban these weapons that have such terrible consequences — that cause superfluous injury and unnecessary suffering to those unfortunate enough to be exposed to them. While many of these sentiments were undoubtedly genuine, the principal motivation for concluding the Convention had less to do with deleterious consequences of the weapons from a humanitarian point of view, and more to do with other strategic security factors — most importantly the growing concerns about horizontal proliferation of chemical weapons and the recognition by both the USA and Russia that they did not need to retain their chemical weapons stockpiles following the Cold War.

Biological Weapons

As already mentioned, the 1925 Geneva Protocol prohibited *inter alia* bacteriological methods of warfare. However, as with asphyxiating, poisonous or other gases, the Geneva Protocol prohibited neither the production nor the stockpiling of biological weapons. Again, the limitations of the Geneva Protocol resulted in extensive use of biological weapons by Japan against China in the early 1940s, in clear violation of international legal norms. Apparently the biological agents deployed by Japanese forces included cholera, anthrax and plague. Estimates of the number of biological weapons-related deaths in China range from several thousand to "hundreds of thousands".

The Convention on the Prohibition of the Development, Production and Stockpiling of Bacteriological (Biological) and Toxin Weapons and on Their Destruction (BWC) was negotiated between 1969 and 1971 and opened for signature in 1972. It entered into force in 1975. It now has 140 States Parties. The BWC was the first true multilateral disarmament treaty, being the first convention to ban an entire class of weapons. States Parties to the BWC undertook never to develop, produce, stockpile or otherwise acquire or retain biological agents or toxins, or their delivery systems. The BWC has now been in force for over 20 years. Though it constitutes an important landmark in arms control, a number of developments since 1975 have resulted in assessments that the BWC is seriously weak and lacks credibility because it contains no effective verification provisions.

Unresolved allegations of clandestine production or use of biological weapons since 1975 have caused the BWC a serious loss of credibility. In 1980, the USA claimed that an outbreak of anthrax at Sverdlovsk, in the Soviet Union, raised questions concerning compliance by the Russians with their BWC obligations. In 1992, President Yeltsin admitted that there had been an offensive biological weapons programme over the previous 20 years, and acknowledged that the Sverdlovsk anthrax outbreak was the result of military research to make biological weapons.

The recent revelations from the UN Special Commission for Iraq (UNSCOM) concerning an offensive biological weapons programme in Iraq, in which Iraq had spent several years developing, producing, weaponizing and testing a number of biological agents, provides further evidence of the need to strengthen the provisions of the BWC. In addition, intelligence assessments from the USA and the Russian Federation have concluded that about eight countries either have, or are seeking, an offensive biological weapons capability. Most States Parties to the BWC now accept that the Convention does require additional strengthening through the development of verification or compliance-monitoring procedures. Progress towards that goal is well under way. The analysis of the influence brought to bear by humanitarian concerns in negotiations for the BWC is similar to that for the CWC. No one doubts the potentially diabolical effects of germ warfare. Hence it is entirely justified to acknowledge the significance of concluding a multilateral agreement to prohibit any effort to attain an offensive biological weapons capability, let alone to use such weapons. The argument here, however, is that the BWC was not concluded primarily because of the deleterious consequences of biological weapons in humanitarian terms but because of concerns about horizontal proliferation of these weapons and of the difficulties of effective defence against biological attack. Similarly, in current negotiations for a Verification Protocol to the BWC, the principal motivation is national security, with humanitarian concerns a complementary coincidence.

Nuclear Weapons

The devastating effects of the atomic bombs dropped on Hiroshima and Nagasaki stunned the international community and caused many, including the ICRC, to respond with grave concerns for the deleterious effects in humanitarian terms of further use of such weapons. Those humanitarian concerns have not proved to be a major force in encouraging serious efforts at nuclear disarmament.

Following various unsuccessful attempts in the early post-World-War-II years to negotiate a treaty to eliminate nuclear weapons, negotiations focusing on the less ambitious objective of non-proliferation of nuclear weapons were commenced by the Eighteen Nation Disarmament Committee in 1962. The negotiation of the Nuclear Non-Proliferation Treaty (NPT) was concluded in 1968 and the treaty entered into force in 1970. It now has 183 States Parties and can claim broad and diverse membership. It is unique among key global multilateral treaties in that it establishes a discriminatory regime among States Parties. The NPT distinguishes between nuclear-weapon States Parties and non-nuclear-weapon States Parties. Nuclear-weapon States are those States (coincidentally the permanent five members of the UN Security Council) which had "manufactured and exploded a nuclear weapon or other nuclear explosive device prior to 1 January 1967". Under the provisions of the NPT, the former are entitled to retain their existing nuclear weapons stockpiles and are not prohibited from developing new weapons systems or from testing and stockpiling any such weapons. The only NPT obligation purporting to limit the right of States Parties possessing nuclear weapons to continue an indefinite nuclear arms build-up is the obligation to undertake negotiations for an agreement for nuclear disarmament.

The NPT has proved largely successful as an effective regime in controlling horizontal proliferation of nuclear weapons. A former Australian Foreign Minister, Gareth Evans, has described the NPT as "the single most effective and widely supported arms-control agreement in existence: without it we would by now be facing a world with perhaps twenty or thirty nuclear weapons States." It should be noted, though, that the NPT has clearly not prevented horizontal proliferation altogether. A number of key States have been able to produce nuclear weapons or have at least reached a "threshold nuclear weapons capability" outside the NPT regime. Subsequently, there have been calls for the strengthening of the NPT safeguards regime established by the International Atomic Energy Agency, although these calls have been made primarily for security reasons rather than out of humanitarian concerns. The conclusion of the negotiation of the Comprehensive Test Ban Treaty (CTBT) in 1996 was seen as a positive development in promoting the non-proliferation of nuclear weapons.

In contrast to the situation with chemical and biological weapons, there has still been no agreement on a general prohibition on nuclear weapons. Many of the non-nuclear States parties to the NPT, particularly many non-aligned States, had become frustrated with the lack of progress by the permanent members of the Security Council in fulfilling their obligations under Article VI of the NPT towards a comprehensive treaty ban on nuclear weapons. The UN General Assembly resolution requesting an advisory opinion from the International Court of Justice on the legality of the use or threat of use of nuclear weapons was adopted by a substantial majority. The request for an advisory opinion was a controversial strategy but one clearly designed to advance the cause of nuclear disarmament. In July 1996, the International Court of Justice handed down the long awaited advisory opinion.

The Court determined that, despite the lack of a specific prohibition on the threat or use of nuclear weapons in conventional or in customary international law, the general principles of customary law, particularly the principles of international humanitarian law, would apply to any use of nuclear weapons or threat to use them. Although the Court was able to conclude that the use of nuclear weapons "seems scarcely reconcilable with respect for such requirements", the judges felt compelled to reach a qualified conclusion because of their perceived lack of "sufficient elements to enable [the Court] to conclude with certainty that the use of nuclear weapons would necessarily be at variance with the principles and rules of law applicable in any circumstance". The unwillingness of the majority of the Court to declare the use or threat of use of nuclear weapons illegal in all circumstances only serves to emphasize the need for a comprehensive multilateral treaty prohibition — a fact not lost on all fourteen judges in the case.

Paradoxically, the lack of agreement on a comprehensive treaty prohibition of nuclear weapons contrasts with, and yet is entirely consistent with, the situation in relation to chemical and biological weapons. Humanitarian principles may have had some influence in the negotiation of treaties to comprehensively prohibit chemical and biological weapons but those humanitarian principles have always been secondary to strategic national security concerns. The major world military powers have been prepared to forego the possession of chemical and biological weapons but are not yet prepared to do the same in respect of nuclear weapons. In this respect, the influence of humanitarian principles has been consistent across all three categories of weapon.

Anti-personnel Landmines

The ICRC has estimated that as many as 27,000 people are either killed or severely injured by anti-personnel landmines every year. The overwhelming majority of these victims are civilians because most landmines remain active in the ground long after the cessation of armed conflict — in some cases for sixty years or longer. It has also been estimated that there exists unknown millions of landmines laid in 64 countries around the world. While these landmines are being cleared at a rate of 100,000 per year, millions of new landmines are being sown every year. Even if from today no new mines were laid, at current rates of clearance it would still take at least 1,000 years to remove the mines currently in the ground, at a cost of approximately US$ 33 billion.

Concerns were expressed during the 1970s about the problem posed by anti-personnel landmines and there were calls to negotiate a treaty to prohibit both them and other "inhumane weapons". In 1973, the ICRC convened a group of experts on weapons and humanitarian law. In response to requests, the IC RC subsequently organized a conference of government experts, held in two sessions — in Lucerne in 197451 and Lugano in 1976.52 At the conference, some experts advocated total bans on specific weapons. Others considered that total bans were beyond reach and that more progress would be achieved if the conference were to concentrate its efforts on restrictions of use. This more pragmatic view was shared by the ICRC.

The reports of these meetings formed the basis of a special UN conference convened in 1979 to discuss the problem of 'inhumane weapons'. At the conclusion of its second session in 1980, the UN conference adopted the text of the Convention on Prohibitions or Restrictions on the Use of Certain Conventional Weapons Which May be Deemed to be Excessively Injurious or to Have Indiscriminate Effects. This Convention, often referred to as the "Convention on Certain Conventional Weapons" (CCW), was opened for signature in New York on 10 April 1981 and entered into force on 2 December 1983 (i.e. six months after the 20th ratification).

Protocol II to the CCW placed restrictions on the use of anti-personnel landmines, booby traps and similar devices. The Protocol also prohibited, in all circumstances, the deployment of anti-personnel landmines against the civilian population; prohibited the indiscriminate use of mines; specified that all feasible precautions must be taken to protect civilians from the effects of mines; restricted the use of mines (other than remotely delivered mines) in populated areas; prohibited the use of remotely delivered mines unless their locations can be accurately recorded or an effective neutralizing mechanism is used; specified that effective early warning must be given of any delivery or dropping of remotely delivered mines which may affect the civilian population, unless circumstances do not permit this; specified that the parties to a conflict must record the location of all pre-planned minefields laid by them and endeavour to ensure the recording of the location of all other minefields.

The CCW may, arguably, have raised international standards regarding the inhumane use of certain types of weapons. However, given the relatively low rate of participation in the CCW, this is less than certain. Furthermore, given the terrible suffering and devastation currently being caused by anti-personnel landmines, the CCW has clearly been ineffective in reducing the deployment of anti-personnel landmines. Unfortunately, the attempts to strengthen Protocol II to the CCW with the Revised Protocol II negotiated through the 1995/1996 CCW Review Conference (e.g. application of Revised Protocol II to non-international armed conflicts; prohibition on the use of non-detectable, non-self-destructive or non-deactivating mines) are unlikely to significantly ease the problem.

Many see the conclusion of the Ottawa Convention on the Prohibition of the Use, Stockpiling, Production and Transfer of Anti-Personnel Mines and on their Destruction as a major victory for arms control, particularly regarding a weapon which causes incredible suffering primarily to innocent civilians. The Convention was negotiated in record time and demonstrates what can be achieved when the requisite political will exists. Others are more circumspect. The Ottawa treaty may be a step in the right direction but it has two major limitations. Firstly, it will not change the reality of the devastation caused by the anti-personnel landmines still in the ground and waiting to explode and, secondly, several significant producers, users and exporters of anti-personnel landmines did not participate in the negotiations and have stated that they will not become parties to the treaty.

In recognition of these limitations, some States, including Australia, which has recently ratified the Ottawa treaty, have suggested that other supplementary measures are required. The conclusion of the Ottawa treaty cannot be allowed to turn attention away from the enormous challenge of mine clearance. Increased resources for mine clearance and rehabilitation for victims are essential worldwide. Additionally, it has been suggested that the UN Conference on Disarmament negotiate a ban on the *transfer* of anti-personnel landmines that might include some States which have refused to participate in the Ottawa process. One thing is certain: future developments in arms control and disarmament that increase protection for the victims of armed conflict will not happen overnight. There is a role for 'creeping incrementalism' as there also is for 'dramatic progress' and one should not be viewed as ruling out the other.

Perhaps the most significant aspect of the Ottawa treaty for the purposes of this discussion is that its conclusion represents the first occasion on which an arms-control agreement banning an entire category of weapons has been motivated primarily by humanitarian concerns. The instruments of international humanitarian law purporting to regulate the use of anti-personnel landmines were demonstrably ineffective in alleviating the suffering of huge numbers of civilian casualties. Here, complete disarmament has been widely acknowledged as a fundamental step in the process of improving protection for victims of armed conflict. The Ottawa treaty thus represents an unprecedented causal link between the negotiation of arms-control regimes and actual enhancement of respect for fundamental principles of international humanitarian law.

Other Conventional Weapons

One of the most encouraging recent developments in the whole area of controlling the weapons of war has been the new Protocol IV to the CCW, adopted in 1995, to prohibit laser and blinding weapons. This category of weapons was discussed at ICRC conferences convened in the 1970s, but at that time there was no agreement that such weapons should be banned. Protocol IV is unique in arms-control history because the prohibition was negotiated before the weapons were actually used in battle. A number of countries had been developing laser weapons to inflict blindness and in some circumstances these weapons had gone into production. To have reached agreement on prohibition before the weapons were deployed in battle situations is a landmark development. It would seem that concerns about proliferation of such weapons technology and about development of effective defence combined with humanitarian concerns to enable this unprecedented prohibition to be adopted.

By contrast, as noted with concern in a recent ICRC report, achievements in regulating the use of other conventional weapons have been much more modest, despite the increasingly deleterious consequences, particularly for civilians, of the unrestrained transfer of conventional weapons. The UN Register of Conventional Arms is currently the only global cooperative security regime dealing with the transfer and accumulation of major conventional weapons. The idea of an international register may be traced at least as far back as the aftermath of World War I, and such a register was kept for a number of years by the League of Nations. More recently, there have been repeated proposals in the UN to establish a register of arms transfers, but it was only in 1991 that the idea gained wide international support. In December 1991, the UN General Assembly agreed to establish the Register. In December 1992, the details of its initial design were agreed. It first came into operation in April 1993, which was the date by which states were requested to supply data on their arms transfers in 1992.

The UN Register is a transparency measure. Participation is voluntary, includes both suppliers and recipients, and does not involve any controls on arms transfers. The Register aims to improve transparency relating to conventional arms transfers and holdings in the hope that this may achieve the following: contribute to the timely identification and prevention of excessive and destabilizing accumulations of arms; promote confidence and restraint; and provide a basis for regional or global confidence and security-building measures. The rate of participation in the Register has been encouraging. Most major importing and exporting States now provide data. It has been concluded that the Register already has the potential to contribute to regional and international security and domestic accountability, and may have already done so on a modest scale. However, it is far from achieving its full potential.

With respect to comprehensive multilateral treaty prohibitions on other conventional weapons there is little cause for optimism, at least in the immediate future. This point was succinctly made by former Australian Foreign Minister Gareth Evans in 1991:

"It has to be acknowledged that the international community has yet to come to grips with the problem posed by the huge volumes of conventional arms transfers. While agreements are in place or under negotiation to control or eliminate weapons of mass destruction, there is as yet no remotely comparable process for conventional weapons. We need to acknowledge openly the difficulties which stand in the way of conventional arms control: compared with weapons of mass destruction, they are relatively readily available; trade is well established and lucrative; and considerations of national sovereignty, and the legitimate responsibility of any government to ensure national security, mean that countries are reluctant to forgo the right to acquire conventional arms."

Unfortunately, very little has happened since 1991 to warrant a more promising prognosis.

Thus, with respect to conventional weapons other than those specifically covered by the 1980 CCW, international humanitarian law instruments are all that is currently available to minimize the risk of these types of weapons causing superfluous injury or unnecessary suffering. The ongoing lack of a definition for superfluous injury or unnecessary suffering makes the ICRC's current project to define the concept all the more significant.

Conclusions

Historically, humanitarian concerns have initiated the negotiation of prohibitions on the use of certain weapons by international humanitarian law agreements. Unfortunately, these agreements have often failed during actual conflict.

(i) massive casualties caused by chemical weapons during World War I, despite the prohibition of chemical weapons by the First Hague Conference;

(ii) extensive use of both chemical and biological weapons since 1925, despite the prohibitions enshrined in the 1925 Geneva Protocol; and

(iii) extensive casualties caused by the deployment of antipersonnel landmines in methods prohibited under Protocol II of the CCW.

In each case, the humanitarian concern at the massive suffering caused by these weapons, in spite of existing agreements based on international humanitarian law, led to calls for disarmament treaties. However, while the initial motivation for arms control and disarmament has often been based on humanitarian concerns, the actual negotiations of most of the recent arms control an d disarmament treaty regimes have been motivated primarily by national and international security concerns. Arms-control treaties have generally been difficult to negotiate because of the need for balanced reductions and verification of compliance (and the associated concerns about loss of national security or other sensitive information). Thus, despite recent political events including the collapse of the Soviet Union and the end of the Cold War which have provided new opportunities for substantial developments in arms control, negotiation of arms-control treaties is likely to remain a slow, tortuous process through the "conventional" fora of the Conference on Disarmament or ad hoc groups.

Also, in the past, the ICRC has recognized that direct action by it to bring about disarmament is — like any action to achieve peace — difficult, for the choices it implies are open to challenge, which prompts some States to contest the organization's neutrality. So while the ICRC has played a very supportive role in the development of arms-control treaties, it has consistently adopted a position of neutrality on disarmament negotiations, arguing that this is a political question for the States participating in the negotiation process.

However, the recently concluded Ottawa treaty provides a significant exception to previous treaties, both in the way that it was negotiated and in the role of the ICRC. The international community was confronted with the reality that the convention negotiated through the UN machinery (the 1980 Conventional Weapons Convention) had failed to significantly reduce the extent of superfluous injury and unnecessary suffering caused by antipersonnel landmines. This led to a very strong humanitarian quest which resulted in the negotiation of a disarmament treaty (the 1997 Ottawa treaty) in record time, using a "fast-track approach" external to the UN-based arms-control negotiation machinery. In this case, the community of States was subjected to an unprecedented level of influence from humanitarian concerns in the initiation of the negotiation process, and humanitarian concerns remained the major motivating force throughout the negotiation of the treaty. In what was for the ICRC an unprecedented move, the imperative imposed by the devastating consequences for non-combatants of anti-personnel landmines forced the organization to adopt a political position in pushing not just for international humanitarian law standards on the deployment of anti-personnel mines but for complete disarmament — a comprehensive prohibition which extends to transfer and destruction of existing stockpiles.

While the Ottawa treaty has only recently entered into force and has yet to demonstrate a significant impact on reducing the suffering caused by anti-personnel mines, the significance of the impact of humanitarian concerns in the conclusion of the Ottawa treaty deserves special recognition. In particular, it emphasizes the importance of the ICRC and other interested organizations continuing to express their concerns about superfluous injury and unnecessary suffering caused by particular weapons, and continuing to be active in supporting efforts to conclude appropriate arms-control treaties relating to such weapons.

MAJOR ROUTES OF SMALL ARMS PROLIFERATION

Russian weapons are systematically moving to Vietnam, Cambodia and Laos by sea from Vladivostok and Nakhodka to Haiphong and Saigon (Ho Chi Min City) and further through Vietnamese territory. It is also reported that they are often resold by Vietnamese and Cambodian authorities. Certain amounts of firearms might also be transported from Russia to Vietnam by air. We can suppose that some quantities of Russian weapons might be transported from the Russian Far East to Vietnam via Chinese territory, but as of today, no reports on that possible route have been seen.

Considerable numbers of Chinese-made light weapons are regularly passing across the Chinese-Russian border to Russia through two major points:

- Zabaikal'sk (Chita province)/Manchouli (Inner Mongolia) border crossing placed astride Hailar-Chita highway. Since March 1, 1998 (after revamping), this crossing has 14 lanes and is capable of handling 10,000 to 20,000 people and 1,500 cars daily. As of today, about 60 percent of trade between Russia and China passes through this point.
- Blagoveschensk (Amur territory) border crossing astride the Qiqihar-Blagoveschensk highway. This crossing has only eight lanes handling daily not more than 10,000 people and 950 cars. Most Chinese-made firearms are brought to Russia from China by commercial trailers, often accompanied by false papers indicating other types of goods (for example, mechanical toys). Certain amounts of firearms are smuggled by Chinese and Russian private citizens (the so-called "Chelnoks" or "Shuttle-traders"). Actual forms of Russian-Chinese border trade and smuggling in combination with corrupt and under-equipped custom officers and border guards do not permit even approximate calculations of the amount of Chinese-made arms smuggled into Russian federation within the last three years.

We should also mention the secondary direction of small arms (both Russian-and Chinese-made) proliferation in East Siberia and the Far East. This direction runs from south to the north down the rivers Lena, Aldan, Nizhnaya Tunguska, Angara and Yenisey to the cities lying along these rivers and to small rural communities and settlements scattered in their basins.

Some high-quality Russian-made light weapons might be sold to North Korea (at least until 1991 this was one of the regular routes of Russian weapons). Several reported cases of drug smuggling across the Russian-North Korean border (from Korean side) suggest that this might also be one of the routes of small arms trade. (Experience has shown that drug smuggling routes are in most cases the routes of small arms smuggling as well). It is possible that an arms-smuggling route might run through the tiny section of Russian-Korean border Najin-Ungghi (N. Korean side) — Khasan-Posyette (Russian side), limited by the Sea of Japan on the south and the "Kyonghung sack" of Chinese territory on the north. One of the possible sea routes of small arms proliferation might lead from Russian Far East (Vladivostok-Nakhodka) to Central and South America. Another reported sea route goes from Vladivostok to Japanese ports — possibly Osaka, Kobe and Yokohama.

Russian-made assault rifles and submachine guns, as well as ammunition have been reported in Nicaragua, El-Salvador and Colombia. As of today, we have discovered no materials tracing the delivery of the above mentioned arms across the Pacific Ocean. However this assumption does not seem unreasonable. We could also assume that if that delivery really took place, some amounts might be reloaded and stored in some ports at the Pacific coast of the USA and Canada.

Major Recipients of Small Arms in the Area

In Siberia and the Russian Far East, there are at least four groups of regular recipients of small arms coming from both foreign and domestic sources:

- criminals belonging both to highly organized "Mafia" groups ("syndicates" and "brotherhoods") and to smaller, spontaneously organized gangs;
- private citizens interested in purchasing firearms predominantly for self-defence;
- private security formations; and,
- different opposition and separatist groups.

Russian criminal groups in Siberia and the Far East, with their major headquarters in the cities of Vladivostok, Nakhodka, Khabarovsk, Blagoveschensk, Irkutsk and Yakutsk, (as well as criminal groups scattered all over Russian Federation) prefer Russian-and Western-made (American, German, and Israeli) weapons for permanent use and storage.

Those groups regularly purchase a considerable amounts of Russian-made firearms and ammunition which comes either directly from the military plants (from Tula province, the Urals and other arms-producing areas of the country), or is stolen from army barracks and stores. Some small amounts of Western-made (predominantly American and German) firearms have also been detected in possession of criminals in Siberia and the Far East. These weapons, as well as the ammunition they acquire might be sporadically coming from North America (predominantly via Vladivostok and Nakhodka) and/or from Western Europe (probably through the Trans-Siberian railway).

However, for contract killings and for arming the lowest-class recruits, organized mobsters of Russia tend to use Chinese products mainly because of their low price. According to information provided by the Moscow Nizam Research Group, the black-market price for the latest model of Russianmade AKM assault rifles may vary from $US 1000 to $US 1200 depending on the area and season, while Chinese-made AKM assault rifles are sold in the range of $US 400 to $US 600. The similar ratio ($US 6 for one box of 20 Russian-made AKM cartridges to $US 4 for the similar but made in China one) exists for ammunition.

For contract killings, acts of terror and property destruction, the "Russian Mafia" also uses various sorts of mines and explosives, most of which are produced by specialists working in state laboratories and using state equipment. However, some parts and elements are partially stolen from the stores of the Russian Army, or imported from abroad.

Millions of private citizens of the Russian Federation not involved in organized criminal activities, are also regular purchasers of Russian-and Chinese-made firearms. Often illegally, they acquire firearms at their own risk believing that it might protect their lives, their families and property. Urban residents tend to purchase pistols and revolvers, while rural residents prefer to buy rifles, automatic and even assault rifles. Since the end of the nineteenth century, wearing firearms was a tradition and part of a way of life for rural residents of the Russian-Chinese frontier and remote northern areas of East Siberia and the Far East (both descendants of settlers from European Russia/Eastern Europe and Native Siberians). The main reasons for this tradition were:

- hunting as one of the important means of survival;
- the need to protect human lives from wild animals;
- dangerous atmosphere of the frontier with often and unexpected attacks from China;
- petty and high criminal activity, and regular escapes of inmates from prisons and concentration camps; and,
- low density of population in combination with poor activity of law enforcement structures.

After the end of Civil War (1917-1922), the Communists tried to ban the private ownership of small arms in the area, but that policy was not effective, and semi-illegal possession of small arms by private citizens finally became tolerated by the authorities. Thus almost every family residing in the area keeps and regularly updates its own small arsenal of small arms. Although it is absolutely obligatory that every small arm in the country should be registered, most Siberians tend to neglect this legal prescription. In most cases, residents of frontier and northern areas tend to acquire Russian or Chinese arms (depending on the purchasers' wealth), but some copies of American rifles have also been noted. A similar situation is observed with respect to small arms acquisition and registration by various private security and detective companies in the area, as well as in numerous prospectors' and explorers' teams operating in the remote northern territories.

The Russian and international media have been regularly reporting the presence of small arms in the arsenals of various paramilitary opposition groups. Among those groups worthy of mention are several right-wing and nationalist organizations having branches in Siberia and the Russian Far East, namely: Kossacks,

Pamyat', Russian National Union, Skinheads, Young Patriots of Russia, and the leftist terrorist "Revvoyensovet RSFSR" ("Revolutionary Council of Russian Soviet Socialist Republic.") Several representatives of other radical organizations, among them the Liberal Democratic Party, leftist Union of Russian Communists and different associations of Afghan War veterans, have also mentioned in their public speeches that their branches might also have small arms arsenals. Separatist movements in some autonomous areas of Russian Siberia and Far East, namely the Republics of Sakha-Yakoutia and Tannu-Tuva might be also recipients of small arms both from Russian Army stores and from China. Vietnam and Cambodia are still the main recipients of Russian weapons in East Asia. They acquire Russian weapons for their domestic army and police use, as well as for further sale to Myanmar, Malaysia and the Philippines. The North Korean Army might still be one of the recipients of some highquality Russian weapons, including small arms.

Certain amounts of Russian-made firearms are exported from the Russian Maritim Territory to Japan in exchange for Japanese cars. This "business" has been organized by the Kovalsky Mafia Syndicate (with its headquarters in Vladivostok) and supposedly the Yakuza. We can assume that various separatist movements of China — among them Uigur and Tibetan separatists, as well as guerilla movements in Myanmar, Thailand, Indonesia and Philippines — might have been, or will be, explored and approached by Russian arms traders looking for new markets.

Some Tibetan tribes and communities in remote areas of the Tibetan "Autonomous Region" and the province of Qinghai (for example the tribe of Golog which officially has still not surrendered to Chinese communist troops) have been reported to possess arsenals of Chinese-made firearms, including assault rifles, and to purchase ammunition on a regular basis.

At present, there are about 157,000 Russian troops deployed in the area (the forces of Trans-Baykal and Maritim military districts). Keeping in mind the equipment saved for tactical and strategic reserves, together with some out-of-date weapons, there should be deployed at least 1.5-2 million units of small arms at various military stores. Widespread embezzlement of small arms belonging to the army may have resulted in the transfer of at least 5 to 10% of the above amounts to underground stores of criminal groups, as well as into the hands of private citizens. About 350,000 units of small arms (pistols, submachine guns and assault rifles) should be deployed at MVD (Federal Police), OMON (Special Police Forces) and FSB (Federal Security Service) stores in the area.

In spite of widespread corruption and collaboration with criminal structures typical of Russian law enforcement structures within the last years, the stores of the above forces have never been reported as objects of embezzlement. Private citizens (both involved and relatively non-involved in criminal activity) residing in the research area, are expected to hold at least 2,000,000 small arms (rifles, automatic rifles, carbines, assault rifles pistols and revolvers). The possible number of small arms in underground ("Mafia"-controlled) arsenals in the area is estimated at 3,000 to 10,000 items including Kalashnikov assault rifles and machine guns, TT and TM pistols, Uzi rifles and submachine guns, as well as antitank weapons and grenade launchers (RPG-22-1 "Mukha").

Possible Consequences

Further development of small arms proliferation in the area might boost further escalation of crime and organized crime in Siberia and the Russian Far East, especially regarding new wars between different criminal groups. It may also boost crime in China. As of writing, kept under relative control by Chinese law enforcement structures, criminal activity might strongly escalate in the face of economic reforms, corruption and small arms proliferation. The process of proliferation may also escalate criminal activity in Mongolia, situated between Russia and China and dependent on both neighbours.

Escalation of Corruption

Most salaries paid to Russian policemen, customs officials, etc., do not exceed $US 400 per month while purely subsistence wages for one person are at least $US 800. Further escalation of criminal activity in the Russian Far East and Siberia, in combination with ongoing underpayment of law enforcement officers, makes it necessary for them either to look for additional part-time jobs, or to take bribes and cooperate with criminals. The latter variant tends to seem more attractive to the increasing percentage of Russian law enforcement officers and leading to the formation of what Russian criminologist A. Gurov calls "the Criminal State."

Export of Crime

Further proliferation of small arms in the area together with the escalation of corruption and helplessness of law enforcement structures, leads to accumulation of funds in the hands of organized criminal groups in Russia and China, as well as the growth of their members. As a result, criminal groups are already exploring such prospective "business areas" as Japan, Singapore, USA and Canada. During the last five years, numerous representatives of Russian and Chinese organized criminal groups have penetrated Canada and USA and have started building networks here. Within the next ten years, their influence in North America could significantly increase and drastically worsen the criminal situation here. Canada has already been used by Russian and Chinese criminal structures as a place for moneylaundering and permanent residence. This process might develop further if not brought under control, and turn Canada into a springboard for Russian criminal groups used for penetrating the USA.

Terrorism and Insurgent Groups

Concentration of small arms in the arsenals of the "Russian Mafia" has made contract killings and other acts of terror typical elements of modern Russian life. If not brought under control, this process may expand into new countries and areas. Concentration of small arms in the arsenals of rightist and leftist opposition parties and organizations might provoke political violence, in turn increasing the flow of political refugees to North American countries.

Illicit trade in small arms in Siberia might facilitate separatism and violence in some ethnic "republics" of Russian Federation (mainly Sakha-Yakoutia and Tannu-Tuva). Accumulation of small arms in the hands of citizens might eventually provoke high-scale ethnic violence between native and Russian Siberians on one hand, and Chinese and Korean settlers on the other. This scenario might also create refugee problems.

Accumulations of small arms in the area might activate so-called "Siberian separatism." At the moment, this sentiment is popular among a relatively small number of Slavonic-speaking Siberians, but However it is most likely that small arms acquired by mobsters for their "actions" will lead to an increase in violence when used. the idea of an independent Siberia might someday cause political and even military confrontation in the area.

Possible Policy Options

The challenge of small arms proliferation facing national governments requires international cooperation and coordination. Some of the general tasks which must be addressed, include the following:

- collection and regular updating of accurate information on small arms flows — both legitimate and illicit;
- monitoring the traffic routes;
- locating and confiscation illegal stores and depots; and,
- identifying the leaders of criminal and paracriminal groups involved and interested in illicit proliferation of small arms.

More international coordination in the field of exchange information and tracing, as well as the intercept of the illicit movement of small arms are among possible options. However, experience suggests that these options do not work well either in China, or in Russia because of corruption and traditional mistrust towards foreigners/westerners in both countries.

Accumulation of information and tracing might work better if a considerable number of competent law-enforcement officers in the area would serve as direct sources of information for law enforcement structures of Canada and USA. This might work well in Russia for two reasons: In spite of traditional mistrust, there exists a stereotype of a "Mighty American Cop" among Russians including Russian law enforcement officers, and that stereotypical figure is respected. Russian law enforcement officers are underpaid and open to part-time jobs for other employers (among them criminal gangs).

Thus many of them might also work for non-criminal employers overseas representing, for example, Canadian or American law enforcement structures. It is presently an opportune time to recruit them, as they are relatively free of old communist ideology, while new radical nationalist ideology is still not strong enough to prevent them from being hired by foreign structures. Other East European backgrounds, i.e., the descendants of "white settlers" who first came to Siberia at the end of the 16th century.

12

The Social and Economic Impact of Small Arms in Warring Nations

Small arms trade plays a prominent role in the economies of nations at war, and particularly in intrastate conflicts. The availability of small arms makes war possible, and their continuing availability fuels the protraction of war. War economies require continuing violence for sustenance. In many protracted civil wars, the availability of weapons exceeds that of soldiers, leading to the mushrooming prevalence of child-soldier "recruitment" by kidnapping (Sudan, Uganda, Sierra Leone, Sri Lanka, and elsewhere).

Thus, the small arms market helps to drive the diverse disabling economic and social effects of war. Wars fed by small arms supply divert economic investment and energy from normal productivity, and suck up resources otherwise available for domestic services and infrastructure (education, health care, social welfare, and productivity-related infrastructure like roads, energy provision, and water supply). "War interrupts, and indeed reverses, economic development." War destroys physical and social capital, and erodes what Sen calls the "capacities" and "entitlements" of people's lives.

Small arms warfare is intimately connected to poverty and arrested economic development in conflict-affected areas. Agriculture suffers both from the loss of opportunity to work in fields and from the weapons themselves, especially land mines. Looting and the ruination of croplands are common tactics. Commerce suffers as well; necessary safety, reliable transportation, and open communication become extremely difficult in areas infused with small arms. Industry and international trade suffer for all these reasons, plus the increased risks of loss to combatants. The stability of government and policy, required for the smooth function of economies, suffers in the presence of active violence. When war concludes, conflict-damaged societies must then face the economic burdens of both weapons disarmament and disposal and the education and employment of habituated combatants.

The ready availability of small arms enables conflict economies of robbery and looting, extortion systems, and kidnapping. Lives lost to small arms violence are a major economic loss to societies torn by conflict, with long-reaching adverse effects on the economic function of families and communities. Small arms violence results in major dislocations of refugees and internally-displaced persons, who are rendered both severely needy and unable to be productive. And the supply of small arms stimulates drug-running and other smuggling economies. Finally, when active warfare abates, the presence of abundant small arms and abundant ex-soldiers fosters the escalation of crime rates and the development of organized crime that has been a virtually constant sequel to recent wars.

Even the ability of outside humanitarian donors to ease the suffering of people in conflict-infected regions risks being hijacked for economic gain by warring groups empowered by small arms. In many situations, armed independent gangs or unofficial militias derive significant funding from regular looting or "taxation" of humanitarian aid providers.

The Case of Sudan

The individual case of the complex, protracted intrastate war in Sudan clearly exemplifies the terrible hazards of the global small arms market. In Sudan, the genocidal campaign of the Sudanese (Muslim) government against native Muslims living in the newly-discovered oil field lands of Darfur has been actively pursued through government-assisted militias, primarily the

Janjawid. The Janjawid are able to carry out their program of mass terror, murder and intentional starvation by virtue of their wealth of small arms provisions — Kalashnikov AK47 assault rifles, rocket-propelled grenades, and jeep-mounted machine guns — despite the UN adoption in 2001 of Article 16 of the UN International Law Commission's Articles on Responsibility of States for Internationally Wrongful Acts. The agreement is binding on *all* states, and forbids any assistance of another state in the commission of "any internationally wrongful act." The Janjawid's atrocities clearly surpass international definition as "Internationally Wrongful Acts," and the Sudan government's claims to be uninvolved and opposed to the arbitrary and indiscriminate killing, "disappearances," systemic rapes, and torture fly in the face of heavily documented evidence of the government's supply of and government troop participation in the atrocities. In 1994, the European Union joined in an arms embargo against all non-governmental entities in Sudan in order to "promote lasting peace and reconciliation within Sudan," but the world weapons industry has continued to sell arms to the Sudanese government without restriction. Given the clear evidence of the Sudan government's programmatic support of and participation in the Darfur genocide and crimes against humanity, any sale of arms to Sudan violates Article 16 of the UN International Law Commission. Every nation fully understands this, yet the world community of weapons exporters have continued to feed small arms into Sudan, fueling the Darfur genocide. In March, 2004, The UN Security Council voted 13-0-2 to demand that Sudan disarm its paramilitary militias, but issued its demand without teeth. Further, small arms shipments to other East African countries from the USA and Germany, among others, is certain to bolster Sudan's stockpile of weapons. It is estimated that 85% of the personal assault weapons in Africa originate in the five countries of the UN Security Council: the USA, the UK, Russia, China, and France.

Finally, only two weeks ago, the UN Security Council approved a total weapons embargo, targeted economic sanctions against atrocity perpetrators, a 10,000-person peacekeeping force, and an International Criminal Court investigation and prosecution of criminals against humanity in Sudan. Principal exporters of small arms to Sudan appear to be Iran, China, France, Saudi Arabia, Switzerland, and the UK (this tally excludes further volumes of arms sales in terms of fighter jets, helicopters, etc.). The fact that UN Security Council nations have stakes in the illegal arms supply of the Janjawid/Sudanese government genocide in Darfur (and China's strong oil-supply relationship with the Sudanese government) helps explain the Security Council's failure to act to stop the war. In November 2004, Amnesty International revealed densely documented details of the uncontrolled arms exports that have fueled massive human rights abuses in Sudan, including the killing, rape, torture and displacement of more than a million civilians since the Darfur conflict escalated in February 2003 after the discovery of Darfur oil deposits.

The inability (or unwillingness) of the Swiss, paragons of organization, to regulate their own export of weapons demonstrates the degree to which the weapons market is out of control. After being told by the Geneva-based Graduate Institute of International Studies that Swiss small arms exports to Sudan totaled more than $4 million in 2002, the Swiss Finance Ministry promised that Switzerland would review its weapons exports. The Swiss government records reveal less than *$4,000* worth of handgun exports to Sudan, to be used "for use as personal protection or sporting purposes." "Such trade would not have been approved by us," stated Ottmar Wyss, responsible for export control. "Either there is illegal export trade going on, or the numbers are wrong." Reason and experience suggest that the wrong numbers are those of Mr. Wyss.

The Sudanese government estimates that "two to three million" landmines cover 32 % of the country; the original exporters of the landmines were Russia, China, the UK, Iraq, Iran, the USA, and a list of others.

While Sudan's population is impoverished and has been victimized by its two decades of civil war, and although Sudan is one of the 38 "Heavily Indebted Poor Countries" eligible for favourable borrowing terms, Sudan is also sitting on major oil reserves — a resource pool that could possibly deliver economic stability and domestic freedoms to the people of Sudan. Instead, oil production is bankrolling the government's pursuit of genocide against its own people, through the purchase of small arms and other weapons, a political economic decision founded on abuse of one part of its population for the benefit of a relative few. The main foreign direct investors in Sudan are companies from China, Malaysia, and India.

HALTING THE GLOBAL SMALL ARMS MARKET

What measures might effectively govern the worldwide small arms market and reduce the likelihood of violence? Given the present prevalent system of deregulated trade and finance, and the monstrous productive capacity of a profusion of nations to produce the weapons that fuel conflict, it is hard to be sanguine about the prospects for real change.

Rhetorical advocacy for peace and human rights is often a smokescreen to cover the transnational corporate "national" interests of weapons producers.

The following measures must be pursued as part of an aggressive world response to the calamity of the global small arms market system and its contributions to the Sudan civil war:

1. The UN Security Council must aggressively pursue all of its new measures against Sudan's criminal war against its own people, and apply this same standard to all conflicts.
2. The United Nations, regional interstate security unions, and individual weapon-producing nations must be aggressively and resolutely pushed to reform policy in order to reduce and govern weapons manufacture and export. The economic benefits of the global small arms market enrich a few while impoverishing the interrelated economies and lives of most of the world. Targeted financial sanctions against non-compliant producers might enable this reform, if the Security Council permanent members can find the political and moral will to curtail their own weapons industries. Real change will take determination, and will not be a short-term project.

3. All weapons should be given international registry marks, so that manufacturers and countries of origin can be determined.
4. A fund should be created to pay for the purchase and destruction of small arms, initially in areas of conflict and then globally, in order to reduce the massive world stockpile of such weapons.
5. The neo-liberal system of economic globalization itself must be progressively reformed. It is time for the world to again implement regulatory governance of trade, finance, labour, environment, and community, on state and transnational bases.

This essay allows space only for an introductory analysis of the global small arms system of manufacture, export, trafficking, and use in violent conflict; and economic bases and effects of this system. Small arms, and the broader concern of all weapons production for sale, are a major piece of the conflict and peace puzzle. Weapons manufacture and traffic, and particularly that of small arms, is a beast that will require taming if the world's wildfires of violence are to be contained.

EVALUATION OF MEASURES ADOPTED BY THE SOUTH ASIAN STATES

This chapter will briefly evaluate the different legal and administrative measures so far taken by South Asian governments to curb the proliferation of SALW in their countries. Four out of six countries have a common legislative history as a colonial legacy which is the Arms Act of 1878. That each country has a legislative framework, rules and regulations regarding issuing of licences and documentation for the legal export and import of firearms and ammunition. All five countries also have provisions regarding domestic production, markings, record-keeping, seizures, penalties and security, safety and management of the stockpiles in custody. However, the scope and stringency of these stipulations varies from country to country.

Bangladesh has made no amendment to its 1878 Act so far, and its current legislation is unable to cope with the present challenges of SALW and, therefore, is considered the weakest in the region. The Sri Lanka Firearms Ordinance has the strictest limitations on exports and imports in South Asia but it does not clearly define what a 'firearm' is and still facing the problems of SALW proliferation from its rebels. Despite provisions for a manufacturing licence, Bangladesh, India and Pakistan have a growing problem with small arms from cottage industries falling into the hands of non-State actors. In Nepal, licensing requirements for manufacturing small arms are very weak. Even a Chief District Officer can issue a licence to favourite persons by his discretionary powers. In India, a police report is not absolutely necessary for the issuing of a permit to own a locally-manufactured firearm. The Government of Sri Lanka, on the other hand, is planning to put a moratorium on the licensing of small arms.

Provisions for the seizures also vary from country to country. In Bangladesh and Pakistan, a magistrate determines if possession is illegal. In India and Nepal, the government has the discretion to seize arms in order to protect public peace and safety. Sri Lanka has the toughest laws, wherein the threshold for seizure is the lowest; any authorised officer can confiscate a weapon on the suspicion that the holder does not have a licence. As far as markings are concerned only the Indian and Sri Lankan gun laws require every firearm made to bear the name of the manufacturer, a serial number and the place of production. Detailed marking allows for weapons to be traced back to the individual manufacturer and serial number, and serves to check illicit possession and to prevent illegal transfers.

All the South Asian countries except India make it mandatory for gun-dealers to maintain proper records of the numbers of firearms in its possession or control. These national laws allow government officers, at least in theory, to ask weapons-dealers to account for the firearms in their inventory at any time. All five South Asian countries' legislation contain penalties for contraventions of restrictions on manufacture, possession and transfer. Punishment ranges from six months imprisonment to death, and the imposition of a fine, alone or concurrently. As a part of their international commitment, the South Asian states also participated in the 2001 UN Conference on Illicit Trade of SALW and agreed to implement the UN PoA, which is a politically binding document endorsed by consensus, as the central global agreement on preventing and reducing trafficking and proliferation of SALW. In practice, the UN PoA establishes an international programme of relatively comprehensive scope, including almost the full range of issues specified in the 1997 and 1999 Reports of the UN Groups of Experts. Thus, it contains substantial agreed-upon norms, standards and programmes on a number of issues, including:

- Preventing and combating illicit SALW production and trafficking;
- Ensuring effective controls on the legal production, holding and transfer of SALW;
- Weapons collection and destruction;
- Management and security of official and authorised SALW stocks;
- SALW control in post-conflict situations; and
- Information exchange and confidence-building.

From a South Asian perspective it is also necessary to have an overview of the implementation of the UN PoA in order to draw a coherent regional approach which in turn would contribute towards building a base for an effective international mechanism to curb problems associated with SALW in all its aspects.

In implementing PoA no coordinated regional action has been taken by the South Asian states. Although attempts were made to implement the PoA at national level, but no major legislative change has been made by any government since the introduction of PoA. However, comparative analysis and evaluation of governmental efforts indicate that in key areas existing laws are not adequate enough in terms of implementation to control the proliferation of SALW in all its aspects. South Asian states are also lacking mechanisms to implement the existing regulations and procedures in order to control illicit trafficking and use. States also lack consistency and coordination to monitor legal trade and enforcing penalties for illicit exchange. Cottage industries are not strictly regulated and as a result smuggled exports to non-state actors are also increasing. The existing framework of the UN PoA is also unable to deal with domestic production. All South Asian states lack standardised export and import licensing and documentation mechanism, especially when corruption is prevalent within the governments and societies. States also lacks control over the political use of SALW. However, Nepal is the only country where legislation explicitly deals with weapons and elections. Above all there is need for a comprehensive regional approach to deal with all theses problems associated with proliferation of SALW in such a way that each state can benefit from its results nationally as well as regionally.

A Coherent Regional Approach

In the field of arms control and disarmament much more needs to be done, not only in the context of nuclear, biological and chemical weapons but also to prevent the proliferation of SALW in all its aspects. In the South Asian context such proliferation of SALW exists mainly due to poor governance and mis-management of law and order as well as the inability or unwillingness of governments to address security-related reforms. South Asian states should take drastic initiatives at national as well as at regional levels to formulate a coherent national and regional approach to curb SALW in all its aspects, in order to assure greater human security. Any future initiatives should be guided by the principles and purposes of the UN Charter, International Humanitarian Law (IHL), human rights, human security, political stability, law enforcement, social and economic development and de-weaponisation of societies. For the success of any regional initiative taken, confidence, trust and understanding, cooperation and information exchange, social and economic development and reduction of poverty are necessary elements. States should collectively identify the hurdles in their way to undertake any interlinked initiatives.

In order to draw a coherent regional approach the following measures should be adopted by South Asian countries to curb problems associated with SALW within their territories;

- Strengthening through modernisation, law-enforcement and intelligence agencies including Police, Customs and Border Control, and enhancement of judicial capacities.
- Establishment of national commissions to check the illicit proliferation of SALW. Such a Commission should serve as a forum for dialogue and discourses among political parties, law-enforcement agencies and civil society to devise and achieve consensus on effective strategies for curbing the proliferation of SALW and related regulations. Furthermore, establishing of a national co-ordination committee would help bring together relevant officials and departments for intra-provincial interactions.
- The unlicensed cottage arms industries could be strictly regulated. However, this has to be done by recognising the prevalent socio-economic conditions and providing viable alternative incentives which would probably work better than taking punitive measures. For example, the domestic producers could be designated the official small arms-makers to complement the bigger manufacturing units, which presently are all government-controlled.
- By making the domestic process more transparent, political influence should be checkmated by which political vested groups resort to the use of small arms for violence. Political parties should be held responsible for any use of armed militia by its members, or display of weapons.
- Checks on civilian possessions of small arms and control over weapons designed for military should not fall in the hands of civilians.
- South Asian states should re-enact their existing legislations to eliminate loopholes and ensure its proper implementation to reduce the unauthorised use of small arms. Legislation should stipulate registration of brokers, transactions and penalties for illicit activities.
- Proliferation and illicit use of small arms can never be understood in isolation of economic and social development. Therefore, concerted initiatives involving South Asian countries need to be taken.

- All five countries should require legislation for proper markings for both locally manufactured and imported firearms;
- South Asian states blame each other for spreading small arms, however, possibilities of regional cooperation are there but a uniformity of ideas and efforts are needed. Pakistan's seven-stage de-weaponisation campaign is a good example and South Asian states would benefit by adopting similar strategies.
- SAARC is presently unable to discuss SALW concerns in order to avoid any bilateral wrangle. Its role should be expanded to cover problems of SALW. SAARC should evolve an integrated regional action programme for curbing proliferation of SALW. SAARC member states should set up a comprehensive regional convention on small arms and light weapons to investigate, expose and curb illicit arms trade and trafficking across South Asia. All states should be brought under a common legal umbrella for working towards non-proliferation of SALW.
- Collection, safe and secure stockpiling and eventual destruction of small arms should be ensured so that SALW do not get recycled back to criminals, organised groups and non-state actors. States should improve management of authorised stocks at the point of production, transportation, and storage and record must be kept at every stage. Efficient record-keeping and databases of these stockpiles could serve as a basis for possible future co-operation and information sharing among states. It would be useful for all the countries of the region to extend mandatory record-keeping rules on small arms manufacturers to government agencies and their own stockpiles, as well as to individuals holding licenses to possess guns for private use.
- Money-laundering and safe havens abroad are the main factors behind the proliferation of small arms. In this regard a South Asian police force should be established to stop

trafficking of small arms and its widespread use in the region.

- Public awareness and involvement of civil society is also necessary for curbing the element of violence in South Asian societies and prolonged awareness campaigns would serve to source the public apathy into civic action. To this end, informal exchanges, seminars and workshops at the level of non-governmental organisations, academics and media representatives could serve a useful purpose. Governments and civil society need to work together to implement the UN Programme of Action on small arms.
- Member States need to take stock of the challenges of effectively controlling their long porous borders and of associated problems of smuggling, narcotics trade, which in turn are closely linked to the illicit trade in SALWs. In this regard sharing of intelligence on known smuggling networks and illicit arms markets is required. The South Asian states have to muster their will for bilateral and regional co-operation to combat smuggling, the finding and destroying of arms caches.
- Proliferated small arms are mostly manufactured in western countries. There is a need to trace out their routes.
- There is a need to strengthen the Anti-Terrorism Convention adopted by the UN in April 2005. However, there is the need also to clearly distinguish between legitimate right of self-determination and terrorism for political ends.
- SALW should be redefined to cover other traditional weapons such as knives, swords, machetes and hatchets which have been widely used during civil conflicts and riots by organised crimes. Rwanda and Burundi massacres were done by such weapons.

Strengthening of International Mechanisms

South Asian states are profoundly concerned about the problems associated with SALW and need to devise and adopt international legally-binding mechanisms, based on national, regional and international considerations for curbing proliferation of SALW. The mechanisms should enable South Asian states to control and prohibit the use of millions of SALW circulating in their territories. Any regional, sub-regional agreements and initiatives would in turn complement and reinforce global efforts to prevent, combat, and reduce the proliferation of SALW and their misuse. In this regard South Asian states should take concrete efforts to implement fully the UN PoA, and other related efforts for controlling SALW.

The proposed Draft Framework Convention on International Arms Transfer, 'the Framework Convention', is one example which can provide a legal framework within which further issues can be addressed over time, such as building up a series of interlocking instruments, and subsequent initiatives which could either take the form of protocols to the Convention or self-standing instruments associated with the Convention in some other way.

According to this Draft Convention, international arms transfer should be authorised through licensing. States should ensure that any arms transfer should not violate international law, the Charter of the UN, UNSC resolutions, customary international law, International Humanitarian Law (IHL), human rights, and international norms and treaties. It also states that the use of arms should also be prohibited which are capable of distinguishing between combatants and civilians, or which cause superfluous injury or unnecessary suffering, in serious violation of human rights, for genocides or crimes against humanity, and against violations of IHL. An international registry of international arms transfer should be maintained on an annual basis by the respective national report of every country. Generally this Convention covers almost all kinds of technical, procedural and theoretical aspects to curb proliferation of SALW in all its aspects.

The scope of traditional arms control and disarmament approaches should be extended to cover SALW as weapons of mass destruction, and on a priority basis a strengthened international binding mechanism to control SALW should be established. There is a need to adopt human security-centred policies. Emerging weapon technologies should be analysed as to how they undermine human security and strict state regulations ensure that they do not fall into the hands of non-state actors. Controlling proliferation of SALW is not only a multi-layered work, but also a multi-sectoral effort requiring the formation of partnerships based on national, regional and international levels. The 1997 anti-personnel Land Mines Convention is one such example. Implementation of existing norms, such as the Basic Principles on the Use of Force and Firearms, the UN Code of Conduct for Law Enforcement Officials, and the Firearms Protocol of the Transnational Crime Convention on priority basis is necessary for security and survival of human beings. Curtailment of civilian possession of small arms, security sector reforms, exchange of information between states, inter-regional and intra-regional cooperation, financial and technical help to weak countries are some of the measures which can give strength not only to a legally-binding mechanism, but can also heal the disrupted social fabric.

NUCLEAR POLICY IN PUBLIC DISCOURSE

Discourse on security issues in Pakistan is determined by the lack of transparency in the formulation of policy and the absence of an informed public debate. The lack of debate is the result of deliberate state policy and a by-product of the political system. For most of Pakistan's history, political power has been exercised by the military through the civil bureaucracy. Not only has the military attempted to maintain complete control over policy in areas of particular sensitivity, it has also endeavoured to ensure that its interests and perceptions are not challenged by political rivals. Although successive military regimes have failed in their attempts to gain domestic legitimacy for authoritarian rule, they have succeeded in attaining popular acceptance of their security policies, particularly in the nuclear realm.

Pakistan's decision-making authorities have been assisted in their quest for acceptance of their perceptions and policies by a number of factors. In the external sphere, the uneasy relationship between India and Pakistan and the disparities in size and resources between the two mutually antagonistic states have enabled Pakistan's state managers to acquire domestic support for measures to manage the perceived threat. Not only do most Pakistanis accept the need to buttress the country's conventional strength *vis-à-vis* India; official efforts to depict the nuclear capability as an effective deterrent against the Indian threat also seem to have won popular acceptance.

For a state with a troubled history and fragile political foundations, the acquisition of nuclear capability has also served a useful domestic purpose. Not only is the country's threshold status projected as a symbol of Pakistan's sovereignty and prestige; external pressures on Pakistan to renounce its nuclear capability have been used to rally a deeply divided people behind state authority. In the internal context, moreover, the external threat is a particularly useful tool in gaining political legitimacy and diverting domestic discontent from unrepresentative rule and authoritarian practices. Thus internal threats to the political, economic and social status quo are often depicted as inspired and assisted externally—that is, by India. In a similar fashion, internal questioning of the direction of external security is officially equated with sedition or even treason.

A majority of the population, however, tends to accept official security concepts voluntarily since its access to information is limited, as is its exposure to alternative views. Thus, in the nuclear sphere, official definitions of deterrence have won popular acceptance and support, even though there is little understanding either of the concept itself or of its potential economic, political and strategic risks and costs.

Official endeavours to restrict and control the parameters of debate are assisted by the unrepresentative nature of the decision-making process itself. All aspects of policy in the nuclear field remain the military's sole prerogative. While some input is provided by the civil service, its main role is to ensure that the internal and external developments do not interfere with the military's policy objectives. Thus, in the external sphere, officials assist in the acquisition of technology and in the mitigation of international pressure. Internally, official control of the broadcast media in a country with a largely illiterate population has played a major role in the popular acceptance of policy. The security debate is, therefore, restricted to official rhetoric and its echoes.

Public opinion

Most Pakistanis in any case have no role in the making of policy. They are illiterate, poverty-stricken and subjected to systemic economic, social and political constraints. Pakistan's small educated élite has the means to influence public opinion and hence official policy.

Its acceptance of official policy and rhetoric on the nuclear question is essential for policy makers. This segment of public opinion is systematically targeted with a sophisticated but dependent academic debate and manipulation of the independent print media.

So far as academic discourse is concerned, the debate is easy to manipulate since most institutions of higher education in Pakistan function under the direct control of the civil service. Academics, for all practical purposes, are government functionaries. Career incentives and the fear of punitive action make it easy to limit academic dissent. Since all important think-tanks, particularly in the fields of defence and security, are also financed by the government and under governmental control, official rhetoric becomes the academic discourse.

The nuclear debate in the print media plays a more important role in influencing the perceptions of Pakistan's educated élite. Although the independent print media have resisted state control, independence of thought is seldom demonstrated *vis-à-vis* security issues. The absence of a vigorous debate on nuclear policy can be attributed, in part, to the plethora of retired civil and military bureaucrats who dominate the media's security discourse. Most media personnel, however, uncritically accept official postures and justifications on nuclear policy since they have little independent knowledge of the subject.

Civil–military relations

Neither the restricted nature of the domestic debate nor the unrepresentative character of the policy-making process was changed much by the transformation of the political system in 1988, when power was transferred to civilian hands after 11 years of direct military rule. Security policy remains the military's responsibility, and elected civilian leaders continue to play a limited role in either the formulation or the direction of Pakistan's nuclear policy.

This continuity in the policy-making processes is the result of the political order which was devised in 1988, when the military high command decided, reluctantly, to turn formal power over to civilian hands. The transfer only took place after the elected political leader- ship accepted the military's continued guidance in sensitive areas of policy making, including defence and foreign affairs. The military has retained its political predominance since, continuing to play an interventionist role and dismissing and forming governments at will, both at the centre and in the provinces.

Since no elected government has been allowed to complete its term of office, the two main political parties, the Pakistan People's Party (PPP) and the Pakistan Muslim League (Nawaz) (PML-N), believe that the military's continued support and approval are an essential precondition for attaining or retaining power. Hence elected governments as well as the political opposition not only tacitly accept the military's dictates on security issues, but even use their political platforms to further the military's perceptions, priorities and policies. All major political actors, including the Islamist parties, use nationalistic rhetoric to bolster their support and to attack the legitimacy of their opponents. This use of rhetoric further reinforces domestic support for official nuclear policy, which is strongly associated with Pakistani sovereignty and prestige. At the same time, the political risks entailed in questioning support for the nuclear weapon programme contribute to the one-sided nature of the debate.

THE NUCLEAR ISSUE AND REGIME LEGITIMACY

The nexus between public opinion and the nuclear programme has been strengthened over time. Care has been taken to introduce changes in the directions of Pakistan's nuclear policy in such a manner as to retain public acceptance and approval. The history of the programme, which dates back to the 1960s, illustrates the domestic determinants of security policy in Pakistan.

From Partition to the first military government

A combination of hostility towards India and the need to address domestic challenges contributed to the inception of the nuclear weapon programme in the 1960s. This particular mix of internal and external factors has, in fact, existed since Pakistan's creation as an independent state. As early as 1948, Pakistani policy makers opted for anti-Indian rhetoric and the threat or use of force to advance their dual goals of regime legitimacy and external security.

By 1958, when the military took direct control of the state after a decade of indirect control in alliance with the civil bureaucracy, the role of the military as guarantor of national security had begun to bear political fruit. Although the military's political legitimacy was questioned and rejected, Pakistani decision makers proved more successful in manipulating anti-Indian sentiment, the by-product of a bitter partition and of the continued existence of territorial disputes. As a result there was general acceptance among most sections of the population of a security policy based on two assumptions: an unremitting Indian threat and a reliance on military (as opposed to diplomatic) means to counter it.

This approach suited the domestic political interests of the now- dominant armed forces. Pakistan's participation in Western security alliances, justified by the putative Indian threat, was generally accepted by the public, while the military became the beneficiary of Western economic and military assistance. Nor did the public question the emphasis on military expenditure at the cost of development.

With respect to nuclear policy, Pakistan's first reactor started up in 1965, but the weapon option was not yet an important activity. India's nuclear ambitions were condemned, but key officials disclosed their intention to counter a potential Indian nuclear threat with a similar capability. Thus, General Ayub Khan's politically ambitious Foreign Minister, Zulfikar Ali Bhutto, could declare in January 1965 that if India developed an atomic bomb Pakistan would also have to because there was no conventional alternative.

In the wake of the Indo-Pakistani War of 1965, Pakistani policy makers faced new and more serious domestic challenges. The miscalculations of the military regime, combined with heightened public expectations, led to widespread opposition to authoritarian rule.

In the regime's attempts to divert domestic attention away from an unpopular cease-fire in the West wing of the country and disillusionment with the prospects of a stable and secure East Pakistan, anti-Indian propaganda reached new heights in the officially controlled print media.

Despite the intention to develop a nuclear option, the military's main priority was the resumption of security links with the USA and access to US arms, disrupted during the 1965 war. The 1970s were to lead to a change in nuclear policy as decision makers faced new inter- linked internal and external challenges.

The civilian government after the 1971 war

Following its defeat in the 1971 Indo-Pakistani War and the independence of Bangladesh, the Pakistani military opted for a strategic withdrawal from politics, handing over power to civilian hands.

Under President, later Prime Minister, Zulfikar Ali Bhutto, the new government faced the onerous tasks of restoring domestic legitimacy and providing a new sense of identity to the truncated state. At the same time, conscious of the military's resentment at their loss of power and prestige, the civilian leadership had to ensure that the interests and goals of the armed forces were given priority in policy making.

In the domestic realm, the PPP Government relied on the tried and tested approach of using the external threat to foster internal unity, exploiting anti-Indian sentiment and suspicions, which also served to legitimize a gradual military build-up in both the conventional and the nuclear realms.

The nuclear aspect became more important following the Indian nuclear test in 1974. The Bhutto Government embarked in earnest on an ambitious nuclear programme aimed at providing

Pakistan with an equivalent nuclear standing, and nuclear policy was justified on the ground of the Indian threat to receptive internal audiences.

Although the programme clearly had a weapon orientation, the Pakistani authorities insisted that it was peaceful in nature as they attempted to acquire the necessary technology and hardware from external sources, including a French nuclear reprocessing plant.

Pakistan also attempted simultaneously to justify its nuclear pro- gramme and discredit its Indian adversary by proposing a nuclear weapon-free zone for South Asia, an offer which was promptly rejected by India.

Although official offers of regional disarmament and their rejection by India reinforced Pakistani public perceptions of the Indian threat, they did little to reassure the USA of Pakistan's peaceful nuclear intentions.

The return to military rule after the 1977 coup

The nuclear programme became even more of a symbol of Pakistan's national prestige and sovereignty when the French rescinded the nuclear reprocessing deal under US pressure.

Following the military coup which brought General Zia ul-Haq to power in 1977 and led to Bhutto's execution, nuclear policy still proved to be a successful tool in providing a degree of legitimacy to an unpopular military regime, since it projected itself as the guardian of Pakistan's national security and sovereignty.

Although domestic legitimacy continued to elude the Zia regime throughout its 11 years, there were no significant internal divisions on the issue of the nuclear weapon programme. While the successful use of the government-controlled broadcast media and the co-optation of the academic community helped in creating a domestic consensus on the issue, the regime's role in Afghanistan during the second cold war helped it to acquire external legitimacy and substantial economic and military support.

Deliberate US inattention helped Pakistani decision makers in their clandestine quest to acquire an independent ability to produce fissile material, which was achieved by the mid-1980s. When Under-Secretary of State James Buckley was questioned by the Senate Government Affairs Committee on Pakistan's nuclear programme, he said that he had been 'assured by Pakistani ministers and by the President himself that it was not the intention of the Pakistani government to develop nuclear weapons', stating even more categorically on another occasion, 'I fully accept the statement of President Zia that Pakistan has no intention of manufacturing nuclear weapons or acquiring nuclear weapons'.

A State Department memorandum in 1983, however, disclosed that Pakistan had shifted from 'procurement of weapon components themselves to procurement of machinery necessary for their manufacture'. Certain of Western economic and military assistance, the military regime continued to expand and consolidate Pakistan's nuclear capabilities.

Nor were any attempts made to resolve tensions with India, exacerbated by the tendency, on both sides, to exploit internal tensions.15 As relations continued to decline, war was narrowly averted in 1985 and 1987.

These crises were, however, used in the internal Pakistani context to justify the directions of both security and domestic policies, including the forcible repression of dissent in the province of Sindh.

In a deteriorating regional climate, Pakistan's achievements in the nuclear field were also used to buttress the legitimacy of the military regime. Although ambiguity remained Pakistan's nuclear policy, high-profile figures within the nuclear establishment revealed that Pakistan had acquired the ability to produce weapon-grade uranium, joining the select club of nuclear-capable countries. Abdul Qadeer Khan, head of Pakistan's uranium enrichment programme, admitted that Pakistan had a nuclear capability in an interview with a visiting Indian journalist, Kuldip Nayar, in March 1987, an interview which could only have been held with the military regime's approval and connivance.

Thus the nuclear programme was presented to domestic audiences not only as the ultimate means of ensuring Pakistani security against aggressive Indian intentions, but also as a symbol of national prestige and sovereignty. Zia stated, for instance, 'We are among the five countries in the world who know and practice this technology', that is, the production of reactor-grade enriched uranium; while Khan, in an interview with a widely read Urdu-language daily, *Nawa-i-Waqt,* declared that 'Pakistan had broken the western countries' monopoly on the enrichment of uranium'.

Conscious, however, of the need to divert international attention from the rapid progress of the nuclear weapon programme, Pakistani policy makers offered proposal after proposal for regional nuclear disarmament to an unresponsive Indian establishment. India's rejection of Pakistan's diplomatic offensive was then used to undermine Indian credibility in international forums and to strengthen the domes- tic consensus in favour of Pakistan's nuclear capability.

13

Arms Trade: Difficult to Define, Measure, and Control

The international arms trade apparently has weathered the financial crisis quite well. Available data indicate that the impact to date on the volume of orders and deliveries has been limited.

As has been shown in the past, financial resources—from domestic budgets or foreign military assistance—are not the only factor that influences arms acquisitions. Perceived internal or external threats to national security, the need to replace or upgrade military inventories, demonstrations of international status, development of domestic arms industries via licensed production and offsets, the desire to strengthen ties with suppliers, and the influence of the military play important roles in the arms acquisition process. Before permitting exports of arms and military equipment, suppliers will assess the potential economic gains and the potential impact of the transfer on their strategic interests and foreign policy. Will the transfer harm or help friendly states or the supplier's international commitments, reputation, or standing?

For several reasons, there is no straightforward answer to the question, "How big is the international arms trade?" First, there is no globally agreed definition of "arms." States and international organizations that seek to measure or control the arms trade use lists of items that vary in their complexity and coverage, most notably with regard to their inclusion of "dual-use goods," items with both military and civilian applications. Second, there is no common agreement on what types of activities constitute the arms trade. Examples of areas where differences exist include arms leased to other states; gifts and donations; the transfer of technology to produce arms and military equipment; and upgrades, parts, and services related to the transfer of arms and military equipment. Third, the lack of openness and transparency by many arms suppliers and recipients regarding the value and volume of their arms exports and imports makes it difficult to collect accurate data. As a result, a variety of different definitions of the international arms trade and estimates of its scale exists. This has implications for efforts to establish controls on arms transfers via a future international arms trade treaty (ATT). This chapter will outline some of the challenges in defining, measuring, and controlling the international arms trade.

Definitions and Estimates

The national lists of arms and military equipment to be subject to export controls (control lists) maintained by most states and all major arms exporters provide a useful starting point for defining "arms" and the international arms trade. The Munitions List and Lists of Dual-Use Goods and Technologies of the Wassenaar Arrangement on Export Controls for Conventional Arms and Dual-Use Goods and Technologies provide the basis for the control lists of the 40 states that are members of the group. The Munitions List covers a wide range of arms and military equipment, from small arms to ships, as well as ammunition, information and communication technologies, training equipment, and equipment for producing arms. Several significant arms-exporting nonmembers, including China, have fully or partially aligned their national control lists with the Munitions List. As a result, all of the top 10 arms suppliers during 2005-2009 have control lists derived from the Wassenaar Arrangement.

National control lists serve as the basis for national reports on arms exports. As of January 2010, 32 states had published at least one national report on arms exports since 1990, and a further nine states provided information on the value of their export licenses and exports to the 2009 European Union (EU) Annual Report on Arms Exports. These reports vary in detail but, at a minimum, tend to provide data on the financial value of arms export licenses or arms exports. Several major exporters (e.g., Russia) do not produce such reports, but do release official data on the financial value of their arms exports. Using national reports and official statements, the Stockholm International Peace Research Institute (SIPRI) has attempted to provide estimates of the financial value of the international arms trade.

The now-defunct U.S. Arms Control and Disarmament Agency (ACDA) created the following comprehensive definition of the arms trade, which has been widely used by researchers: weapons of war, parts thereof, ammunition, support equipment, and other commodities designed for military use.... Dual-use equipment...when its primary mission is identified as military. The building of defence production facilities and licensing fees paid as royalties for the production of military equipment.... Military services such as training, supply operations, equipment repair, technical assistance and construction are included where data are available.

A similar definition of the arms trade is used to compile the U.S. Congressional Research Service's (CRS) annual report, "Conventional Arms Transfers to Developing Nations." In spite of the name, the report contains estimates for the value of the global arms trade, not just trade with developing countries. The CRS estimated the financial value of deliveries of arms to be $34.5 billion for 2007. Despite using a narrower definition of arms transfers than the CRS, SIPRI's accounting of official financial data contained in national reports and official statements for 2007 generated a figure of $51.1 billion for arms exports, representing 0.3 percent of world trade. This figure is likely to be lower than the true figure because a number of significant exporters, including China, do not release data on the financial value of their arms exports. The difference between the SIPRI and CRS estimates is a further demonstration of the difficulty of estimating the financial value of the international arms trade.

The SIPRI arms transfers database provides information on international arms transfers from 1950 to the most recent calendar year. Its coverage is narrower than that of the ACDA, CRS, and national control lists; for example, it does not include transfers of most small arms and light weapons (SALW). However, it provides information on the number of units transferred and employs a unique pricing system to measure the volume of arms transfers. The SIPRI trend indicator value allows researchers to track developments in transfers to and from different suppliers, recipients, and regions.

Arms Trade Trends

The volume of international arms transfers in the post-World War II period peaked in 1982. Following the end of the Cold War, there was a steady decline in global arms transfers. They reached their lowest point in 2002, when transfers amounted to only 38 percent of their Cold War high. This decline has reversed, and the volume of international transfers of major conventional weapons during 2005-2009 was 22 percent higher than during 2000-2004.

One of the most marked aspects of the international arms trade has been its dominance by five suppliers. During 1980-1984, when global arms transfers were at the highest level, the Soviet Union (37 percent), the United States (29 percent), France (8 percent), the United Kingdom (5 percent), and the Federal Republic of Germany (5 percent) accounted for 84 percent of all exports. The five largest suppliers of major conventional weapons during 2005-2009 were the United States (30 percent), Russia (23 percent), Germany (11 percent), France (8 percent), and the United Kingdom (4 percent), collectively accounting for 76 percent of exports.

The governments of these major suppliers are actively engaged in assisting the export efforts of their domestic arms industries in the competitive international arms market. Some governments also provide military equipment to allies at beneficial rates as a key plank of their foreign and defence policies, something that often has clear benefits for commercial arms manufacturers based in these states. Since 2001, the United States has increased foreign military aid for allies in regions of tension or conflict. President Barack Obama has maintained the Bush administration's pledge to increase foreign military financing aid for Israel, which is set to reach $3 billion in 2012. Egypt and the members of the Gulf

Cooperation Council have been the recipients of increased assistance as well.

Russia has announced its willingness to develop and produce arms jointly with other countries to help strengthen ties, accept payments through barter, participate in joint economic projects, and offer credit and exchanges of debt for arms. In 2009, Russia extended a $2 billion line of credit to Venezuela for arms purchases. In addition, it agreed to cancel Vietnam's debt to Russia and help modernize its shipbuilding industry in exchange for Vietnam's commitment to purchase 20 Su-30MK combat aircraft and six Type-636 Kilo-class submarines and further expand the involvement of Russian companies in the exploration and extraction of Vietnamese oil.

In 2007 the French government simplified and modernized France's arms export licensing system and began taking a more active role in promoting exports abroad. It has demonstrated a willingness to engage in far-reaching technology transfer agreements in order to win contracts. In September 2009 French President Nicolas Sarkozy visited Brazil to conclude an almost $10 billion deal to supply four conventionally powered submarines and technology to assist in the development of Brazil's first nuclear-powered submarine.

Attempts by countries beyond the traditional major producers to develop their own arms industries and increase their share of global arms exports have typically had limited success, largely because of high technological barriers or an inadequate civilian industrial base. Yet, many countries still seek to increase their levels of autonomous capability in arms production, with some developing state-of-the-art products for particular niche items. For example, Israel is widely recognized as a leading producer and supplier of unmanned aerial vehicles (UAVs), supplying systems and licenses for production for more than 100 UAVs to 18 states, including all of the top five suppliers, during 2005-2009.

In addition, licensed production agreements have led to an increase in the number of states that are capable of manufacturing less-advanced weapons systems, particularly small arms and light weapons. Although licensed production agreements often include controls on who can receive the weapons produced, this is not always the case, or the agreements are not enforced. Soviet Avtomat Kalashnikov (AK) and German Heckler and Koch G3 assault rifles serve as classic examples of cases in which licensed production has led to exports being made without the express permission of those issuing the original license. Russia perceives the production of Kalashnikov rifles in a number of former Warsaw Pact countries to be unlicensed and illegal, claiming that arrangements concluded during the Soviet era have expired. The decision to give designs and information on product technology to Warsaw Pact states and clients during the Soviet era therefore remains a source of concern. Nonetheless, Russia continues to issue licensed production agreements for Kalashnikov rifles, revealing recently that 10 states had applied to build factories. The possibility remains that today's license holders could produce or export Kalashnikovs without the express permission of Russia in the future.

In contrast to the largest suppliers, the largest recipients of major conventional weapons have varied considerably over the years. During 1980-1984, the five largest recipients of military equipment—Iraq (7 percent), India (6 percent), Libya (5 percent), Syria (5 percent), and Egypt (4 percent)—accounted for 27 percent of total imports. The five largest recipients of major conventional weapons during 2005-2009 were China (9 percent), India (7 percent), South Korea (6 percent), the United Arab Emirates (6 percent), and Greece (4 percent), accounting for 32 percent of total imports. After the end of the Cold War, China imported a large volume of aircraft, ships, submarines, air defence systems, and missiles from Russia, but Chinese arms imports from Russia have declined dramatically in recent years. One explanation for this drop is that China appears to have overcome many of the problems that have dogged its arms industry and is now able to manufacture advanced weapons systems domestically. There are persistent allegations that many of China's "indigenous" weapons systems are actually copies of other countries' designs. It continues to rely on imports of components and subsystems for a number of its weapons systems, but is regarded as an example of a country in which arrangements for licensed production and technology transfers as part of arms import deals have helped with the development of an indigenous arms industry. India has sought to develop its own arms industry and decrease its reliance on arms imports but with limited success to date. It is expected to replace China as the largest arms importer in the coming years.

Recent acquisitions by states in Latin America, the Middle East, North Africa, and Southeast Asia indicate the possible emergence of reactive arms acquisition patterns that could develop into regional arms races. The volume of deliveries to Southeast Asia nearly doubled during 2005-2009 compared to 2000-2004. Deliveries were 722 percent higher to Malaysia, 146 percent higher to Singapore, and 84 percent higher to Indonesia. In 2009, Malaysia received six Su-30MKM combat aircraft with advanced missiles from Russia, two Scorpène submarines from France and Spain, two MEKO-100 frigates from Germany, and 21 PT-91 tanks from Poland. Singapore received eight F-15E combat aircraft with advanced air-to-air and air-to-ground missiles from the United States, two La Fayette frigates from France, and 40 Leopard-2A4 tanks from Germany.

There is limited empirical evidence to suggest a direct causal link between an increase in the volume of arms imported and the outbreak of conflict or an increase in the intensity of conflict. It has been suggested, however, that states that acquire significant quantities of military equipment may be more prone to use armed force to resolve disputes. For example, the recent conflicts in Sri Lanka and Georgia, both of which are relatively minor arms importers, were preceded by significant increases in transfers. In both cases, governments sought to restore what they perceived to be their state's territorial integrity against forces that were seeking independence and had established high levels of autonomy to some degree within clearly defined regions.

As the graph on this page demonstrates, the volume of Georgian imports of major conventional weapons in the years preceding the August 2008 conflict in South Ossetia increased significantly, with the largest volume of arms imports for Georgia, excluding acquisitions by forces in Abkhazia and South Ossetia, taking place in 2007. Significant increases in arms imports and military spending were perceived by some as indicating that the

Georgian government was preparing to use force to restore Georgia's territorial integrity.

TRADE CONTROL EFFORTS

At present, UN Security Council arms embargoes are the only global, legally binding prohibitions on arms transfers. Since 1990, the United Nations has imposed 28 arms embargoes against targets in 17 countries and one nonstate entity (Osama bin Laden and al Qaeda). The most recent new arms embargo was introduced against Eritrea on December 23, 2009. Recent UN arms embargo resolutions recognize that nonstate actors play an important role in the contemporary arms trade and in the facilitation of arms transfers to "undesirable" end-users. States retain primary responsibility for enforcing arms embargoes and controlling the activities of arms brokers and dealers operating from their national territory or registered with their national authorities.

Sanctions committees and panels of experts charged with monitoring arms embargoes have documented the role different states have played in violating arms embargoes, such as in the case of Eritrea's involvement in transfers to Somalia. Also, states have been accused of giving shelter to individuals and entities accused of violating embargoes and of failing to investigate alleged violations but in such instances have not been sanctioned themselves. Stronger transfer control policies and increased political will are of central importance for preventing violations of UN arms embargoes.

States have long been reluctant to give up any element of national control in the field of arms transfer controls. Yet, the Iraqi invasion of Kuwait in 1990 and the scandals involving Western states and companies in the arming of Iraq prompted the development of the guidelines for conventional arms transfers, under which the permanent members of the UN Security Council agreed to exercise restraint in exports of conventional arms transfers. Suppliers were required to ensure that exports met only the "legitimate self-defence" needs of the recipient and did not contribute to conflict or regional instability or introduce "destabilizing military capabilities in a region." There is no international agreement on what constitutes legitimate self-defence or "destabilizing military capabilities."

Efforts to improve controls on international arms transfers have primarily been driven and directed by suppliers in North America and Europe. Motivations have included protecting national industries by preventing the spread of technologies and limiting potential adversaries' access to key technologies. The prevention of conflict and human rights abuses also has long been at the heart of efforts to control the arms trade. States, export control regimes such as the Wassenaar Arrangement, and regional organizations (e.g., the Economic Community of West African States, the EU, the Organization for Security and Cooperation in Europe, and the Organization of American States) have developed various sets of best-practice guidelines and model legislation to help ensure that arms exports do not provoke or exacerbate conflict and are not used to commit violations of human rights and humanitarian law. In addition, efforts have been undertaken to prevent the diversion of arms to terrorists, criminals, and armed groups.

Experience with existing regional mechanisms and export control regimes demonstrates some of the problems that an ATT is likely to face when it comes to ensuring harmonized interpretations of the criteria it puts in place. Despite developing agreed export criteria and mechanisms of consultation and information exchange, members of the Wassenaar Arrangement have demonstrated contrasting attitudes toward exports of arms and military equipment to a range of destinations. Although the EU and the United States have arms embargoes against Iran, Myanmar (Burma), Sudan, and Zimbabwe, Russia continues to supply weapons systems to these states. Meanwhile, Russia has repeatedly called for restraint on arms transfers to Georgia, but Wassenaar Arrangement members the Czech Republic, Turkey, and Ukraine have continued to supply arms to Georgia. It appears that bilateral pressure on nonmembers Bosnia and Herzegovina, Israel, and Serbia led to some deals to Georgia being canceled.

Even within the EU, where states have agreed that their export license decision-making should be guided by eight criteria relating to issues such as conflict prevention, human rights, and economic development, there appear to have been differences of opinion among members regarding exports to Georgia. EU member states reported issuing licenses worth more than $180 million between 2004 and 2007 for exports of arms and military equipment to Georgia and making exports worth almost $96 million during that period. Also during this period, EU member states denied 41 export licenses for arms and military equipment for Georgia because of concerns about the potential impact of the transfer on the possibility of conflict within Georgia. In several cases, EU member states denied an export license for the export of a particular type of military equipment that other EU member states had exported.

Researchers have found evidence of a correlation between the introduction of the politically binding EU Code of Conduct on Arms Exports in 1998 and a decline in arms exports from EU member states to countries in conflict or considered violators of international human rights and humanitarian law, but differences in decision-making on "responsible" recipients continue within the EU. In this regard, the impact of the EU arms exports code and the legally binding Council Common Position 2008/944/CFSP, defining common rules governing the control of exports of military technology and equipment, which replaced the EU arms exports code, continues to illustrate the challenges of reaching agreement on how to interpret and implement a set of agreed common standards among (supposedly) like-minded states. Disagreements in the Wassenaar Arrangement show the difficulties in achieving similar objectives when the group is composed of states that hold very different opinions on what constitutes a responsible end-user.

RECENT TRENDS IN EXPORT CONTROL MECHANISMS

Arms export policies are policies that govern 'The dispatch of conventional weapons, weapon platforms and related equipment (that would normally be found on a military list of controlled goods) from one country to another'. Along with other defence- and security-related issues, the development and implementation of such policies is almost universally considered to be the exclusive prerogative of states. States have traditionally pursued widely divergent arms export policies and, with the exception of multilateral arms embargoes, have been reluctant to give up any element of national control in this area.

Nonetheless, numerous states have also sought to increase the level of coordination and harmonization in this area—as a means of both increasing international standards and off setting the commercial costs of maintaining a more restrictive system than other states.

Such efforts have intensified in recent years. While they have largely focused on regional organizations such as the Organization for Security and Co-operation in Europe (OSCE) and the EU, the UN has also made extensive and long-standing efforts. Numerous UN Security Council and General Assembly resolutions have reiterated the importance of states maintaining functioning controls on the export of military goods. For example, under the 2001 Programme of Action to Prevent, Combat and Eradicate the Illicit Trade in Small Arms and Light Weapons in All Its Aspects (POA), states have agreed to ensure that they have adequate laws, regulations and administrative procedures to control transfers of SALW.

Transfer prohibitions and guidelines

At present, arms embargoes imposed by the UN Security Council are the only global, legally binding prohibitions on arms transfers. UN arms embargoes are imposed by resolutions adopted under the authority of Chapter VII, Article 41, of the UN Charter. Like all Security Council resolutions, embargoes require the affirmative votes of at least nine of the 15 members of the Security Council, and each of the five permanent members (China, France, Russia, the UK and the USA; the P5) has a veto. As of 1 January 2009 there were 11 mandatory UN arms embargoes in force. However, according to the sanctions committees and panels of experts monitoring these embargoes, many UN arms embargoes have been repeatedly violated, by both states and private individuals.

The development of regional and global guidelines for conventional arms transfers has been on the international agenda since the 1920s. In 1925 the League of Nations produced a draft convention on the arms trade, but it was never adopted. While global conventions govern the transfer of nuclear, biological and chemical weapons, there is currently no equivalent, global mechanism covering the transfer of conventional weapons. During the cold war the two competing blocs and individual countries used conventional weapon transfers in order to establish or maintain spheres of influence. At the regional level, the coordination of export control policies was mainly focused on preventing transfers to members of the opposing bloc. For example, in 1949 the Western bloc formed the Coordinating Committee for Multilateral Export Controls (COCOM) to manage an embargo on transfers of arms and related technologies to the Eastern bloc. COCOM was disbanded in 1994.

In the early 1990s states concluded that the accumulation of major conventional weapons in Iraq in the period preceding the 1990 invasion of Kuwait had contributed to Iraq's decision to invade. Partly as a result, during the early and mid-1990s different state groupings developed several sets of guidelines or principles on arms transfers. Rather than targeting specific groups of states, they sought to lay down rules that would apply to all conventional arms transfers, regardless of their destination.

In October 1991 the P5 adopted a set of guidelines for conventional arms transfers which called on the P5 and other arms exporters to export conventional arms only in line with the legitimate self-defence needs of recipients and appropriate and proportionate responses to security threats. It was also agreed that transfers that were likely to prolong existing conflicts and tensions, introduce 'destabilizing accumulations' or contravene international commitments, such as arms embargoes, would be avoided. In November 1993 the OSCE reaffirmed its commitment to a similar set of principles governing conventional arms transfers.

Other principles emphasized in these guidelines include the need to prevent transfers that might contribute to destabilizing military build-ups, prolong or aggravate an armed conflict, or fall into the hands of terrorists. However, the guidelines lack enforcement mechanisms, and their interpretation has been left entirely at the discretion of individual states. Concerns such as these have played a significant role in the recent push for the development of an international arms trade treaty. A 2006 draft UN General Assembly resolution states that the 'absence of common international standards on the import, export and transfer of conventional arms is a contributory factor to conflict, the displacement of people, crime and terrorism'.

Export control regimes and other regional mechanisms

The post cold-war period has also seen the development of more formal mechanisms aimed at coordinating the policies of supplier and recipient states. These mechanisms involve the application of guidelines and principles, but they also include some level of coordination between the states involved to try to ensure some level of harmonization in how they are implemented. Other mechanisms cover exports of missiles (e.g. the Missile Technology Control Regime), nuclear technologies (e.g. the Nuclear Suppliers Group) and chemical and biological agents (e.g. the Australia Group). The Wassenaar Arrangement on Export Controls for Conventional Arms and Dual-Use Goods and Technologies was established in 1996 in an attempt to replicate some of the benefits of COCOM but on a broader and non-adversarial basis. It currently has 40 participating states, including Russia, the USA, most members of NATO and most former members of the Warsaw Treaty Organization. The Wassenaar Arrangement was designed to promote transparency and responsibility in transfers of arms and dual-use items in order to prevent 'destabilizing accumulations'. Participating states exchange information on their exports and discuss policies on particular regions or destinations.

The EU's Common Rules Governing Control of Exports of Military Technology and Equipment (known as the Code of Conduct on Arms Exports until 2008) was first formally adopted in June 1998.41 It consists of eight criteria on which EU member states should base their export licensing decisions, relating to issues such as conflict prevention, human rights and economic development. Under the EU Common Rules, governments agree to exchange, in confidence, information on any application for an export licence that is denied, including the reasons for the refusal. If a member state is considering granting an export licence for a transaction that it believes might be 'essentially identical' to one that has previously been denied, then it is obliged to consult the state that previously issued the denial in order to clarify the situation. In 1998 members of the Economic Community of West African States (ECOWAS) adopted a moratorium on the manufacture, importation and exportation of SALW. A 2002 evaluation report highlighted a number of weaknesses in the moratorium and cases where certain states had failed to uphold its principles. In response, the ECOWAS Convention on Small Arms and Light Weapons, Their Ammunition and Other Related Materials was adopted in June 2006. The convention retains the moratorium's prohibition on SALW imports, but states can apply to the ECOWAS Commission for exemptions 'in order to meet legitimate national defence and security needs, or to participate in peace support or other operations'. The convention also requires that participating states provide detailed information to the ECOWAS Commission on any SALW import.

THE IMPACT OF ILLICIT SMALL ARMS ON HUMAN SECURITY

Terrorism and Insurgency

The number of insurgency movements in Southeast Asia receiving frequent supplies of small arms is limited. These movements exist in Indonesia, Myanmar and the Philippines. As well, there is continued fighting among different political factions in Cambodia.

The insurgents in Indonesia (Acehnese, East Timorese and West Irian) are among the least likely to receive small arms from abroad. Their numbers are small and they do not have the mechanisms to raise adequate funds for weapons purchase. The Indonesian government and military have been effective in isolating these movements and preventing any contact with the outside. The East Timorese resistance, for example, mainly uses weapons taken from Indonesian soldiers. Therefore, although the demand for small arms may exist in these insurgent areas, the threat of actual acquisition is minimal. This argument is strong especially considering that profits have become the main goal of today's small arms trade.

The most likely recipients of small arms in Indonesia are criminal elements. And even this situation is questionable because there is not a network of organized crime, such as the Triad in China or the drug cartels in Myanmar, that have the resources to sustain any form of arms transfer. In the Philippines, separatist groups on Mindanao have engaged in sporadic armed confrontation with central government forces for years. The insurgents have admitted to obtaining weapons from foreign sources. Photographs of rebel soldiers show them to be well equipped with small arms and ammunition, and it is unlikely that these are solely from stealing and confiscating weapons from government forces. Further fighting not only threatens human security in the Philippines, but also could have a significant impact on the country's economic growth.

Since last year's coup in Cambodia, incidents of political violence have been high. "Hundreds of [Hun Sen's] oppositions remain in Thailand in exile or are fighting in the jungles." Although Hun Sen's faction has been accused internationally for committing such violence against Norodom Ranarindh's supporters, the latter often are perpetrators as well. Prior to the coup, during the United Nations sponsored peacebuilding process, it was feared that disarmament efforts would result in small arms moving out of the country and into neighbouring states. However, while the movement of small arms from Cambodia to places such as northern Myanmar is possible, the demand for weapons in Cambodia is rising. Small arms are probably re-circulating within the country and foreign sources may be involved in further re-supply. While Hun Sen's faction could be receiving small arms shipment from Vietnam, Ranarindh loyalists could be receiving theirs from China. To make things even more complicated, the Khmer Rouge is still actively seeking ways to become involved in this political power play.

Criminal Activities

Criminal elements have profited most from easier access to illicit weapons, and there are signs of increasing gun related violence. In China, there is a steady growth in gun-related crimes since 1994 and the government warns of the threat this poses to public security. The problem is intensified by the growing brutality of such crimes. As numbers and levels of criminal violence escalate, citizens seek security through acquiring small arms for personal use. In turn, this trend exacerbates overall conditions as it allows the small arms trade to flourish by raising the demand for such weapons. This becomes the case especially when the government is perceived to be slow and ineffective in implementing measures to manage the problem. Such a situation is not unique to China and can be observed throughout East Asia. The links between small arms proliferation and criminal activities in Southeast Asia is especially problematic when one also factors in the estimated high volume of drug trade in the region. In Myanmar, the sales of small arms to drug lords such as Khun Sa have allowed them to strengthen their power. With easy access to such weapons, the drug cartels have formed well-equipped private armies, which increasingly pose serious threats to state sovereignty. The state monopoly on violence — one of the main characteristics of the modern state system — is increasingly undermined. Through the flourishing illicit trade in small arms, these private armies occasionally appear at least as well equipped and trained than the national security forces. This situation provides drug cartels with the tools to strengthen their grip over communities of peasants who are enslaved by the trade. Small arms proliferation is also associated with the drug trade in the form of common channels of supply.

The transfer of small arms may be different from that of drugs because the former carry more bulk and are easier to trace in their origins. However, the manner in which they are transported is comparable. For example, drugs and small arms transfers across the Thai-Cambodian border are sometimes carried out by concealing these products inside the gas tanks of shipping trucks. In addition to the similarities in methods, these goods are moving through similar patterns of supply channels. This argument is supported by reports claiming that weapons and drugs are often exchanged along such supply lines. The trades in small arms and drugs complement each other; the flourishing of one trade certainly induces growth in the other.

While the small arms/drug trades model also applies to illicit maritime activities, piracy is the more serious problem at sea. The most recent International Maritime Bureau (IMB) report shows that Southeast Asia remains the region with the highest rate of piracy in the world. These criminal activities are frequent in the South China Sea (especially within the Hong Kong-Luzon-Hainan triangle), the Strait of Malacca and the Gulf of Thailand. While trends have been on the rise for the last five years or so, last year's report indicates another problem; the level of violence committed during pirate attacks have dramatically increased.

Acts of piracy in the region are usually carried out using homemade explosives and small arms such as rifles and machine guns. The increasing level of violence during pirate attacks could possibly be linked to the growing availability of small arms. Considering that the number of pirate attacks reported did not increase dramatically, the surge in levels of violence which accompany these acts can only be explained by the widening use of small arms. Consequently, in addition to facing the fear of being robbed, the personal security of ship crews is also increasingly threatened.

Implications for State Sovereignty in the Region

The most predominant threats to security caused by the growth in illicit small arms trafficking are of non-military nature. Insurgency movements, factional fighting and criminal activities flourish with easy access to small arms. While regional states may not see these threats as serious in the short term, their implications in the long run may cause disruption in state legitimacy and stability.

One of the most important features of the modern state is its monopoly on internal violence. However, as non-state, non-military elements gain power, they pose a challenge to the norm. Having just gained their independence from European powers in the latter part of the century (except for Thailand, which was never ruled by a foreign power) countries in Southeast Asia are still undergoing statebuilding processes. Most of them are still concentrating on developing mechanisms against encroachment from other countries (especially considering the existence of historical animosities and unending territorial disputes among the regional countries). As a result, small-scale insurgencies and criminal activities are often overlooked as possible threats to the state.

The growth of drug smuggling and piracy poses threats to the region's economic activities. As the current economic downturn deepens, there is a strong possibility that these activities may grow even faster. For example, the tough anti-drug policies in Thailand, which has been responsible for the declining production of opium on the Thai section of the Golden Triangle, could lose its effectiveness as officials try to relieve their economic hardship through corruption. Also, the hundreds of Indonesians who are fleeing to the Malaysian peninsula could become easy targets for pirates operating in the Malacca Strait. These descriptions are mainly speculative, but they are important considerations for governments in the region. The current economic meltdown represents a tough challenge to statehood in Southeast Asia. The erosion of state legitimacy by internal, non-military, non-state elements renders the task of overcoming the meltdown more difficult. Therefore, it is in these countries interest to attribute more attention to the trafficking of illicit small arms, which enhances the power of these non-state actors.

POLICY OPTIONS

UN Based Efforts

The United Nations remains one of the best institutions for promoting efforts to manage the problem of small arms proliferation. Former UN Secretary General Boutros Boutros Ghali's Agenda for Peace was important as a beginning, and last year's Report of the Small Arms Panel provided some guidelines to further treatment of the issue. The greatest advantage to UN based efforts is its inclusiveness, especially when considering that illicit small arms proliferation is a global security problem as much as it is a regional or national one.

One of the most talked about suggestions is the possible expansion of the UN Register of Conventional Weapons to promote transparency about the legal trade in small arms. However, since its creation, the UN Register has had mixed results. Not all states have submitted reports of their weapons acquisitions, but the leading arms exporting countries have responded. The export/ import information provided by states often contain discrepancies, but it has revealed some previously unknown data as well as represents a modest step towards enhancing transparency. The expansion of the Register (beyond the seven original weapon categories and to include small arms) seems an efficient and logical progression, however the goal will be difficult to achieve. The creation of the Register in the first place was a difficult enough process and some states are unhappy about its current scope and coverage (hence, the lack of universal participation). For a number of states, the current situation represents the limit of their willingness to cooperate in transparency measures. Although the expansion of the Register may be the most desired goal for countries such as Canada, its actual realization is difficult. Nevertheless, this should not deter attempts to proceed with such an approach.

Bibliography

Allison, Graham: *Nuclear Terrorism: The Ultimate Preventable Catastrophe,* New York: Times Books, 2004.

Backman, Jules. *War and Defense Economics.* New York: Rinehart, 1952.

Bhatia, Shyam: *India's Nuclear Bomb,* Ghaziabad: Vikas Publishing House, 1979.

Buzan, B.: *People, States and Fear: An Agenda for International Security Studies in the Post-Cold War Era,* Harverster Wheatsheaf, London, 1991)

Frederick B.: *Protection and Security on the Information Superhighway.* John Wiley & Sons, Inc.: New York, 1995.

Grimmett, Richard F.: *Conventional Arms Transfers to Developing Nations, 1993–2000.* Congressional Research Service Report to Congress. Washington, D.C., 2001.

Harkavy, Robert E. *The Arms Trade and International Systems.* Cambridge, Mass., 1975.

Harold Glenn. *Fundamental Economic Issues in National Defense.* Washington, DC: Brookings Institution, 1941.

Hasan-Askari Rizvi: *Nuclear Terrorism and South Asia,* Albuquerque, NM: Sandia National Laboratories, February 2003.

James L. *The Economic Impact of the Cold War: Sources and Readings.* New York, 1970.

Karanjit Siyan: *Internet Firewalls and Network Security.* New Riders Publishing: Indianapolis, 1996.

Krause, Keith. *Arms and the State: Patterns of Military Production and Trade.* Cambridge, U.K., 1992.

Laurance, Edward J. *The International Arms Trade.* New York, 1992.

Lens, Sidney, *Military-Industrial Complex.* Philadelphia: Pilgrim Press, 1970.

McGrath, R. *Landmines: Legacy of Conflict,* Oxfam Publication, 1994.

Nininger, Robert D. *Minerals for Atomic Energy*. New York: D. Van Nostrand Company, Inc., 1954.

Pierre, Andrew J. *The Global Politics of Arms Sales*. Princeton, N.J., 1982.

Posen, B.R.: *The Sources of Cyber Crime,* Ithaca, 1984, Cornell Univ. Press.

Rhodes, Richard, *The Making of the Atomic Bomb,* New York: Simon and Schuster, 1988.

Robert E. Harkavy, eds. *Arms Transfers in the Modern World*. New York, 1979.

Robert H. *The Navy and Industrial Mobilization in World War II*. Princeton, N.J., 1951.

Schroeer, Dietrich, *Science, Technology, and the Nuclear Arms Race,* Ontario: John Wiley & Sons, 1984.

Sherwin, Martin J. A World Destroyed: *The Atomic Bomb and the Grand Alliance*. New York: Vintage Books, 1977.

Sivard, R L.: *World Military and Social Expenditures,* World Priorities, Washington D.C, 1993.

Smith, C.: *The Diffusion of Small Arms and Light Weapons in Pakistan and Northern India,* Centre for Defence Studies, Brassey's, London, 1993.

Thayer, George. *The War Business*. New York, 1969.

Van de Goor, L.L.P.: *Conflict and Development: The Causes of Conflict in Developing Countries,* The Netherlands Institute of International Relations, The Hague, 1994.

Index

I

L

M

N

P

R

S

❑❑❑